MOVING TOWARD LIFE

MOVING TOWARD LIFE

FIVE DECADES OF TRANSFORMATIONAL DANCE

ANNA HALPRIN

EDITED BY RACHEL KAPLAN

Wesleyan University Press

Published by University Press of New England

Hanover and London

Wesleyan University Press
Published by University Press of New England, Hanover, NH 03755
© 1995 by Wesleyan University Press
All rights reserved
Printed in the United States of America   5 4 3 2 1
CIP data appear at the end of the book

Sections of this book have been published previously. All pieces copyrighted by Anna Halprin in the year of publication. Original publication dates and places of publication are as follows:

"Three Decades of Transformational Dance" (interview with Nancy Stark Smith), *Contact Quarterly*, Winter 1990.

"Movement Ritual I," *Movement Ritual I*, Written by Anna Halprin, illustrated by Charlene Koonce. Tamalpa Institute, 1979.

"Yvonne Rainer Interviews Ann Halprin," *Tulane Drama Review*, vol. 10, no. 5, Winter 1965.

"What and How I Believe," *Arts in Society*, Spring/Summer 1968.

"Mutual Creation," *Tulane Drama Review*, vol. 13, no. 1, Fall 1968.

"Ceremony of Us," *Tulane Drama Review*, vol. 13, no. 4, Summer 1969.

"Instructions to Performers/Microcosm in Movement," *Tulane Drama Review*, vol. 13, no. 4, Summer 1969.

"Community Art as Life Process," *Tulane Drama Review*, vol. 17, no. 3, Fall 1973.

"Citydance 1977," *Citydance 1977*, Dancers' Workshop, 1978.

"After Improv" (interview with Nancy Stark Smith), *Contact Quarterly*, Fall 1987.

"Circle the Earth: Peace Dance, A Philosophy," *Contact Quarterly*, Winter 1986.

"Anna Halprin: A Life in Ritual" (interview with Richard Schechner), *The Drama Review*, vol. 33, no. 2, Summer 1989. Permission courtesy of the MIT Press.

"The Planetary Dance," *The Drama Review*, vol. 33, no. 2, Summer 1989. Permission courtesy of the MIT Press.

"Life/Art Workshop Processes," *Taking Part*, by Lawrence Halprin and James T. Burns, MIT Press, 1974.

Moving Toward Life is a registered servicemark of Dancers' Workshop/Tamalpa Institute.

For more information regarding the Halprin Life/Art Process and related publications, contact: The Tamalpa Institute, Box 794, Kentfield, CA 94914 (phone: 415-461-9479).

Edited by Rachel Kaplan
Designed by The Office of Michael Manwaring
Set in Garamond Stempel and Univers 75
Cover photo by Paul Fusco

Frontispiece: Anna Halprin, The Prophetess, *1955. Costume designed by Lawrence Halprin and Martha Graham.*

Photo by
Imogen Cunningham.

Facing page: A. A. Leath, Four-Legged Stool, *1962.*

Photo by
Warner Jepson.

THIS BOOK IS DEDICATED TO MY HUSBAND, LAWRENCE HALPRIN,

TO HONOR MANY YEARS OF COLLABORATIVE CREATIVITY

CONTENTS

LEANING INTO RITUAL

APPENDIXES

As I leaf through these pages of Collected Writings, I'm sitting on a bench overlooking my dance deck and studio, surrounded by redwood trees and shadowed by the constant presence of Mount Tamalpais. I realize I have been here a very long time. Each tree, each flight of a bird, rustle of a deer, feel of the breeze, or sound of a foghorn holds a memory of a dance born in this place. My life and work are interwoven with the rhythms, changes, and subtle shifts of this land.

I left the Midwest of my childhood and my budding professional dance career in New York City to move to California in 1945. World War II was over, and I set off to San Francisco to join my husband who had just returned from the Pacific. I was twenty-five years old. Six years later, we had two daughters, Daria and Rana, and our young family had moved into a new home designed by Bill Woorster in collaboration with my husband, Lawrence. Both men are primary influences in the Bay Region style of architecture and landscape architecture, a movement that influenced me and my art on a daily basis. Their style allowed for a free-flowing connection between inside and outside, a major theme in my own work which would develop through explorations of dance both inside and outside the theater. At my new house, sliding glass walls opened onto tan-bark terraces and led into the surrounding redwood groves, and the views reached to the bay and the slopes of the majestic mountain. My new house in the country felt like an integral part of nature, and increasingly it was a contemplative environment, free of the distractions of the city. At this time I shared a dance studio with Welland Lathrop in San Francisco, but I felt a gradual and steady pull to spend more and more time at my home studio.

Lawrence and the modern-dance lighting designer Arch Lauterer designed a dance deck that meandered among the redwood trees below our house. The pull was getting stronger. I did not want to be away from my two daughters, and I was ready to make the final break. I left the city and began to dance in this invigorating outdoor environment. I cut my ties with modern dance and began to search for new directions. I offered experimental workshops for dancers and invited visual artists, musicians, actors, architects, poets, psychologists, and filmmakers to join. I called the group Dancers' Workshop, an idea from the experimental Bauhaus school of pre-Nazi Germany. At Dancers' Workshop we were looking for ways to rediscover the basic nature of our materials free of preconceived associations and concepts. We were interested in avoiding the predictability of cause and effect. As a result of our many experiments, we created theater pieces and gave performances on the dance deck and the surrounding wooded area for invited audiences. As people became interested in our work, we were invited to international art festivals, both here and abroad.

The three aspects of my work I wish to illuminate are, I believe, unique trajectories; they have been of the greatest importance to me over the years. The first is that the experiments Dancers' Workshop and I did in the 1960s and '70s with new *forms* of dance led to new *uses* of dance. Dancing outside the confines of the proscenium theater and in the environment—the street or the natural world—had unexpected results. As it came closer to the environments where people lived, dance became more connected to people's lives and more responsive to people's needs. The image-making and sleight of hand common to the theater dropped away and we were left with the raw material of our lives to make our art. The boundaries between art and life, and between performer and audience, shifted and expanded, and the uses and applications of dance followed suit. Some larger force, which I believe has to do with the ancient roots of dance and its primary importance to human beings, was set into motion.

A second aspect developed as we researched new uses of dance and movement, and our forms became accessible to more people and began to exist outside the theater and in the daily lives of ordinary people. As the forms expanded, the kinds of people who participated became more diverse, which brought about profound changes in dance. New methods of communication and a creative process encouraging pluralistic involvement developed as we sought to create an art form speaking directly to various ethnic groups and nationalities, and people of different economic backgrounds, age levels, or physical abilities. Just as we had discovered a total, holistic theater, we needed a well-trained holistic dancer-performer. I began to generate forms in which the physical, emotional, mental, and spiritual bodies functioned in greater relationship to one another. My search was for the whole person, and my criterion was the meaning in each individual's life.

My early work focused on new forms and uses for dance; later I became concerned with the meaning of the works I was creating, in order to reinvest these forms with emotion and personal motivation. In the process of stripping away all pretense in the theater and then engaging the whole person, we found that an unexpected synthesis occurred. We began to work with real-life themes, so now the dances we made had a real purpose in people's lives. We were tapping into our own personal stories, and the dances we made had transformative powers. I began to call them rituals and identified the materials that created them as myths. This was a turning point for me in terms of how I viewed dance and its potential uses.

The third aspect of my work, and the part that has challenged and nurtured me all these years, has been the ways dance has been instrumental in developing community through the expression of these myths and rituals. It seemed an inevitable direction—the experience of community—and as community became my theme, larger symbols, or archetypes, emerged. The driving, pulsing life force that motivates us all became the inspiration of my later works. The shock of having cancer and the changes it wrought on my life and my work led me to explore the relationship between dance and healing. I began to work with dance as a healing art, and with people who are challenging life-threatening illness. Compassion, health, love, catharsis, life, death—the full spectrum of humanity's striving—needed to be contained in my evolving forms. And over and over again, returning to the mountain, or to the sea, I was fed with images and resources and power which I recycled back into the work of making vital community.

As many of us struggle to find our spiritual identity, we can, I believe, return to dance to recover an ancient tradition that will serve us in today's culture. The wisdom of dance and the body contains resources that can provide us with tools for the survival of life on this planet. Our connection to the earth and to one another as forms *of* the earth is our crucial next step. I believe that this is the wonderful possibility for dance today. Through dance we can rediscover a spiritual identity and community we have lost, and the work of making this dance current, immediate, and necessary continues to be of the greatest importance. At the moment, nature is the greatest teacher for me, the clearest voice guiding my dance. To feel and experience the earth helps me find my own deepest human nature, and I am directing much of my dancing toward this timeless, infinite theater.

As I sit on the bench overlooking my dance deck, a flood of questions arises. What next? Where am I going? What is my work now that I am seventy-five? What do elders in other cultures do? Teach the young, heal the sick, care for the land, hold the rituals, speak with the ancestors, maintain the family. I take all these actions, and call upon the spirits, wherever they may be, whatever that might mean, and however they may appear, to lead me further into this evolution of dance to which I have committed my life. I continue to believe in the shining potential set forth by all of this work, in its evolution from rebellion to expansion to community to healing and back again to the natural world.

Anna Halprin
Kentfield, California
June 1994

ACKNOWLEDGMENTS

The events, performances, and workshops described in these writings are the collective result of many, many good friends and colleagues with whom I have collaborated since 1948. I have been challenged, inspired, supported, and enlightened by their contributions, and their creativity and commitment have shaped the form and development of my work in incalculable ways.

Often ideas and attitudes have a profound yet indirect influence for many years. For that reason, I want to pay special tribute to Margaret H'Doubler, with whom I studied at the University of Wisconsin from 1938 to 1941. H'Doubler led me to explore an objective and universal path that lives within my work to this day.

I have immeasurable gratitude for the creative input of the dancers and collaborators who helped me in the creation of my early theater works, John Graham, A. A. Leath, Simone Forti, Josephine Landor, and Patric Hickey. Norma Leistiko played a multitude of major roles for over twenty-five years as a dance performer, teacher, researcher, secretary, manager, and friend.

The students and participants in my workshops over the years who have been the source of much of my experimental work are too numerous to mention. However, they include Meredith Monk, Trisha Brown, Yvonne Rainer, Kei Takei, Soto-Hoffman, Coni Beeson, James Broughton, Terry Riley, LaMonte Young, Charles Amirkhanian, Morton Subotnik, and Pauline Oliveros.

I want to thank Alice Rutkowski, Jamie McHugh, Allan Stinson, Jasper Redrobe-Vassau, and Joseph and Eeo Stubblefield for their contributions as co-workshop leaders and collaborators of *Circle the Earth*.

James Hurd Nixon deserves special thanks for his ongoing dialogues which have provided inspiration for over two decades.

But most of all, thanks go to my husband, Lawrence, and my two daughters, Rana and Daria, for enabling this work to come to be in endless ways. My daughters inspired me to initiate the Marin Dance Cooperative, and they performed with the Dancers' Workshop Company from its inception. They performed in every major dance and tour and substituted many hours of rehearsal time for play time. My husband has had a tremendous impact on my work, particularly in environmental and architectural awareness and the use of the RSVP Cycles. When the dance deck and studio were built on our land, I didn't anticipate that the boundaries between work and home would be so blurred. I want to thank my family for tolerating this infringement on their privacy for these many years.

Final notes of thanks to Janice Ross and Sally Banes for contributing essays to this collection, Rachel Kaplan for her work as the editor of this book, Suzanna Tamminen of Wesleyan University Press for her generous assistance, and the Flow Fund for its support.

Anna Halprin

For the past three years I have had the pleasurable task of being Anna Halprin's personal assistant. This means I have answered phones, typed correspondence, written and filed articles, wandered through her extensive archives, reminded her to breathe, and listened with delight to the many stories she has to tell. I have been moved by Halprin's expansive curiosity about the work to which she has so completely committed herself, and its relevance in so many spheres, and I wanted to help her create this collection which articulates, in her own words, her many thoughts, stories, visions, and scores for dances, classes, community rituals, and events. Hence this book, which spans the range of her career, from her early work as a modern dancer and teacher of children; to her challenging proscenium-breaking theater pieces; to the community-based events which marched right out of the theater and into the streets; and her later, more contemporary works, concerned largely with ritual and the healing power of dance and movement. These essays have been edited for repetition, but otherwise are printed as they were written.

A book of this nature allows us to see the evolution of an artist's thinking and approach. The writings in this volume span many decades, and consequently, some of Halprin's thematic concerns are defined in different ways over the years. For example, in 1973 a myth is a "tribal happening" created from the unification of collective energy and group consciousness; in 1974 a myth is simply an "audience participation event." In 1986 a myth "embodies a personal and collective vision of how we see ourselves and the world," and by 1993, myth is more specifically defined as "a narrative pattern giving significance to our existence, whether we invent or discover its meaning. When expressed in words, a myth is a story; in sound, it becomes music; in visual images, a painting or sculpture. Through the shaping of matter, myth becomes a dwelling, a village, a temple, an altar; through physical movement, a dance or drama." As a central quest throughout Halprin's career, the search for myth is defined over and over again in myriad ways. Because these variations give depth to the resounding themes of Halprin's long journey, the integrity of each essay has been preserved, although in the 1990s Halprin radically departs from some of her earlier beliefs. Essays exploring similar themes from different vantage points are reprinted here to create a larger portrait of Halprin's evolution as a dance artist.

Like all art, Halprin's work can be seen in light of a few simple themes which branch out in different directions but continue in a familiar refrain. To highlight these themes, the essays are not arranged chronologically but divided into three sections. Halprin's continual quest has been for a dance of meaning, one that comes from the authentic center of the person dancing. In addition to the theatrical pieces she conceived, she has also developed a number of systems for generating creativity and understanding the creative process, which have come to be called the Halprin Life/Art Process. The first section of this book, "The Halprin Life/Art Process: Theory, History, and Practice," addresses the theoretical foundations of her work, including the RSVP Cycles (developed by Lawrence Halprin), Movement Ritual, the Five Stages of Healing, and the development of community through art-making. Both the now defunct San Francisco Dancers' Workshop (1955–78) and the fully operational Tamalpa Institute (1978–present) were founded to ensure the development and deepening of the Life/Art Process. Sally Banes has contributed an introductory essay that places these discoveries within the larger context of dance history.

A unique aspect of Halprin's career has been her unfailing ability to remain contemporary—to shift her concerns to match the concerns of the time. In that light, it is no surprise that her work of the late 1960s and early '70s reflects the social upheaval of that American landscape and is concerned with racism, the development of multicultural community, and issues of power between women and men, elders and children, performers and audience. At this time, the Dancers' Workshop began to create what Halprin called Events—nearly synonymous and synchronous with Allan Kaprow's Happenings—group experiments in which audience members were an integral and creative part. Simultaneously, the Dancers' Workshop was exploring various body-centered therapies, altered states of consciousness, and shifts in lifestyle, and their work was reflective of this research. Halprin also initiated numerous street theater events and formed a multicultural dance company. The section of the book which describes this work is titled "The Work in Community." Janice Ross has contributed an essay to this section, contextualizing these developments.

During these convulsive years, Halprin discovered a convulsion of her own—cancer. This traumatic experience has changed her life and her art, and continues to determine, in large part, the direction of her activities today. After this encounter with her own mortality, she became more committed to making a useful art rather than a decorative one, and she became interested in the significant healing functions of movement as well. Large-scale experiments in community theater and healing grew out of this impetus and are described in the third and final section, "Leaning into Ritual." In an essay introducing that section, I discuss the ramifications of this direction in Halprin's career.

A portrait of Halprin's lifework would show a true search for place and meaning—for the individual and the community—in the body, in the family, and in the world. Halprin's work has grown and developed, as she has grown and developed, from the individualistic search of the "creative" artist to the more expansive search of a community leader working in service to the collective. I hope the essays in this book will give you insight into the heart and mind and work of Anna Halprin, an artist whose vision has significantly stimulated and fed generations of dance, theater, and visual artists. Her continuing challenges to become embodied, to tell our stories, to feel our lives through the center of our bodies and come together in community, represent, I believe, central human strategies for our survival.

Rachel Kaplan
June 1994

MOVING TOWARD LIFE

THE HALPRIN LIFE/ART PROCESS:

THEORY, HISTORY, AND PRACTICE

*Movements were of the
everyday sort that every-
one could identify with.
They were task oriented.
For example, build a
scaffold and when
you've built it, go up to
the top.* Parades and
Changes, *1965.*

Photographer
Unknown.

INTRODUCTION

Sally Banes

When Anna Halprin turned her back on the dance establishment in the 1950s, modern dance was at its pinnacle of achievement. Among Martha Graham's dances of that decade were *Seraphic Dialogue* and *Clytemnestra*; Doris Humphrey choreographed, taught at the Juilliard School, and wrote *The Art of Making Dances*. Charles Weidman, José Limón, Pearl Lang, Pauline Koner, Helen Tamiris and Daniel Nagrin, Anna Sokolow, and others had successful companies. Even Ruth St. Denis was still performing, and Ted Shawn still ran the Jacob's Pillow Dance Festival. Generations of younger dancers and choreographers were trained each summer there, at Hanya Holm's summer dance school at Colorado College, and at the American Dance Festival at Connecticut College. American modern dance had established itself, but the entrenched and the status quo were not Anna Halprin's metier.

Educated as a dancer under Margaret H'Doubler at the University of Wisconsin–Madison, Halprin had moved to California in 1945 with her husband, Lawrence Halprin, making a career as a New York dancer a virtual impossibility, although she had danced in Humphrey and Weidman's *Sing Out, Sweet Land* in 1944. She could have made a career for herself as a modern dancer on the West Coast: Lester Horton worked in Los Angeles until his death in 1953, and Bella Lewitzky founded her own company after leaving Horton in 1950. But Halprin chose another path.

Although her way was unique, in the 1950s she was not alone in hewing an individual path, nor was she entirely unprecedented. The tradition of modern dance itself had been founded on individual experimentation—on antiacademic principles.

NOTE

This introduction is based, in part, on information gleaned from my conversations with Anna Halprin and Janice Ross, and also from Janice Ross's forthcoming book, *Anna Halprin: Revolution for the Art of It* (Berkeley: University of California Press), as well as Anna Halprin's writings.

But to Halprin and many of her peers, what had once been a dramatically new and eloquent art form now seemed hidebound. On the East Coast, Merce Cunningham, Alwin Nikolais, James Waring, and others looked for various methods—chance, technology, collage—to escape the new academy.

At the University of Wisconsin, H'Doubler had stressed personal creativity and the scientific study of anatomy and kinesiology over the values of dance as an art form in performance. Forsaking the stylized, expressive movements and pre-scribed structures of traditional modern dance choreography, Halprin did not start from scratch; she had the H'Doublerian repertoire of movement studies at her dis-posal. But her gift was to bring these ideas to a new pitch and to place them in new contexts.

Cunningham and Halprin shared an interest in reflecting in art the arbitrari-ness of modern life through radical juxtapositions of disparate activities, undercut-ting narrative logic. Both also reacted against the emotional coloring of the modern dance establishment. If Cunningham rejected the expressionism of mod-ern dance by looking outside the self to chance procedures as a way to generate and structure movement, Halprin at first chose the opposite extreme—going deep inside the self through improvisation. This was not, as she has said, for the pur-pose of self-expression. Rather, it was to plumb the depths of the human corporeal imagination, to discover capabilities that had been stymied by the conventions of modern dance.[1] Halprin penetrated the interior of the body/mind, guiding her dancers and students to scrutinize individual anatomical workings as well as unconscious needs and desires, in the voice as well as with movement. This led to a surrealistic effect in which untrammeled psychological and movement behavior rubbed against the cool tasklike performances produced by scientific kinesiological explorations.

After thoroughly investigating improvisation with her group, however, Halprin felt the need to discover external stimuli and frameworks. This she found through various approaches, including collaborations with other artists throughout the 1960s, and a crucial abiding framework—the use of scores, which allow for individual input within an ordered collective whole.

Halprin's interest in community and the rituals that create and sustain it even-tually led her away from dance as a theatrical art and toward dance (or simply movement) as a healing art—whether in social terms, as in the healing of racial divi-sions, or in physical/psychic terms, as in her work with persons confronting cancer and HIV/AIDS. This interest in the creation of community, in turn, led her from

NOTE

1. "Yvonne Rainer Interviews Ann Halprin," this volume, p. 75.

the incorporation of ordinary life in her avant-garde dance/theater pieces toward the appreciation of the dancer in every person, whether trained to move or not. Both her commitment to community and her architectural collaborations with Lawrence Halprin steered her to the creation of environmental performances.

In many of these arenas, Halprin has been an unsung pacesetter. She disowned the modern dance world—both its technical apparatus and its production system—early on. She used nondancers in her performances. She forsook the proscenium stage, and even the familiar dance studio. Many of the new generation of iconoclasts who revitalized dance in New York in the early 1960s—including Simone Forti, Yvonne Rainer, Trisha Brown, and Meredith Monk—were inspired by their studies on the West Coast with Halprin. So were important visual artists and musicians of the next generation, including Robert Morris, LaMonte Young, and Terry Riley. Her outdoor performances in both urban and pastoral landscapes prefigured the environmental pieces that swept New York by storm in the 1970s. Since the late 1960s, she has worked with multicultural groups specifically to struggle with racial and ethnic tensions. In the 1980s and '90s, her work with men and women challenging HIV/AIDS and cancer, as well as her large group dances for the environment and for world peace, once again showed visionary thinking coupled with compassionate action.

This first section of Anna Halprin's collected writings lays out the history and theory of her lifelong exploration of dance and movement. It shows a lifetime of intelligent analysis, courageous innovation, unwavering commitment, and, above all, a passion for dance, art, and life.

THREE DECADES OF TRANSFORMATIVE DANCE

INTERVIEW BY NANCY STARK SMITH

NANCY: *Today is April 13, 1989, we're in Kentfield, California, at Anna's house. We're having a talk about work that Anna's done over the years that relates to social and political issues.*

ANNA: Dealing with issues has many layers. It's only political when it begins to affect our economy. But it can affect us culturally. It can affect us deeply emotionally. We can say that the Watts riots, which I'm going to get into later, was a political issue, but it was much more than a political issue. It was a cultural issue of a dominant Anglo-Saxon society over a subdominant minority culture. It was an issue of prejudice which is a psychological, emotional issue. So when I think of issues I really tend to think of them on all those layers simultaneously. When they are deep enough in our culture they will ultimately affect our economy and then they become political and social. So that's a good landmark to know when something has gone that deep.

I think of the late '50s and up to the mid-'60s as being a very crucial time in the arts for dealing with one of the most prevalent issues of the time which was anti-establishment, and which led to the hippie movement. During that period we were often referred to as avant-garde. Though we were doing things that were new or against the common values, we were really attempting to search out what was authentic, what was real, as opposed to accepting what was the conformity of the time.

NANCY: *Artistically or socially?*

ANNA: Both. Because they were completely connected. Simple things, like modern dance had become accepted. You had the three or four major dance companies. All

NOTE

Nancy Stark Smith is the editor of *Contact Quarterly* in collaboration with Lisa Nelson. She is one of the leading innovators of Contact Improvisation.

the Graham dancers looked alike. All the Humphrey dancers looked alike. You looked like the person who was leading your company, who in a sense was a guru. Your movement style, your philosophy, everything. You wore the same kinds of costumes. And you always went with bare feet. It wasn't just me who felt that rebellion. Musicians were rebelling, like Terry Riley and LaMonte Young, against Stockhausen or whoever was the traditional modern musician of the time.

NANCY: *On what level do you think you were challenging the tradition?*

ANNA: Movement, particularly. There was the Graham style, etc. And that became very much a conformity. So all of that had to be reexamined. You had to find new compositional forms as well as new movement. That's how the whole idea of task-oriented movement and my particular interest in Mabel Todd and her approach in her book *The Thinking Body* arose at the time. I was interested in going back to my roots with my original teacher, Margaret H'Doubler, where we really looked at movement from the point of view of anatomy and kinesiology with a strong emphasis on creativity. And so I started doing improvisation as a way of getting away from the a-b-a forms. Looking at space differently. Why did we have to be in a proscenium arch? If you did perform in a stage area then you used the aisles, the ceiling, and you used the pit, all the inside and the outside spaces. And along with that you began to take issue with what your role was as a dancer. Who said we couldn't speak, sing, build environments? You didn't have to go around with bare feet, you could wear shoes, dresses, or no clothes at all and go naked.

When we did *Parades and Changes* in New York City and used nudity, I was very surprised when we started getting the kinds of reviews we did. It was made fun of by the *New York Times*: "The no-pants dancers from San Francisco." We were not self-conscious about what we were doing. It seemed to us a very natural thing to do. It was very natural to the other artists we were working with. That was a time when there were all these interdisciplinary connections, we were breaking down the narrow role of the dancer. The dancer could be a musician, a musician could be a dancer, the audience could participate. And we were so dead serious about it, it seemed so absolutely normal to us. Also I was surprised because we had gone to Sweden where there was nothing radical about what we did. The use of nudity was accepted as a ceremony of trust.

It occurred to me that we were doing something very anti-establishment in New York when we started taking our clothes off and we could hear people in the audience whisper, "Oh, they're not going to do it . . . Oh my God . . . they did it." And I saw policemen backstage. Before *Parades and Changes,* we had done other kinds of smaller performances but this was the first major full-length piece by the Dancers' Workshop.

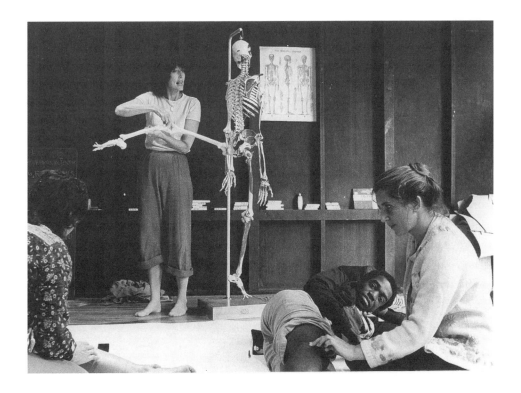

We look at movement from the point of view of anatomy and kinesiology. Norma Leistiko teaching in the training program, 1974.

Photographer
Unknown.

As we began to perform some of our smaller pieces, we began to notice that the audience was getting very unglued. They either wanted to do it with us, at us, or somehow or other be involved. And so they started throwing things at us, yelling and shouting and really getting very [*laughter*] involved.

NANCY: *What were you actually doing?*

ANNA: We were doing things that were very unexpected. Breaking rules without letting them in on it. Going into their territory. I mean I buy a ticket and I sit in my seat, somehow or other I'm buying my space. And what are you doing in my space? What are the boundaries now? You're getting me all stirred up; does this give me permission to react any way I want? So I began to realize that we were breaking tradition, that we were involving other people who weren't in on the process. And so as a result of that, they're telling us something, which led us to do scores for all the people to perform.

In a way, that kind of audience reaction had its own excitement and certainly on a social level was making a statement about "anti"; anti-this, anti-that, react, make your voice felt. What was instructive about that response was that it was part of the times. People rebelling and being very dramatic, saying, "I want to be heard!" But it stopped right there. We felt there was a lot of power there and it wasn't being channelled in a creative way.

NANCY: *Would you say that audience reaction was the issue, the driving force?*

ANNA: Absolutely. It was a great driving force. Without that reaction I think we would have gotten stuck in our own indulgent way of just doing our own exploration, forgetting that the audience is who you are performing for.

NANCY: *What were you actually exploring in that work?*

ANNA: Well, we made everything absolutely visible. The stage was completely visible, stripped of curtains, flats. The light sources were completely visible, movements were everyday movements that everybody could identify with. They were task-oriented. Like "build a scaffold and when you've built it, go up to the top." They were risky and they made people excited and created a kind of a tension. The music was live by people we collaborated with who sometimes became dancers, like sometimes we became sculptors. So that was very unfamiliar, people would get charged up. Emotionally insecure.

NANCY: *It sounds like you started out with the kind of mood of the times, of challenging the assumptions that were in your field, and in the process you realized that you were cutting across more than artistic boundaries but also social taboos. Was there political content in any other way?*

The automobile created a wonderful environment for movement. I was attracted to it as a prop with so many possibilities—visual, audible, kinesthetic, symbolical. From Automobile Event, *A. A. Leath and Lucy Lewis, 1620 Montgomery Street, San Francisco, 1968.*

Photo by
Rudy Bender.

Automobile Event, *Norma Leistiko facing camera, John Graham on car, 1968.*

Photo by
Rudy Bender.

ANNA: In a sense, yes. There were very few grants in those days, and they were very small. One of the reasons we took to the streets, just went outside, was that this was a place to perform. A place where you could have ready-made audiences. You didn't have to go through the expense and the machinery of putting out brochures, getting the press and renting halls. And audiences would be wherever they were. We wanted to perform. So we went to the streets, to beaches, to bus stops, to abandoned buildings, to anywhere.

Well, this became a political issue as we found ourselves getting arrested over and over again. It became a political issue regarding the right of using the street territory. When were we obstructing the peace? We were behaving in a way people were unfamiliar with and people would get irritated about it. So finally we did a march with blank placards, as a procession through the city. Well there was an ordinance that you have to have a permit if there were more than 25 people in the group. So we would have 24 people go at a time and then we'd leave a space of about a block between us, but we kept it going. We had a hundred people or so doing this.

What we were really trying to build up to was a dance throughout the whole city. You could get permission to perform in a park, but we wanted to be able to use the whole city as we wanted to. So in a way we were rebelling against the restrictions that were put on artists performing in the environment.

NANCY: *So it wasn't that the piece was a political satire, but the doing of it was challenging some political definition. Where did it go from there?*

ANNA: Making scores for an audience to perform. We did a series at the San Francisco Museum of Modern Art, open to the public, where we led 100 to 500 people in performing various scores. This led to the development of *Citydance*, which was performed from sunrise to sunset, in subways, neighborhoods, parks, plazas, hillsides and the ocean. We did *Citydance* for three years as a statement that the city was a place to be creatively enjoyed by all its inhabitants.

Then in '64 and '65 we began to go back to exploring on a personal level, and the workshop modality became very important for us. We wanted to withdraw and look at a more inner world within the person. Really study the social terrain of the

We began to pay atten-
tion to the feedback
process between move-
ment and feeling. Circle
the Earth, *1985.*

Photo by
Paul Fusco.

person, the whole person. This was at the time of the human potential movement. This was the time also that we began our first serious training program.

NANCY: *When you say "whole" person, what do you mean?*

ANNA: The emotional life, which dancers rarely study. Dancers studied movement. But movement is related to feeling, and we had no system for looking at those feelings that were evoked through movement. Nor did we have any idea of how the mind was really functioning in relation to movement or feeling.

During that period in the '60s, there were all these conferences on body-mind-spirit, as if they were separate. But in terms of what we were exploring, we said there is no separation. They're in a single impulse. There is the mind working in terms of images which think faster than the linear verbal thinking process. But images are like dreams. They go instantaneously with the movement, with the impulse to move, and the feeling. And so we were working with that integrated power. And at the same time realizing that was also taking us to the connection between artistic growth and personal growth, and that the two went hand in hand. And this was, again, part of a larger issue going on: the Human Potential Movement, which has had an incredible impact, all over the world.

Now what that led us to was dealing with real-life issues. And it's as if all the work up to this point was laying the groundwork to deal with real-life issues. All this was the foundation.

NANCY: *You've got the context of the society and then you've got the individual.*

ANNA: And we've got the tools. We developed a system of movement, a system of working with emotions. We studied eight years with Fritz Perls, who worked with Gestalt Therapy, which is "the whole is greater than the parts." He worked specifically with our company. So we had this system for working with emotional material that came up and also with imagery. This is called the PsychoKinetic-Visualization process, which we use now with people challenging AIDS and cancer. But we developed that then.

NANCY: *When you say you developed "a system of movement," what do you mean?*

ANNA: Simply that if you do not teach people a traditional or idiosyncratic style and instead you set up a situation to move in, you systematically give people the opportunity to develop a full range of original movement. You set up movement situations that evoke emotional responses, situations in which the movements may be extremely assertive or very passive, or with partners in intimate contact. This will tend to bring up a lot of emotional material, which we then process. We do a lot of drawings of images and dance them. That's called the PsychoKinetic-Visualization process.

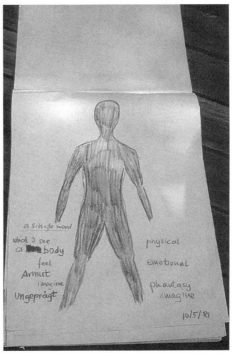

In dealing with real-life issues, we had to find a way of moving, feeling, and making images. These three images show the development of the self-portrait work done by Nicolette Uta, 1987.

Photos by
Anna Halprin.

In dealing with real-life issues, to be totally authentic, we had to find a way of moving, feeling and thinking that would become new tools. Like when I got cancer, and I wanted to deal with that issue on a level of healing. I had to have an open-ended vocabulary. How did I know what I was going to do until I worked with it? If I had a stylization of movement, it would have been predictable. I could not have gotten past what I already know.

One of the things about working with real-life issues is that it can be transformative. You work with an issue because it is unresolved, and through the dance, we hope to discover new possibilities. It's not about the dancers and it's not an interpretation of a theme, it is real. And by doing it you get to a different place with that issue, and in your life. The dance changes the dancer.

The purpose is to create change. That's when we started using the word "ritual." To distinguish that from dance as entertainment, dance as spectacle. Not that it couldn't be a spectacle or it couldn't be entertaining, but that is not the purpose. So that became a very important shift for me. And so we developed the RSVP Cycles in which people were able to learn how to score in a very direct and simple way. And this made it possible for us now to deal with groups of people. Because an individual can kind of feel things out, be intuitive, but if you're dealing with groups of people, you can't just feel things out and be intuitive.

Through the RSVP Cycles people can validate what they are doing in terms of their own experience. I wanted to create something for a group of people to do in which they're given the opportunity to explore the theme and find out what's real for them, find out what our differences are and what our commonalities are. It's a particular way of being a choreographer. It allows for social impact in process as well as in the final product.

We did ten myths for small audiences. It was really a research process because I wanted to find out what were the natural forms that groups did. If you got a group of 50 people together and you gave them a very open score, what would they do? Because finding order is biologically how we're made. We can't exist in a totally random form.

NANCY: *What are you hoping to change as people are finding their own creativiy and moving through these various forms that arise?*

ANNA: In those exploratory myths, the purpose was to empower people to create together and to impart the experience of the power that comes from cooperating through movement as a collective body and find out what are the collective forms and perhaps even the archetypes.

This led to another issue that was coming up. I was invited to the American Humanist Psychology Conference on androgyny. And this was about the time,

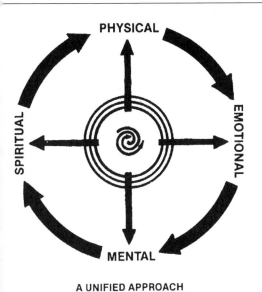

A UNIFIED APPROACH

DEEPENED LIFE EXPERIENCE

EXPANDED ART EXPRESSION

1. BODY/MOVEMENT & DANCE   2. PEOPLES   3. ENVIRONMENT

TECHNIQUES (partial list)

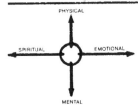

PHYSICAL
Anatomy & Kinesiology; Structural intergration; Movement Rituals I, II & III and variations; Movement exploration; Rhythmic & Movement Analysis; Space, Time & Force studies; Improvisation; Tamalpa Bodywork; Passive/Active, Blending; Partner & Group Interactions.

EMOTIONAL
Gestalt Processes; 5 Part Process; Emotional Scripting; Attitudinal studies; Visualizations

MENTAL
Theory; Journals; RSVP Cycles (Collective Creativity); Communication Skills; Scores; Movement Sciences.

SPIRITUAL
Personal rituals; Social rituals; Environmental rituals; Meditation

PROGRESSIONS

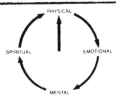

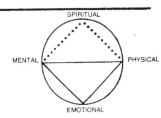

MOVEMENT AWARENESS, CONNECTED TO FEELINGS, CONCIOUSLY UNDERSTOOD, THEN TRANSFORMED TO UNIVERSAL PRINCI-PLES — REINTERGRATED FOR ONGOING DE-VELOPMENT.

© S.F.D.W. 1980   Anna Halprin

Principles of a creative process.

about 1967 I think, when the feminist movement was just getting hot. And the whole question of male and female differences or alikeness, the concept of androgyny, was on everybody's lips. I felt that what was going on at that time was creating a tremendous cultural upheaval. Families were being drastically affected by the feminist movement, the workplace was being affected, people at that time felt that the feminist movement was the biggest cultural and economic and political issue that would hit us in this century.

So I had an opportunity to deal with that issue at this conference. I just had the men dance alone. And had the women just watch. Then I had the women dance alone and I had the men just watch. And after this whole conference in which everybody was intellectualizing about the male and female issues and that we're alike and that the only reason that we're different is because of conditioning processes and so forth, we did this dance. They had exactly the same score. And it was just astonishing. I mean, it was funny, we all laughed at ourselves. We cried, we got so excited, because it was such a relief for the men to be together, to do their work and to work as a team, and to do their kind of movement. And the women were so delighted to be together as women and they had a totally different tone about what they did. Then when the men and women came together, they came together with mutual respect. That was truly a transformative experience.

The issues we had been dealing with at the conference were not the real issue. The issue was—we are different and it doesn't matter that we're different. What matters is that we're able to respect our differences and bring those differences together and find our commonality.

NANCY: *Where did you go from there?*

ANNA: About this same time I got a call from James Woods in Watts asking if I would do a performance at the Mark Taper [Theater] with my company. This was at the time they were having the riots in Watts in 1967. His idea was that the Studio Watts, the black community, would bring us down to the Mark Taper, which is like the Opera House. It's the big theater in the middle of Los Angeles. And Watts is in the ghetto. And I said, "No, no. Instead of bringing me in as a symbol, we're going to take on this issue of the separation that you feel in a ghetto from not being part of the mainstream and the cultural life. I will come down and work with an all-black group in Studio Watts for a year." Which I did, every Saturday. And I said I'd work simultaneously in San Francisco and start a new company, all-white. We'll start exactly at the same time and it'll just be two new groups doing the same scores.

At the end of the year I brought the black group up to San Francisco and the two groups essentially spent 24 hours a day together for 10 days. We developed a dance based on our encounter, our prejudice. We performed it at the Mark Taper Theater in Los Angeles. It was called *Ceremony of Us.*

The dance showed the whole process of how these two groups came together. We started separate and then we showed the conflict and confrontation and so forth. And then at the end, the performers came out and did a procession and gathered the audience. And when we went outside to the Mark Taper Plaza we were all dancing together. So the transformation was not just in the performers. But our purpose was to bring it out into the audience.

NANCY: *Do you wait for an actual transformation in the workshop process to show you what forms to use, or do you just lay out a symbolic structural transformation and let it happen in the performance?*

ANNA: I know what you're saying. No, you can't score a transformation. In the Watts/S.F. workshops, I had each group work separately on the same score. It was a simple follow-the-leader type of score. When we came together for the first time, the Watts group did the black dance for the whites and then the S.F. group of whites danced for the blacks. Then the next score was to do these two lines, the black and the white, at the same time so you both have to use the same space. But what happened is that they started interacting. Cutting through lines. They tried to take the people out of one line and seduce them to their group, and all hell broke loose. It became very competitive but in a charged and creative way. Issues of how far you would go with the movement came up. The degree of outrageousness was a big issue. All the issues came out that first day, and most of them were unresolved. So then we had to deal with setting up situations where we could explore issues of competition, leadership, sexuality, abandonment, issues of self-esteem. We had no notion beforehand what the outcome would be. It took its own form as we danced the issues that emerged.

NANCY: *In what way does the RSVP Cycles allow people to participate in the creation of the event?*

ANNA: You see, the RSVP Cycles wasn't developed when I first was doing the black and white *Ceremony of Us.* We developed it *because* of that, because we didn't have a common language for communicating. Our way of speaking, and our language and our images were so different we weren't hearing each other. We didn't know how. So we developed this RSVP Cycles so that we could listen to each other and find a way to respect our differences and find our commonality.

The RSVP Cycles is so simple. You take the creative process and you look at it in four different ways. One is collecting Resources, the other is Scoring, the other is Performing, and the fourth is Valuacting. Now, when you collect resources, you collect them objectively or subjectively. That includes what we are trying to achieve by it, what are the changes we want to create, what is the theme? What are our resources, our people resources, our movement resources that we might use in this, our space resources, our prop resources, whatever . . . it's like an inventory. What is possible? Everybody chips in. This is my idea. My ideas are resources. And then we take those resources and we start to score them. We score them in relation to activity, over time, in space, with people. Now we know where that score came from. The score is graphic and absolutely visible. We put the score up and we try it. We perform it. And then after we perform it we valuact it. We say, it didn't work, or it did work. Or I liked this, or I didn't like that. What new resources do we need, how can we change the score? So we're very involved in it.

NANCY: *How are you making decisions together?*

ANNA: There's always a facilitator. Sometimes in scoring, it's done totally cooperatively. Other times, I'll come in with, "These are the resources I got from watching you. This is the score I think will work. Do you have anything to add to that?" And then we will valuact it. But they still feel invested in it because they've been able to take those themes and explore them and understand what it means to them on a personal level. They've been able to validate those scores in terms of their own personal experience. That's how it works.

What happened in Watts was that through the workshop and by doing these movements together and by dancing together and drawing and making our images, we developed into a loyal group. We started out being scared to death of each other. And curious. It's hard to believe this but in '67 this was the first time that this particular group from Watts had ever been in any kind of an intimate relationship with a group of white people. And vice versa.

It was also an issue of economics. I would say that the black group was essentially poor. The white group may not have been individually affluent, but we had resources. It was a totally different economic situation between groups. That was an issue too. And in 10 days we became absolutely loyal as a group. Not separate. We kept saying, "If we can't solve our differences and our problems, do you think the world out there can? We've got to do this and we've got to show the world that we can do this." When we performed it at Mark Taper it was like—See, we can do this. We can live a different life. And we did do it. There was an interracial marriage, there were lifelong friendships.

That was our first big real political issue, social issue, that had a huge impact. Not only in Watts but up here [in the San Francisco Bay Area]. We started a multiracial company as a result of that, which was called the Reach Out Program and was funded by NEA's Expansion Arts Program for 12 years. Then we toured all

kinds of places, including the American Dance Festival, Soledad Prison, neighborhood theaters, schools and colleges, and began to take on Chicanos and Asians,
American Indians. It became very apparent to me that dance had been dominated
by an Anglo-Saxon culture. I was just astonished at the prejudices that I didn't even
know I had. I didn't know a damn about this scope of movement on an ethnic level.
The company began to develop classes in black dance. Not like Harlem ballet, but
rather out of the origins of black dance.

Each member of the multiracial company went through a training program,
and they developed their own form of dance which came right out of the street—
the Asians developed their form of Asian dance, and American Indian dance, and it
just was wonderful.

We had to develop a new criteria for movement, and we did this through a
new theater piece called *Animal Ritual.* Because I found that if we used animal
imagery, we could all use our own cultural background and it wouldn't matter. We
did this dance at the American Dance Festival.

So that went on for 12 years. The impact lasted for 12 years. Until Reagan
came in and Expansion Arts guidelines changed completely and we lost our support.

NANCY: *Really! Was that a natural cycle for it or do you think it was cut off?*

ANNA: It was cut off. Prematurely. There was a lot more work we could have
done. A lot of these people in the company were developing themselves as artists,
they just needed another boost. However, many of them to this day are doing their
own thing. Just today somebody called me from the company and said, "I've just
been reading about the drug warfares that are going on in San Francisco and it's getting so bad that black people are saying that the young people are killing each other
off and I can't stand this any longer. I'm going to see if I can set up some workshops in the Hunters Point area and start some activities there based on the RSVP
Cycles, and see if I can be a force in turning this thing around." So it seems like it's
recycling.

There was continuous development and research around our processes that we
were constantly sharpening. Every time we'd do something there were always new
challenges that we'd then try to incorporate in our training and in our work, try to
understand a little better. So we always were having our workshops going on and
trying to develop our systems.

And then I would always have these projects I personally was interested in.
Somebody came to me and said, "Would you do something at our gerontology
society?" and suddenly I became interested in the whole issue of the aging process
and realized that that was a big issue. Economic and political. In preparing for the

workshop, I thought, "What are the issues for them?" For me, the issue was that old people, again, are isolated. The same issues come up over and over again: isolation, separation, and fear. It comes down to that every single time. The issues with the blacks, the issues with *Citydance,* male and female—isolation, alienation, separation, and *fear!*

Then for quite awhile I didn't do anything because I didn't have anything that excited me, that seemed real, that was a real issue, till we had the murder on the mountain [Mt. Tamalpais]. Then that started this generic cycle which we now call *Circle the Earth.* It started in 1981 with a two-day and night dance called *In and On the Mountain* and the issue was the killer on the mountain.

There was a trailside killer who'd been on Mt. Tamalpais and killed seven women on the trails over the course of two years, and so the trails were closed, and this became a spiritual issue, because the mountain was closed to us. I felt that the issue there was violence in our society, and the attack of our spiritual dimension, because the mountain is the spiritual symbol in our landscape. It's where people go to meditate, where people go to return to nature, where people go for the sense of returning to their roots, their nature. It's the highest spot. It has this symbolic shape to it of yearning, of seeking, and that really got to me. I really got enraged over the sense that this was being taken from our community at a time when I felt this is what our search was. In the '80s, our search was for spiritual meaning, for the purpose of our life. We were facing extinction, on every level. What was the meaning of our life? What did we have to live for? I felt that was the most crucial issue.

I didn't start out by saying, "We're going to dance about the killer on the mountain." I just said, "What's the myth in this community?" What are our myths to live by? I just put it out in the community that we were going to do an exploration of, a search for, living myths, and we were going to do it through movement and the environment. One hundred people came, and we worked for nine months and sure enough the mountain kept reappearing in everybody's drawings. I said, "What is this saying to you?" And all of a sudden, "Phew," big explosion. We are enraged, we've been disempowered, we have no channel to express our feeling. So that became the myth and the issue—the violence on our mountain.

That first time, the Tamalpa company did the dance for the community, using the resources we developed in the workshop. But we were still dancing in the theater. Then we went up to the mountain with 80 people and did various activities at the top—planted trees, read poetry, sang songs. We defied the killer and we walked down the mountain. Our purpose was to reclaim the mountain. A few days after the performance the killer was caught. The tip came from someone in the community. Now the community felt they were part of it.

Then Don Jose Mitsuwa, a Huichol Indian, came to me and said, "The healing of the mountain will not work unless you do it for five years."

So we did a series for five years. Always with the company. I never particularly felt the performances worked. We would take a different theme every year. The big change came when it became a peace dance. The idea was that we would exemplify a peaceful way of being through the way we created the dance. And also, I said, "We can't do a peace dance with a company. It's got to be done with 100 people." I just knew that it had to be a huge scale. And 100 people had to learn how to work together in nine days. That fast. Because there was urgency behind it.

What I required was that they find a conflict in their personal life, in their family life, in a community or in a relationship and that they find a way to resolve that peacefully, and find peace in themselves. After the dance they were required to make a specific application, in their life, and in the world. They were to join a group, or make a donation, or they had to do a peaceful act, in the world. It wasn't enough to just dance it.

We took the dance to different places in the world and different groups would have different visions and different ideas. I'd pick up an idea from people who did it in Switzerland and share it with the people in Australia. And the people in Australia introduced the didgeridoo and I would bring that back here. So it was wonderful because by the time I'd bring the dance back home it was totally different because of the input I'd gotten from everywhere I'd been. Then that led to the idea of wanting to be able to all connect at the same time. So we began the *Planetary Dance.*

By 1988, we had 73 groups in 36 countries performing a score called "The Earth Run," from *Circle the Earth,* every spring at the same time. That brought up for me the need and the importance of a planetary consciousness as another issue. That we needed to expand and find new ways that we could link together so that never again could we feel ourselves as nation against nation.

Then, this year, 1989, was perhaps the most challenging, the most rewarding performance which I've experienced in my whole life. This was dealing with the AIDS issue. It was the AIDS issue, but the myth is—how do we deal with death. This has been my personal issue since I had cancer in 1972. And this is where my personal research and my competence was put to test. Because for me, this dance was the ultimate test of dance. First of all, the alienation and fear around AIDS in this area is intense. People with AIDS are feeling totally isolated and discriminated against and fearful. I said, what we're going to do is get people with HIV positive, ARC and AIDS, and I'm going to work with them for a year, which I have been doing. I'm working with a women's group called Women with Wings, Women with AIDS. I've been working with the Steps Theater Company, People Challenging AIDS. We've been working with the men since last June ('88) and with the women for about six months. Separate, because the women originally were working with the men but they said that they had separate issues.

Then I said, "It's time now to invite the community to come and dance with us. To join us. To support us." Up until one week before the event, we only had 40 people. It was like people got cold feet. They're afraid of getting AIDS. And even the people with AIDS weren't registering—"Can I trust this process? I'm making myself totally visible." I was just freaking out, they won't do it. Only 40 people, I can't believe this. So I did a massive telephoning. I just called everybody and all they needed was reassurance. Finally, by the last week we had about 35 people with HIV, ARC and AIDS dancing in the workshop with 70 people who didn't have it, totalling over 100 people.

The issues were so real and so devastating, and so powerful. We were dealing with death as a way of living life fully now. And we were dancing with people who are in fact facing the issues of death. And people who were scared, "Will I get AIDS?" And the dance, which was *Circle the Earth*—this time called *Dancing with Life on the Line*, totally changed. You couldn't recognize it as the same dance.

I asked each person with AIDS to come forward onto the space and call a support person that doesn't have HIV or AIDS, that you've made friends with, call them out. Then I said, "Why did you call them, what are they to you?" Each person had a different issue, and they used it in the performance. For example, a young man called out, "Andy—I've fallen in love with you. Will you still love me with the AIDS virus?" One girl called Urike out and said, "Urike, are you still afraid of getting AIDS from me?" And Urike faced her and said, "I was at the beginning, I'm not now. Now I'm afraid that I don't have any purpose in my life. And that I will die without any purpose." Somebody else called someone out and said, "Will you be there for me if I get really sick?" and she answered, "I will love you, I will support you, I will not let you out of my sight!"

It was really touching. These were real issues that they were dealing with, put into performance. And at the end of the performance, people felt so empowered, so together. The people in the audience, the witnesses, would cheer them. The performers started the dance by running forward and shouting, "I want to live!" The witnesses were with them and so supportive—crying and laughing and clapping and cheering, tears just streaming from their eyes.

A parent came up to me saying, "We didn't know our son had AIDS until the performance. It's his way of telling us."

And so the dance did work. It transformed. It brought people together, they overcame their fear and isolation. We did a restoration at the end of the dance. We invited any witness who had HIV, ARC or AIDS to come into the center and be restored. And anybody who'd lost a lover or a friend or a member of the family, to

*STEPS Theater
Company for People
Challenging AIDS per-
forms a triumphant
dance of the immune
system, San Francisco,
1988.*

Photo by
Margaretta Mitchell.

come and join in the circle, to be restored. And then anyone who chooses to support it. And gradually everybody joined.

I have never had an opportunity to do anything that was so bottom line. This is the real stuff. Where do you go from here? You know, this is dying or living. What people are capable of doing when they're motivated is astonishing. And one man who was scheduled for a blood transfusion didn't have to have one, his T-cell count went up from 40 to 250 in five days which means his immune system has strengthened. So that dance, in terms of dealing with an issue, was for me the most successful because it worked one hundred percent.

NANCY: *How is an event both successful on the level of the issue, and to you artistically? It has to be meaningful and authentic, and at the same time it has to "work."*

ANNA: That's right. My greatest challenge is to confront issues authentically and at the same time develop scores that generate powerful creativity for the dancers. I want social issues to be expressed imaginatively and in what to me is good art. I'm terribly concerned that when I take on a social issue it should not completely overshadow the artistic aspect. This has been a problem for me.

I wasn't excited about the first few mountain series dances, because I was still working with a limited company concept. And I didn't feel the form was original or sufficiently reflective of the content. I didn't start getting excited until we started working with groups of 100 people and I could begin working with all kinds of people, dancers and nondancers who were totally committed to the issues of peace and healing. And working under the pressure of five days to create and perform the dance meant that participants were required to cooperate at a very high state of alertness. And by necessity the scores had to be essential and archetypal.

I guess I'm also, at heart, a theater person. I've been in theater all my life and I think of myself as an artist, a theater artist. I was at a dance critics conference and I was referred to as doing religious dance. I don't do religious dance! It's not religious, it's not political, it's not therapy, it's not anthropology, it's not sociology, and yet it's all of those things. I've come to trust that because I am an artist, and come from that perspective, that what I make is art.

THE MARIN COUNTY DANCE CO-OPERATIVES:

TEACHING DANCE TO CHILDREN

I began to teach dance to children in 1940 as a student intern at the University of Wisconsin where I was getting my undergraduate degree. In Boston (1942–43) I taught children again, both at a settlement house for impoverished youth and at a private school for children from wealthy families. I learned an important lesson during these years about the environmental influences on movement, socialization, and childhood development. When I moved to Marin County I became instrumental in developing the Marin County Dance Co-operatives (1947), and through the Dance Co-op I taught dance for the next twenty-five years to children in the community where I lived. I loved teaching children, although I did not value it in the same way I valued my life as a performing artist, and I learned many things about creativity and spontaneity from children, which later found their way into my work as a performer and teacher of other artists.

The following text is excerpted from my writings of 1949–57.

THE MARIN COUNTY DANCE CO-OPERATIVES

The Marin County Dance Co-operatives are a collective enterprise, fueled by the energy of the parents, children, and all the communities involved. The mothers assume the responsibility of management. Together, they design exhibits and posters and plan special events to keep the whole community informed of the activities of the dance cooperatives. The purpose of the Dance Co-ops is to give Bay Area children and adults an experience in creative dance and an awareness of the potential of rhythm and movement as they are manifest in daily life. The co-operatives are entirely independent organizations functioning under the management and supervision of community members. The Dancers' Workshop faculty provides qualified instruction and assures the maintenance of the highest possible educational standards, but it is the voluntary participation of the parents and friends which makes these classes

The children are fully participating on all levels: they're making music; they're in their own circle; they are supporting one of their playmates; they're being given responsibility to create their own experience.

Photo by
Ernest Braun, 1953.

From the response of the children, the teacher gets her cue whether to dance about fairies and flowers or fire engines and scribbly houses.

Photographer
Unknown.

possible at a minimum cost and well within the means of the average family group.[1]
At this time, there are fifteen dance co-ops functioning in various communities in the
area and it has been estimated that these co-operatives provide direct opportunities
for dance training to more than two thousand people each year.

The Marin County Dance Co-operatives are a fascinating and successful
example of the organic development of dance within the life of a modern community. To my knowledge, these co-operatives constitute a unique experiment in the
United States. After three years, they have grown in size, number and general community acceptance. Every indication exists that they fulfill a real need in the life of
this California community. We believe the story of the Marin County Dance Co-
operatives is applicable to other communities and other areas of life.

The immediate stimulus for beginning the co-operatives was a children's
demonstration of dance that I coordinated. Some Marin County parents were present and pounced on the idea of dance classes with great enthusiasm. They decided
at once that Marin should have dance classes of that sort and determined to organize the classes themselves. Meetings were called by the parents, and almost
overnight, a space was allocated for classes, which started naturally enough with the
little girls. Soon there were demands for boys classes, and the mothers bought
themselves leotards. Classes grew and grew, and the co-operatives became more
active. Soon dance concerts and demonstrations were sponsored and dance litera-
ture was made available to the community. The moving force behind the whole
organization are the hardworking mothers who, having organized the classes, collected tuition, checked on attendance, and arranged for classrooms, keep the co-
operatives functioning. They have not only kept the classes active and alive, but
have made the whole idea an important element in the life of the community.
Through them, dance has extended its influence throughout the whole fabric of
Marin County.

What is the significance of the Marin County Dance Co-operatives? First,
they are symbolic of the possibility of re-establishing a community's direct participation in an art form. Second, the dance artist and teacher has been given the digni-
ty of place within her own community. Third, because of the non-profit element of
the co-operative, large numbers of people can afford dance classes. This will, it is
hoped, raise the level of excellence in the dance product.

Probably the most exciting aspect of this experiment is to see art fuse with the
life of a community, to watch its influence on children and adults, and to see it

NOTE

1. Classes cost fifty cents apiece. Teachers for the co-ops were trained at Dancers' Workshop and included A. A. Leath,
Norma Leistiko, John Graham, and many others.

*The children are tuning up
their senses.*

Photo by
Ernest Braun, 1953.

*Children using streamers to
experience the visual patterns
of their movement.*

Photo by
Ernest Braun, 1953.

grow from something alien and esoteric to something very alive and close and fun to be part of—truly a co-operative, communal enterprise.

THE ROLE OF THE TEACHER

It is important that the child's everyday experience be brought into focus by the teacher in the dance class. It is also an enhancement that the teacher add to whatever is lacking in the child's realm of experience. The teacher can bring this approach to class by knowing the characteristics of the child's age level, being aware of her background influences and keeping up with the subjects she is learning in school. The teacher must also have established a friendly and sympathetic atmosphere in the classroom so that the children are free to respond. From the response of the children, the teacher can get her cue whether to dance about fairies and flowers or fire engines and scribbly houses, or just a wiggly movement with a sudden stop. In teaching this way, you never know exactly what will happen in advance of a class. The teacher must plan, but the plans need to be flexible. Therefore a children's class is never repeated the same way twice. Each class should be a creation in itself—a completed dance drama that captures the essence of a child's life in that one moment.

DANCE EDUCATION AND TRAINING

We can think of training, first of all, in terms of a learning process. For a child to learn and to progress in technical training, she must have a desire and interest in this direction. What an enthusiastic student she will become if she is aware not only of "what" she is doing but "why" she is doing it. If her technical training is grounded in a kinesthetic awareness of movement, it will be a pleasurable experience. If, in the presentation of a movement idea, the teacher permits the student to take an active role in its development and she is given the freedom to try for herself until the movement "feels right," she will be able to find meaning in what she is doing.

The child strives for perfection because she understands what she is doing. Her effort takes on purpose, and her attitude will be alert and inquisitive. Over a period of time, she develops initiative and self-discipline. She finds a zest and joy in the learning process. She must be continually activated in her learning in order to develop. A wise teacher will give increasing demands and challenges with very careful respect to the child's level of development, thereby avoiding discouragement and frustration by not forcing the child beyond her capacity. The child, when ready to meet these new demands, can then work with concentration for the desired control and refinement. Her achievement of these ideals will give her the motivation to continue.

In addition to the process of learning, there is a question—"*What* is she learning?" She is learning the science of body movement itself, rhythmic factors, elements of force and space, and the relationships of moving with other people, among other things. She is also learning how to discover dance ideas from what she feels, sees and hears. She learns how to use the materials of dance to shape movement experiences into patterns and to create forms for her dance ideas. The result is that her knowledge is not limited to rigid techniques but rather to fundamental materials of dance that draw upon the vast potential resources of the child herself and the principles of art.

A technical training of this nature will enable the child to acquire aesthetic values of images of beauty that emerge out of her own well-spring of responses. What one child has created is shared with others in the class, what they have created as a group is shared together, and in this way, the children gain from each other a breadth of aesthetic values. Because each child has formed her expression in her own way, there are individual differences. Seeing these differences helps all the children be flexible and open-minded, and appreciative and responsive to the feelings and attitudes of others.

A training which integrates technique with expression at every level of the child's growth will bring forth a child who dances with spontaneity, the freshness and vitality of the expressive mind flowing through the muscles and nerves. When children are trained in the disciplines of intrinsic art principles, they dance with great grace and freedom.

MOVEMENT RITUAL I

Try this experiment: *Make a list of your senses, and put them in the order that you first think of them. Avoid looking at my list until you have made your own. Did your list go something like this:*

1st *Sight*
2nd *Sound*
3rd *Smell*
4th *Touch*
5th *Taste*

THE KINESTHETIC SENSE

There is a good chance that you did not mention the kinesthetic sense at all. Most people do not. What is the kinesthetic sense? The kinesthetic sense has end-organs and nerve endings in our muscles, tendons, ligaments, bones and joints that make it possible for us to have any awareness of our movements. Nerve endings in the inner ear allow us to know our body placement in space and our body directions. All of these are part of the proprioceptive nervous system. I can conceivably imagine living without any one of the senses listed above, but can you imagine living without any awareness of your movement? You'd bump into everything, stumble and fall down all the time. You wouldn't even be able to eat because you couldn't get food into your mouth. If you can imagine what it would be like to live *without* a kinesthetic

NOTE

This article is the introduction to the book *Movement Ritual I*, published by San Francisco Dancers' Workshop in 1975 and illustrated by Charlene Koonce. As a movement form, *Movement Ritual I* is an attempt to organize and structure a basic range of ordinary movement within the human body, with the hope that this structure will provide a useful and valid approach for body consciousness. *Movement Ritual I* is the first part of a four-part series and is performed primarily lying down. *Movement Ritual II* is performed standing up using falls, lifts, swings, rebound, and balance. *Movement Ritual III* is performed moving through space using walks, runs, crawls, leaps and various ways of shifting weight. *Movement Ritual IV* combines the variety of possibilities in *I, II* and *III*. We have found that there are as many combinations of movement elements as there are people to discover and invent them.

sense, imagine how exciting and ALIVE you would be if your kinesthetic sense were to
be heightened and cultivated way beyond its present consciousness. Just as a painter
cultivates a keen sense of vision, a musician a keen sense of sound, a cook a fine sense
of smell and taste, so the dancer, the athlete, the acrobat, and the actor need to develop a sharp kinesthetic sense. Since movement is the basis of life itself, and since we
move all the time, then why shouldn't all of us develop this heightened awareness so
that all of us may live a more ALIVE life and become dancers.

Let's do another experiment to give you a chance to experience what is meant
by the kinesthetic sense.

. Blindfold (or close) your eyes so that you may rely on your movement sense, then . . .

. Move around the room for 5 or 10 minutes.

. Afterwards, write down quickly your sensations and feelings.

. Read aloud what you wrote.

. Share what you discovered with someone else.

. With your eyes blind-folded or closed, try another set of movements like pushing, pulling,
crawling, walking backwards, etc.

When you begin to isolate and pay attention to yourself moving you have begun
the process of developing your kinesthetic or movement awareness sensibilities.
You can do this as you walk down a street, carry a load, or shake hands. Your daily
pedestrian life is a potential dance.

SPACE, TIME AND FORCE

However, there is a way to make the process of awareness more complete and
thorough and that is through understanding and paying attention to elements and
ideas of movement. For example, all movement exists through or in SPACE, takes
TIME, and is performed with a degree of FORCE.

Let's take a gesture with a different awareness each time. First move your arm
forward in SPACE and focus your awareness on the spatial aspects of the movement.
Do the same as you go back with your arm. Imagine you had lights attached to
your shoulder, elbow and hand and you could see the visual pattern of the movement in space. Do it again and change TIMING . . . perhaps you could move your
arm forward very slowly and fast coming back. Do this several times until you
notice how the movement begins to take on a rhythmic pattern. Do you "feel" how
the movement is changing? Now again, and this time try moving your arm forward
making a fist and using intense resistance, and come back slowly letting the
resistance go and your arms drop. Do you see how the dynamics have changed?

You could continue to explore changing the ways that you use SPACE, TIME and FORCE in this movement and come up with a variety of qualities. As you learn to focus more keenly on the "feeling" of these qualities another set of responses will be generated. These responses of feeling plug into very personal feeling states that are directly associated with your life experiences. For example, reaching forward and drawing back fast with your arms may have all kinds of associations and feelings attached to the movement. Try it again and pay attention to those associations and feelings. When I do it, I imagine I'm reaching to give and suddenly pull back in fear. When you do the same movement you may feel something quite personal and different. Although the movement is OBJECTIVE we each have a SUBJECTIVE response. We can explore any movement and this same process, inherent in all movement, will occur. It is a NATURAL process and is the basis through which we can communicate and create with movement. This process is the basis through which we can empathize, communicate and share feelings with others.

To summarize this process:

1. The kinesthetic sense is your special sense for being aware of your movements and empathizing with others.

2. Your movements take place in SPACE, are measured by TIME and performed with a degree of FORCE. These elements determine the QUALITY of your movement.

3. When you pay attention to the QUALITY of your movements, FEELING STATES are aroused.

4. These FEELING STATES are what constitute your ability to experience yourself in movement.

The movement may be OBJECTIVE in that many people can do the same movement and SUBJECTIVE in that each person will respond according to personal associations and feelings.

I consider this a NATURAL process, having a biological base and being inherent in all human beings.

GRAVITY, INERTIA AND MOMENTUM

Another important source for developing a keener use of the kinesthetic sense is the consciousness of movement in relation to GRAVITY, INERTIA and MOMENTUM. These three elements operate on our bodies from the outside, whether we are in rest or motion. The human body is subject to the pull of gravity as is any other object on earth. When you move you are moving in two polarities—one is going with gravity, the other is going against gravity; there are all shades of yielding or resisting that lie in between. For example, let's go back to your arm. Lift your arms shoulder height and hold them there until they get tired. Then let go and gravity will cause them to drop.

INERTIA is the desire to continue moving in the same direction. Try running full speed ahead and then suddenly turning to go the other way. This is difficult but also very exciting. Changing direction in movement is overcoming inertia. Have you noticed that when you are lying down at rest, it is often difficult to get up? You need to apply a great deal of will and often have to force yourself up—not just because you are tired but because you are overcoming and resisting inertia and gravity.

MOMENTUM is also constantly operating on the body. You can experience momentum by doing a swing with your arms. The higher your arms drop from space, the more momentum you will build up; the shorter the drop the less momentum you will experience. What I have found fundamental in using gravity, inertia and momentum is a keen sense of awareness of these forces. In this way you can use the energy from an inter-dependency of these elements to give your movement ease, pleasure and excitement.

For me, it is like giving my controlling mind over to these forces and letting the movement take on more energy. Running is much easier if you lean forward and go with gravity, inertia and momentum than if you are upright or leaning backwards and resisting. Try this out for yourself and see if it is true for you. Perhaps swinging on a swing is such a pleasant experience because of the harmony of the body giving over to gravity, inertia and momentum. Children feel this and love to swing. A rocking chair gives this same kind of comfort. In such movements gravity, inertia and momentum are *moving you*. I often say to myself, "Let the movement take over and move you."

And so we have another set of universal laws that govern our movement which I call NATURAL. It is according to the nature within us all, the nature of how our bodies operate, that we respond to these forces.

Rhythm

The basis of a rhythmic movement lies in the alternation between contraction and release of muscle groups over bones. As you contract one set of muscles, you release another set in order for the bone to move. For example, get that arm out again for some more experimentation. Put your arm straight out in front of you. Now bend at the elbow joint. What happened is that your flexor muscles contracted, bending (flexing) your arm. At the same time your extensor muscles released, allowing the bend to occur. Now this time, resist the bending of the arm by contracting your extensor muscles too. If the opposing muscles match the degree of contraction the arm will not move but stay in place. This principle applies to every joint in the body.

Each joint has a different set of ranges: elbow and knee is hinge-action, the shoulder and hip is circular, the head is pivoting, the spine is rotating, etc. It is important in our consciousness of movement to be aware of the opposing forces and of how we manipulate the degree of resistance, or the release, as well as the particular joint range. The use of this principle is what determines your ability to move efficiently and according to the intention of the movement you wish to perform. An uninformed use of this principle causes strain. The implications of this fundamental principle are very great. Just one implication is that contraction and release in alternating intervals give a sense of RHYTHM. Think of rhythm as inherent in the balance and consciousness of activity and rest. Think of rhythm as the way in which you consciously organize these opposing forces within your movement, which is itself a basic and perhaps determining ingredient of rhythm. Once again go back to your arms. You need to experience and try these ideas out for yourself and through your own experience accept or reject what I'm saying as valid or not. Work with muscular contraction and release in your arms. Explore different relationships between contracting and releasing and see what happens.

This time use the trapezius muscles (the large muscles over your shoulder blades) and the pectoral muscles in front (the muscles over the front of your chest) as well as the muscles in your arms. Release the pectoral muscles and contract your trapezius muscles and notice how your arms are drawn back. If the chest muscles are tight and not capable of releasing, the movement is at an impasse. Now move your arms, paying attention to the intervals of contraction and release. Do you feel the inner core of the movement? Find a movement that you can repeat several times using the same dynamic or the same use of tension and release. Do you feel the rhythmic phrase established by the time intervals between contraction and release?

Rhythm and RELAXATION are interconnected yet different. Whereas rhythm is the dynamics of timing between intervals of contraction, release and various types of opposing forces, relaxation is the equilibrium and balance between rest and activity. Rhythm is sensing your harmony, ease, and free flow of energy. Relaxation does not mean going limp or collapsing. Relaxation is using the appropriate sets of muscles to perform a movement without bringing in other sets of muscles not needed. Relaxation means moving efficiently. It means resting while you are moving. The most essential gift of life that we all have is energy. The conservation and creative use of this energy is controlled by the rhythm in the way we move our bodies.

The inability to relax is often so enmeshed in emotional blocks that we are unaware of making relaxation the most difficult skill to achieve. Bad habits unconsciously reflected in our movements and body also prevent us from experiencing relaxation.

As we discover how to move naturally, operating out of universal principles that govern all bodies, we will gradually replace old tired habits with rhythmic and relaxed movement. As we discover how to reach every part of our body we will break up these emotional blocks that drain us of so much energy; instead we will experience rhythm and relaxation, and the enormous pleasure, harmony, and satisfaction in ourselves through sensitive movement awareness.

I believe natural movement has many values for you: you can be yourself and discover your own style rather than being like someone else or taking on an imposed style. You can learn about yourself. Natural movement leads to the potential of self-realization. You can heal yourself. You can increase your range of movement and your range of feelings and experiences and thus grow and develop on a personal level. Natural movement is a reflection of the life force.

In the larger work *Movement Ritual I,* from which this article has been excerpted, I have presented a series of movements which I call Movement Ritual I. In this brief essay I can't give you the entire set of movements, with the accompanying drawings.[1] Up to now I have given you my general approach to movement. I now want simply to stress the importance of doing a set of natural movements every day. I will describe some aspects of Movement Ritual I and then will give you the transitional movements which can lead either into the full ritual or into the daily tasks of your day.

Commonalities in Bodies

Movement Ritual begins with an awareness of *breathing*—a most natural way to begin since breathing is important both to the physical efficiency of our movements and to our psychic behavior. This point cannot be stressed too much.

At present, the diaphragm is the least understood part of the human body. It is tied up with every living function, from the psychic to the structural, and affects the most remote points of the body. Like the equator, it is the line of two great halves of being: the conscious and the unconscious, the voluntary and the involuntary, the skeletal and visceral. Improper use can divide these two halves, whereas an awareness can connect and make your movements whole.

One of the essential aspects of breathing that applies to movement is your mind observing the breath cycle.

The rhythmic cycle of breathing is in three intervals:

1. As you inhale, draw a fullness of air into the lungs deeply and effortlessly; allow the rib case to expand, be soft and resilient.

2. As you exhale, the air departs from the lungs until they are empty and the rib case sinks.

3. Between the inhalation and exhalation there is stillness. Linger in this stillness, wait, and the air will return of its own accord.

NOTE

1. The entire set of movements and drawings can be found in *Movement Ritual I*, illustrated by Charlene Koonce. See Bibliography.

The breath will always lead; it is involuntary. There is no one proper way to organize breathing in relationship to movement. Each movement, according to its intention, will relate to breathing differently. Throughout Movement Ritual you will become aware of how to use your breath to make your movements more efficient and effortless.

As the breath is the flow of all the movements in Movement Ritual, the *spinal column* is the organizer. Imagine your body in this manner: the axial skeleton is the spine with the head, ribs, and sternum (the pelvis, arms, and legs all being outgrowths).

Along the spine are all the essential systems of the body including the nervous system, the digestive apparatus, the circulatory, respiratory, urinary and reproductive systems. It is for this reason that the movements of the spine become central for your attention and care. To understand how your spine operates, you need to understand that the spine has four curves.

In order to lighten and support your body you need to lengthen the spine. To increase your range of movement, to release tension, and to maintain healthy tone in the body, you need to become flexible and strong in the muscles surrounding your spine. You need to cultivate an accurate balance of the parts in your skeletal framework. Movement Ritual I is structured to emphasize this. Every movement is organized around spinal action. Drawing towards or away from the spine is inherent in every movement.

The lumbar or lower back region has the greatest built-in flexibility and capacity for strength, and consequently demands our greatest attention. Your ability to support the entire spine and shoulders, arms and head from your lower back makes this area sensitive to strain. Dr. Rene Calliet has written a book on the lower back-pain syndrome and in it claims that 80% of the members of the human race at sometime in their lives are affected by low back pain or injury.

Your spinal column is also central for the integrity and consciousness of your pelvic region. Through the use of your pelvis, hips and thighs, the balancing of parts, mobilization of weight bearing, shifting directions, and lifting takes place. The pelvic area has long been considered by the Chinese to be the body center, a holy and spiritual center, and visualized as the color red, symbolizing energy.

Differences in Bodies

Although our similarities are obvious, our differences are many and need to be taken into account, in terms of self-expectations and for deriving the most personal benefits. There are general differences that have to do with racial and cultural customs as well as age, occupation and sex. These differences have hardly been tapped as a source of study. Anthropological and sociological information would make valuable resource material for artists and educators. Racial and cultural differences I have

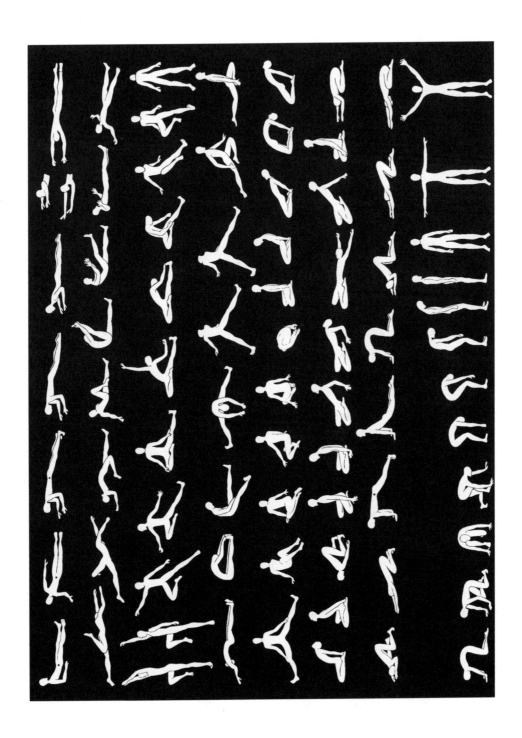

noticed within the multi-racial community at the Dancers' Workshop are that people of Asian ancestry tend to have flat-looking backs and a strong earth grounding. The Black members of our community tend to have short strap muscles and a sharp curve in the lower back, with enormous fluidity in the spinal column and pelvic region. (I carefully use the word "tend" to indicate a *tendency* rather than a stereotype.) Architects who lean over drafting boards have a tendency towards hunched shoulders, and people who are under continuous pressure tend to have forward heads and tension in the neck. I have danced with children for twenty years and was amazed to observe that youngsters tend to be just as tight and have similar postural problems as oldsters, and the people fifty years and over very often are as capable in movement as those twenty years and under. (T'ai Chi masters reach their ultimate perfection between eighty and ninety years of age.) Although men tend to be tight in the hip joints, with practice they can loosen up. Women are sometimes open around the hips but just as often are as closed as the men. Shorter people and children have an ease with gravity that taller people with long limbs may have to develop. Wiry types tend to be fast and darting in movements. We have all noticed that obese people can be light as a feather.

Differences are fascinating and can be appreciated and valued as positive ways of enriching movement with unique experiences and styles. Preconceptions of how one is supposed to move based on a preconceived belief system rather than true understanding, leads to conformity, uniformity and blind acceptance of arbitrary aesthetics. This type of prejudice is repressive to creative growth.

We can learn from each other's differences. We can broaden our range of movement, strengthen our weaknesses, and create a wide variety of new ways to move that open up exciting possiblities. I recommend you understand your body and move in accordance with your own self-image, and then you can learn from other styles, such as ballet, T'ai Chi, Flamenco, belly-dancing, modern dance, etc.

I have often had the experience of starting out to teach a group of participants a particular skill by using a preselected movement. Then I observe different people with different body types and ethnic and cultural patternings. I observe the many structural variations that are equally valid to achieve the same skill. This diversity is always exciting to me and I treasure each person's input as a truly creative and enriching experience.

In doing any movement you need to study your own body by paying attention to the physical sensations evoked by your movement. Use yourself as your own model. If you notice that you have a sway back (lordosis), emphasize the movements that are based on flexion and avoid the back bends or the hyper-extension. Hyper-extension will only reinforce lordosis; flexion will stretch those tight short muscles that reinforce an arch in the lower back.

If you have a sunken chest, then emphasize the movements that contract the upper back and expand your chest. A forward head needs to lengthen and the muscles in the back of the neck need to stretch. Notice if one shoulder is higher than the other, or one hip down or up. As you move, try to make the necessary accommodations. Since each person is unique it is impossible to predict what you will need to do to adapt a series of movements to your particular body type and personal posture preferences. Study yourself in the mirror; have a friend take side view and frontal photographs of you. Try to get in tune with your body image as it is now and how you would like to alter it.

SOME PREPARATIONS FOR MOVEMENT RITUAL

It is helpful to set aside a specific time every day to do movement just as you set time aside for eating and sleeping and bathing. You are taking care of your body in the same sense.

The first thing in the morning and before you retire in the evening is a good schedule, although each of you needs to determine your own natural rhythm.

Arrange a place, a physical environment that is aesthetically pleasing, comfortable, private, and conducive to your concentration. The air should be fresh. It is especially invigorating to move outdoors. The feel of the sun or a cool breeze can add sensual pleasure. The light wlll affect your eyes and mood. The size of space will influence your sense of body scale. Your physical environment does have an effect on you, whether you are conscious of it or not. Create environments to move in that have a positive effect.

The use of sound plays a part in the environment you work in. Sometimes you might want to use quiet music or simply be aware of sounds in your environment that are already there. There are always the sounds of your breathing, and your body as it moves. Sensitize yourself to the sensory stimuli in your environment. Select ways to use stimuli to create a scene for performing your movements deeply and with pleasure.

What you wear also affects how you feel in your movements. Avoid wearing tights and leotards because you think that is the uniform to move in. Try moving without any body covering or with baggy sweatpants and shirt, or a loose-fitting wraparound. Try different body coverings until you find what works best for you.

Transition Ritual

A transitional ritual can be used to begin Movement Ritual I or can be used as a way of discovering what you need from the day ahead of you. Allow the energy you feel from this transition ritual to carry over to your daily tasks ahead.

It is a process of shifting your attention away from external stimuli toward internal body awareness. You can use your mind to perceive kinesthetic sensations within your body, rather than being influenced by any moral or aesthetic preconceptions as to how you ought to look or feel. This ritual is a process for quieting the mind, letting go of muscles, and neutralizing your feeling states. It is a process of self-caring, or bringing yourself to a receptive attitude, and of opening and heightening your own self-awareness. This process allows you to concentrate without effort and awakens your energy.

This is accomplished by closing your eyes, relaxing all over, giving in to gravity, softening your body resistance, releasing inner preoccupations and voiding the mind.

You also need to get in touch with your breath rhythms and appreciate how your breath operates of its own accord following your own natural rhythms.

Begin this movement by sitting with your body comfortably balanced, knees raised, your elbows resting on your knees, your head dropped into your hands, your feet firmly touching the ground and leaning forward at your hips, allowing your back to be open and rounded.

Palming. While you are in this position, cover your eyeballs with the hollow of your palms, using the rim of your palm like the rim of a cup that contains the heat of your hands and brings your palm's energy into your eyes while keeping light out. Relax your eyes, let go of your face muscles, attend to your breath. Whenever you relax, let go. Breathe out, drop your jaw and let your lips part and hang loosely. Now drop your shoulders and breathe into your back, expanding and widening your back. Breathe out and sink into your pelvis, allowing yourself to feel your weight moving into the ground.

Massage your face. Bring your awareness to your face and your scalp. Use your hands as though they are fine sculptor's tools. Press your fingertips into your scalp and rotate, rubbing your scalp and loosening the skin. Use your fingernails and lightly scratch until your head tingles. Use your fingertips to vigorously stroke your forehead. Use the heels of your hands to press into your cheeks. Explore with your hands, moving them into all the parts of your head and face until you have wiped away all expression and your face becomes relaxed, neutral and ready to receive.

Lie down. Keeping your eyes closed, slowly lower your body to the floor, touching one vertebrae after the other, sequentially. To do this movement slowly and smoothly, you can use your arms to counterbalance your movement. When you sense your lower back on the ground, contract your lower abdominal muscles and slowly unroll your spine with control, letting your legs, arms, and head touch the ground simultaneously. Sink. Sense the full weight of your body letting go. Breathe out—let go—relax.

Breathing. Open your palms; place them above your breast, just below your shoulders, and breathe deeply into your hands, with the movement of your breath rising into your hands as you inhale. Rather than being cupped, your palms are now touching and resting on your body. As you exhale, breathe out and let your chest fall. Soften your rib case. Make room for your lungs to expand as you breathe in and to empty as you breathe out. Sense your movement passing through your body and into the ground. Keep breathing, drawing air through your nostrils and exhaling through soft relaxed lips.

If you are aware of your lower back arching off the ground after you've extended your legs in front of you, then it would be better to bend your knees and draw your legs back so that your entire back can rest on the floor.

Now, pass your hands over your rib case to the sides and continue breathing. Sigh as you breathe out. Slide your hands over your abdomen, bringing them to rest on your lower belly just above your pubic bone. Let your diaphragm softly press your viscera into your lower belly so your belly swells and fills your hands. Breathe out and let your movement pass through your lower back and rest on the ground. Let your sigh become a low relaxed sound of your voice. Now let your arms slide off your body and drop to the side.

Be still and quiet and spend as much time as you need to concentrate on how your body feels. With your inner eye, scan all the parts of your body and be aware of any holding on. Breathe into any areas that feel tight, and let go.

Here are suggested ways you can use the transition ritual of palming. You might consider doing these movements with a friend reading them to you and checking you out.

Does your body feel light or heavy?

Are your eyelids quiet? Heavy? Or are your eyes quivering?

Has your breath slowed down? Is your jaw loose or locked?

Do you have any impulses to stretch, twist, change positions?

Follow your impulses.

Do you want to cry, yawn, go to sleep, curl up?

Do it.

Do you want to shout, adjust your clothing, change your location?

Do it.

After you have done the transitional ritual, remain in this altered level of consciousness and begin a private fantasy. Imagine yourself in a place that you truly enjoy. Imagine that you are looking into a blue sky. Now begin to imagine the ground you are lying on. Imagine each part of your body in contact with the ground. What does the ground evoke in you? How does it smell? What is its texture? Its temperature? Can you melt into the ground, be absorbed by the ground? Can the ground hold you? Can you yield to the ground?

Now come back to yourself. Start with your feet and slowly go through each part of your body until you have covered every part and have felt your whole body in this space. Now breathe from your chest into your belly and when you breathe out, exhale from your whole body and into the ground. Breathe in, and this time imagine your breath turned into flowing movement that goes past and beyond the limits of your physical body and streams through your body and out. Connect the space above and around and below. Breathe through your body into these open spaces and let that energy move back into you and into the pelvic area.

Another possible fantasy is to imagine that the breath movement is like the movement of water—flowing, gathering momentum. Think of your breath as the ocean, gently swelling, and feel your breath rising slowly, gathering volume, then slipping back like a wave. Feel the tides of your breath rhythmically creating the flow of that movement. Let your breath swell slowly and gradually, then passively recede, moving effortlessly in a continuously self-generating motion. Let your mind observe this movement restfully.

Suggestions for Movement Ritual

Movement Ritual is meant to be performed slowly, smoothly and with ease. Always breathe into your movements. Closing your eyes helps you internalize and concentrate on what you are sensing when you move. You will notice that you have a limit to your range of action. Find your limit and then go to the edge. This skill will help you increase your flexibility. Avoid forcing the edge by pushing, pulling or bouncing into your stretches. Breathe out and let go each time you want to stretch further. Avoid pain, seek pleasure.

Use your voice. When you breathe out let sighs and hiss sounds out. Color your breath with vocal sounds. Listen to your sounds and notice how the sounds reflect the movement. Notice where the source of the sound is coming from: the chest, throat, belly, head. There will be times when you will want to be quiet, when you want to withdraw within yourself. Be able to choose to go either way rather than limit yourself by cutting your voice off. Keep an awareness of your movement occupying space, consuming time and being performed with a degree of force. Continuity and phrasing involve the way you connect one movement to the other. I call this the flow of movement. Get in touch with the muscles in parts of your body that need to contract as opposed to the parts that are released. Learn to isolate different parts of your body.

These are a few ways to perform movements on a daily basis, and as you become more familiar with your own movements, you will discover the way that works for you.

Undesired tension and resistance in the muscles take a long time to release. Do not expect any visible results right away in terms of limbering up. However, do expect immediate results in how you feel and respond after a movement session. You may have released a great deal of pent-up tensions and feelings, with the result that you feel tired or sleepy. Sometimes just the opposite may occur and you feel "high" and full of energy. You may feel flooded with emotional states, or unresolved situations may come to mind. You may become sexually or sensuously stimulated. Or perhaps you will feel very calm and centered. Linger with your feelings as long as you need to. Reflect on whatever sensations you are in touch with in your body. Reflect on how this feels. Be present. Let this reflection be your closure.

STRUCTURE NOT PATTERN

It is vital to your own creativity to realize that what I have suggested are organized and structured movements rather than formalized or personalized patterns. There is no single formula for movement. The intention or objectives of the organized and structural approach are rooted in the understanding that there are universal laws that do govern all movement. Let this notion be paramount in your attitude when you learn and perform these movements. You could take the same principles and in response to your experience arrive at a totally different series that would be equally sound and valid—perhaps more so—for you.

The four Movement Ritual series (of which *Movement Ritual I* is the first) derived from my own personal response to needs in my life for ways in which my body could "feel good." What I seemed to need most urgently was to replenish my energy, restore my sensibilities, relax my mind and rest my body while in motion. I have been developing and practicing these movements for many years. I continually alter, refine and change them as my life, my needs, and my body change. *Movement Ritual I* has served me well in a variety of ways: as a form of meditation, as a way to build a strong and flexible body, as a catalyst to get in touch with myself emotionally as well as physically, as a time set aside to "let go," as a means to measure development within my body range, as a way to claim my body as ME, as a form of self-healing of impaired and injured body areas, as a gift to myself of time and space to do something for myself. I hope and desire the same and more for you.

LIFE/ART WORKSHOP PROCESSES

———————————————————

This chapter is an excerpt from a manual called *Taking Part*, written after Lawrence Halprin wrote *The RSVP Cycles* (1969), and incorporating some of the same information. The RSVP Cycles are a specific approach to creativity which engages a collective in activities including architecture, community building, focus groups, and brainstorming; I have applied this approach to dance. Although I had been doing these kinds of activities earlier, in the RSVP Cycles we found a system for our experiments, one that could be used again and again and shared with other people. The "workshop" was a new idea, and many of the processes we take for granted today grew out of these first explorations. The fractured nature of this piece is a reflection of this workshop process in its evolution.

The RSVP Cycles are the most important set of principles I have worked with because they extend and formalize a method of applied democracy. We have been able to explore attitudes, feelings, and personal objectives which are in themselves very subjective and which can be objectified in this form. The RSVP Cycles give people a sense of commitment, responsibility, and self-determination, encouraging them to take part in whatever it is that affects them. In today's world, the people who seem to have power are the ones skilled in technology. The RSVP Cycles are a technology of a different sort, a process that has at its heart human needs and experience. In this way, while the arts are a reflection of life, art can also be its guide.

LIFE/ART WORKSHOP PROCESSES

The life/art workshops of the San Francisco Dancers' Workshop are designed for people interested in movement and the performing arts.

Objectives of these workshops are:

1. To build a common basis of experiences from which we can communicate

2. To experience and learn the techniques of *collective creativity*

3. To use the approach of the RSVP Cycles for collective creativity

4. To maximize diversity—cultural, ethnic, female/male, old/young, rich/poor, sexual differences

5. To create rituals and myths out of common experience

6. To fulfill individual expectations within the group experience

7. To develop group awareness to the environment

8. To recycle the experiences of the workshop into daily life

COMMON BASIS OF COMMUNICATION

The first step is to form a *common basis of communication* stemming from shared experiences. This is essential because "dance" has come to mean so many different things to different people. People in our workshops may have had yoga, belly dancing, ballet, modern, folk, or no formal training at all. Perhaps they have seen "dancing" on TV or on stage and think of dance in these terms. Our first task, then, is to establish a direct, personal experience for everyone using natural movement as the basis for building an image of movement-dance.

Our approach leans heavily on natural movement. This means building and developing an awareness of how you feel your body moving and/or how you can interrelate feeling yourself with the movement of others and/or can feel yourself with others in the physical environment. We try to experience movement in terms of body action, structure, muscle sensation, nerve impulses, and so on, and learn to think or send messages and receive messages through movement that recognizes what the body is doing. What we mean by "natural movement" is quite different from learning specific dance styles.

One of the first things we do is to lead people around in space with their eyes closed or blindfolded so they are brought into direct touch with their kinesthetic sense. This is important in our approach to movement because you need to pay attention to *feeling* your movement with your kinesthetic sense rather than using your eyes to copy somebody *else*.

Sharing common experiences for communicating also applies to all the skills we use in collective creativity—active listening, scoring, recycling, ritual making, daily ritual, bodywork, moving alone and together. These all become part of our way of communicating. During the process this becomes richer and richer and is one of the major methods by which a sense of community is established.

COLLECTIVE CREATIVITY

Collective creativity is particularly useful in relation to an activity like dance, which is by its very nature a social or group experience. The more accepted and usual form of dance and theater and music has been to use the ensemble of dancers-actors-musicians to carry out the choreographer's vision or the directions of the director or composer. However, there are other artists who are exploring aspects of participation in the performing arts, using methods other than the RSVP Cycles, but striving for similar objectives: John Cage by the use of chance; Morton Subotnick by activating sounds through audience actions; Pauline Oliveros through ritual; Grand Union Dance Group by improvisation; and (in the theater) the Open Theater and the Performance Company by creating communal lifestyles. The important point here is that people participating in all of these approaches are viewed as contributing artists, not as tools to achieve the "master artist's" purpose.

Collective creativity is a way to utilize multiple input of all the diverse responses from participants, whether in classroom training or a collaboration of performing artists. We use collective creativity to teach, train, and produce performances of theater works. Although personal growth will take place in this approach, we do not stop at this level, but move on to creating results together that relate to group and community growth.

RSVP CYCLES AND DANCERS' WORKSHOP

We use the RSVP Cycles for collective creativity from the simplest dance class to the most complex group performance. We've been using collective creativity for many years at the Dancers' Workshop: methods of collaboration between artists from different fields, improvisation and chance leading to different free styles, scores, etc. The RSVP Cycles differ in that they systematize and make visible the whole creative process *as* it is occurring.

Resources

I will clarify how we use the cycles in our dance-oriented "Take Part" Processes. For example, *resources* might include:

movement categories and ideas;

spaces: their size, quality, and essential natures;

sounds;

people—density, capacities, talents, ethnic and cultural backgrounds, special interests, their bodies;

feelings;

fantasies.

LIFE/ART WORKSHOP PROCESSES

Scores

Scores can be used to serve many purposes. One is a process for integrating person-al growth and artistic expression. Scores can become a way of externalizing hidden feelings, attitudes, and blocks which, because they are hidden and unconscious, can-not be altered or even used as material for art experiences. Unconscious or hidden feelings become limitations rather than possible creative resources. Scores can be used to bring these resources to the surface and put them into some kind of context. Once performed, a perspective is gained, a valuaction takes place, and change and growth can occur.

For instance, in a recent workshop I was working with passive and active rela-tionships in movement between two or more people. We were working on this material as a skill to cultivate. Some people were unable to let go and be passive while others were unable to be aggressive in their movements. As a followup of this exercise, the group was divided into subgroups and asked to do scores with the objective of designing a score that would dramatize a personal life-like situation, one in which the link between a personal awareness and the passive and active movements as an activity was used.

One person had noticed that any kind of aggressive movement that anyone made toward her or that she attempted to do herself frightened her so much that she avoided these movements completely. The objective of her score then was to put herself back into that situation and stay with it and find out what she would do. The score was that she would adopt vocally and in her movements an attitude of anger and direct this to individual people in the group. These people in turn would respond. This was to be repeated with each person directing anger toward her in movement and voice. When the score was performed, she noticed that she was very limited in the ways she could be angry, that she held back the full energy of anger. Her movement quality was limp, her voice dead. When anger was directed at her she curled up, withdrew and eventually got in touch with feelings of being hurt. Her response was to cry and to want people to comfort her. The score was at one level an effective dramatic piece and on another level succeeded in fulfilling her objectives. Used in this way, scores can be effective tools for the development of personal and artistic growth.

We use *scores* to generate creativity. For example, "Daily Ritual" is a very closed score because through it we are trying to alter a state of consciousness and this depends on repetition and on reconditioning the body into proper usage.[1]

NOTE

1. "Daily Ritual" in this chapter refers to the "Movement Ritual" of the previous chapter.

Translating a movement experience into a series of words on the page is so contrary to the kinesthetic experience that in choosing examples I will pick a daily ritual that is easy to put into words rather than the most typical or interesting movements that we use. For example,

SCORE:

LIE DOWN ON YOUR BACK; CUP THE PALMS OF YOUR HANDS OVER YOUR EYEBALLS; FINGERTIPS SEPARATED AND TOUCHING CROWN OF HEAD; HEEL OF HAND RESTING UNDER CHEEKBONE UNTIL YOUR EYES ARE QUIET; AND VISUALIZE A VOID.

An example of an open score in the same situation with the same objectives:

SCORE:

RELAX YOUR EYES.

Two examples of an environmental score:

1. OPEN: SPEND A DAY EXPERIENCING THE CITY.

2. CLOSED: THE CITY MAP SCORE FROM EXPERIMENTS IN ENVIRONMENT[2]

In the second score we carefully defined time, what space to use, what activities to do, and when people met in groups. Objectives were made clear.

Performance

Performance perhaps differs most of all from the processes that have been described so far, but since we are involved in a performing arts field, we emphasize this part of the cycle. Although performance demands different levels of skill and talent, it is of prime importance. For example, a *myth* is an audience participation event. It is not intended to be a brilliant professional display of unique dance talent, but it has profound implications for the people participating and experiencing directly the emotional and communal effects of doing a score. The word performance in *our* terms means implementing and carrying out the score. It does not mean you are required to exhibit a professional stage presence in the terms many people have associated with dance performance. We are not referring to the kind of performer that we have been conditioned to think of in this field: someone who has trained for ten years or more and has reached the pinnacle of interpretative skill. We are referring by "performance" to that aspect of the RSVP Cycles that implements a score. We don't exclude professional expertise or its importance but we do not limit ourselves by that point of view. The implementation of scores in our life/art processes

NOTE

2. "Experiments in Environment" was a workshop for dancers and architects in the environment (1968). Here I refer to a particular exercise done during the workshop.

can vary and uses a large range of media in addition to movement and dance, such as graphics, sculpture, role playing, drawings, painting, voice, instruments, and building environments. A performance can also be a ritual, myth, an exercise, a massage, a meal, a sensitivity walk, and many acts of communal creativity.

Valuaction

Valuaction for us means what worked (felt right) or did not work (felt bad) for everyone (consensus) according to our objectives. In addition, it means becoming conscious (thinking) of the values of the performance experience and its application to life situations. Since we have such a variety of performances we also have different ways to valuact. For example: In a myth I might bring the event to a silent moment and take the participants through a guided fantasy. This is a transfer device to take feelings into a conscious reflective level through a fantasy which will symbolize the experience. Verbally sharing this fantasy with each other strengthens the awareness of its meaning in a way that makes it possible to apply to self and life situations.

In a life/art process we might analyze the performance from the point of view of our objectives and make lists of our likes and dislikes. The group would compare the lists, recycle, and repeat the performance. Also unique, perhaps, to our kind of performance is the possibility in some instance of valuacting and recycling *during* a performance. This can be an objective built into the score.

For example:

S—Call out an idea to group, like RUN.

P—Group does it.

V—Caller responds to what they do and recycles accordingly, then calls out a recycled version.

S—Recycled version might be: Run and listen to your body sounds, or run and touch each other, or run and spin.

After an hour of a caller or leader directing from outside, going from S to P to V back to S, the group will catch on and continue the process on its own.

Note that the leader was using the feedback from the responses of the group *as it was happening* as resources. The leader was not manipulating the performers to do a specific pattern of movement or choreography. Although the dancers were improvising within each score the overall performance was not an *improvisation* because valuaction was applied and recycled into the score. This activity is related to free association and brainstorming activities as they are used in community planning processes.

The only differences between our life/art processes and professional dance performances are:

1. The cast of characters

2. The valuactions performed by the leader

3. The objectives and criteria applied

4. Accountability of group and leaders (willingness to accept personal and group responsibility).

A vital issue of confusion is the difference between our performances in a life/art process and a "professional" production we perform "on stage" for an audience. Since we use the same RSVP process for both how does it differ? Ultimately the turning point is one of decision making. Who makes decisions about scores, performance, and selection of performers? Is it the leader, or the group or performers, and must there be a consensus? Is there more than one person "in charge"—can there be two, three or a subgroup? In the way we use the RSVP Cycles the ultimate decision on sorting out input and recycling the score can be made in any of the configurations mentioned earlier.

The basic requirement is that the group agree and have confidence that the leadership is competent and qualified and will in various ways inspire high motivation and resources of all concerned. The leader can valuact according to objectives, can score clearly, can inspire and lead collectively and accountably. The cast of performers is well trained in collective creativity, talented and accountable and can follow a score.

DIVERSITY

We like to emphasize diversity, rather than diminish it, and then we seek to use it as a creative force. Many people in our culture have tried to diminish diversity and pretend we are all the same. In most performance companies, especially dance, diversity is replaced by uniformity. Everybody learns to dance like the director or choreographer, everybody is supposed to be young, everyone pretends he is heterosexual, and blacks in white companies have to move like whites or form their own all-black companies.

But people are not all the same. Cohesion is not the same as uniformity, and the melting pot is not our ideal. For that reason we bring out differences in positive ways. We do this by various methods.

1. *Ethnic groups* speak their indigenous languages whenever possible, teach their dances, songs, share feelings of their background and their problems, and confront dominant attitudes.

Kadosh, *1971.*

Photo by
Bruce Davidson.

Kadosh, *performed by Dancers' Workshop mul-tiracial company, at Temple Sinai, 1971.*

Photo by
Alan Becker.

For example, at an art/life workshop, food preparation and entertainment was done as an ethnic score. At times blacks, Asians and Chicanos form their own groups and do a ritual or score. One time we scored an entire theater piece called *New Rites* based on separating the Asians, blacks, Chicanos, and whites in space. The audience was asked to choose which of these areas they were to sit in.

2. *Male and female differences* have been used in many ways. Workshops put aside special days for men and women to work apart, design their own scores, and come together again. They have found it easier to overcome the barriers of defining themselves as heterosexual, bisexual, homosexual. Less sexual dishonesty has resulted, pressure has been lessened, and greater creativity has emerged.

3. Work with *age differences* has released us from the American youth-oriented syndrome by making us sensitive to this problem. The use of nudity is an example. In our workshops the body is our instrument, and we become very at home with the unadorned body.

An older person may feel uncomfortable being nude in the presence of young bodies. We have evolved a score and a ritual to make this negative inhibition of aging part of a larger issue—body differences. We have a score that allows these differences to be open.

4. We work with *religious and cultural differences*. We did a two-week workshop based on scoring a Friday night Jewish ritual for a synagogue with a multiracial group.

RITUALS AND MYTHS

By "creating rituals and myths out of common experiences," I refer to the following kinds of scores: In a workshop where we are eating and sleeping in the same areas and during the same times, these activities could become materials for a score. We had a food ritual in which half the group selected an environment and altered it for the purpose of sharing food together. The other half of the group collected all the food, prepared it, and served it in the environment created by group one. We had a forty-minute time limit for preparation and an hour time limit for presentation and eating.

Another example: We were asked to do a performance at a formal luncheon. Instead, we did a ritual of eating lunch—a "Lunch Dance," which you see here. We have ritualized sleeping by scoring sleep arrangements for a group of thirty-five participants—selecting site, groups to sleep on the site, who will wake up first, how everyone will be awakened, and so on.

A *myth*, on the other hand, is often done with large groups of people in a single evening. The objective of the score for a myth is to find a format using

Lunch, *1968.*

Photo by
Michael Alexander.

Lunch, *1968. Left to right: Gary Hartford,*
Larry Reed, Anna Halprin, Norma Leistiko.

Photo by
Michael Alexander.

movement that everyone can do, compelling and profound enough to trigger a
sense of collective energy that will bring the group together in a new way that
leads them into discovering a sense of their own community. We evolved ten
myths which were presented every Thursday night for a year. The "Trance Dance"
was used as a myth within the larger performance *Initiations and Transformations*
performed at New York City Center in 1972. At the end of the performance, the
audience could, if they chose, join the performers in a simple rhythmic walk. This
"Trance Dance" myth was repeated for five nights, and each night a different
group came together in a totally different way: one in a chant; another with various women doing an aggressive and competitive dance; another fading and gradually emptying the auditorium.

FULFILLING INDIVIDUAL EXPECTATIONS WITHIN THE GROUP

Another objective is that, within the overall aim of collective creativity, your own
expectations be fulfilled, or, if not, that you be able to substitute other expectations
more enriching than the ones you originally anticipated. Through learning the skills
of active listening, the RSVP Cycles, and natural movement, and paying attention to
the links between personal and artistic growth you can develop your personal creativity within the framework of the group. This process *is* collective creativity, a
way to become a useful member of a society, by both giving and receiving. One's
tendency is to respond on the basis of one's own cultural background, which, in a
diverse society, is definitely limiting. By working with people of all ages, economic
backgrounds, and ethnic groups, it is possible to enlarge individual dimensions and
sensitivity.

I recall at the end of a day during the last week of a women's ritual one
woman who stood in the center of the circle and gave us this score: "I want each of
you to pay attention to me in any way you choose." One by one, the women performed this score—some danced with her, others voiced their appreciation of her
qualities, others pointed out weaknesses. She needed something for herself and she
used a score to get it. And *all* the women not only enjoyed the score but learned
from each other's experience.

USE OF ENVIRONMENTS

We use environments in life/art workshops and in production workshops as a major
concern. Everything we do takes place in some kind of environment that affects
how we feel and react, whether we are aware of the effects or not. An awareness of
our environment can not only enhance what we do but become a liberating
resource. I include as environment not only spaces but sounds, smells, temperature,
tactile elements, overall qualities, props, lights, basic character. We use many differ-

ent devices to sharpen participants' awareness to environment. We might repeat a sensory walk score in different environments. We have built a workshop around the notion of having one week in the city, one week in the country in a forest area, another week by the seacoast.

We might design a neighborhood awareness score or a city score; we might use driftwood at a beach to build a "community" in which to move and make music. In our performances we might perform on a theater stage or in a polo field, a street corner, a bus depot, or a tennis court. We are apt to use whatever exists and make the environment a positive force. We performed one of our most delightful scores on a steep slope in a wooded area with a flood of water coming down on the performers as they climbed uphill on their bellies.

RECYCLING THE WORKSHOP INTO DAILY LIFE

The last objective of the process, recycling the experiences of the workshop back into life, can be achieved by bringing these experiences into your family, school work, or whatever your daily life involves. In one case, a couple with children brought the process into their children's school life by helping to make a prosaic event—moving from one building to another—into an adventure in collective creativity, group scoring, and communal performance (*Moving Days*, 1973). Others form their own dance groups, or apply resources in their professions as psychologists, teachers, community activists, or artists. Sometimes the experience has the effect of changing people's lives in drastic ways: they quit a job; start a new profession; move to another environment.

TWO DANCERS' WORKSHOP DAYS

Here I will describe two days from the midpoint of a three-week dance workshop in August 1973, to show how this all comes together in practice.
The process leadership team was:

Co-leader—black man

Co-leader—Jewish woman

Assistant—Filipino man

Assistant—Caucasian man

Assistant—Caucasian woman

The participants were thirty-five people with an age range from 17 years to 55 years, including thirteen minority or Third World people (Asians, blacks, and Chicanos), eight Jews, and one English and thirteen American Caucasians. The

economic range was from unemployed to quite affluent. Education ranged from street-educated to several doctorate degrees. (We deliberately accepted applicants from diverse backgrounds and achieved this by maintaining a scholarship program.) The interests in the group ranged from professional actors and dancers to people with little previous experience; students; a married couple; teachers in training; a social worker; an architect.

The purpose of describing two typical days is to demonstrate the type of scores we use; how they get recycled; the feedback process between staff and participants, participants and participants, and staff and staff; how a community begins to build; how scores are learned; the kind of movement approach we use; how we use disagreement and resolve conflict situations; the use of ritual; various media we use; the way all of the various skills and methods link together to form an integration and synthesis of maximum input.

First Day

10:00 TO 12:00

Daily Movement Ritual

Since this workshop was geared specifically toward dance, we usually began the day with a movement session. One coleader conducted the session while the other participated and two trainees assisted and gave individual guidance. In our movement sessions, it is desirable for leaders to participate.

Direct experience helps in recycling the material. Although that morning's movement session seemed normal, there were a series of signals, like warnings before a storm. A few late arrivals, several people deviating from the score itself, and a disagreement between leaders as to the pace of the performance. These signals were material to be recycled and dealt with as resources during valuaction sessions at the end of each day. We will discuss this process later.

12:00 TO 2:00

Lunch Ritual

SCORE:

DIVIDE INTO TWO GROUPS—WOMEN/MEN.

(A) *WOMEN* SELECT AND PREPARE *ENVIRONMENT* FOR GROUP TO SHARE FOOD IN.

Full Moon Water Event,
1968.

Photo by
Paul Ryan.

Building an environment, Sea Ranch, Experiments in the Environment, *1968. Left to right: Charles Moore (architect), Rana Halprin, unknown person, Bob McKay, Annie Hallet, Douglas Murphy.*

Photo by **Paul Ryan**.

Building an environment, Sea Ranch, Experiments in the Environment, *1968. Lawrence Halprin and Douglas Murphy on the right.*

Photo by **Paul Ryan**.

(B) *MEN* COLLECT AND PREPARE *FOOD* FOR GROUP TO SHARE. BOTH GROUPS HAVE 30 MINUTES TO PREPARE; 60 MINUTES FOR EATING; 30 MINUTES TO CLEAN UP. ENVIRONMENTALISTS MAY CHOOSE A SITE ANYWHERE IN AREAS COVERED IN SENSORY WALK ON FIRST DAY.

The objectives of this score were to continue the male/female separation period that had been started the previous week using different situations, to demonstrate how rituals can emerge from ordinary activities like eating, and to continue experiencing a quality of performance and performing. Since this score had been done the day before with the roles reversed, this repetition allowed for a recycling process. The participants did not do a verbal valuaction.

In our workshops *valuactions* take many forms and often are nonverbal but nonetheless conscious. In this instance we used repetition as the valuaction mode. By repeating what had happened the day before but reversing roles, we made the valuaction a comparison with what had happened previously. A powerful method of valuacting is to learn by observing other people working on the same problem. This provides opportunities for people to say to themselves: "I liked this," or "I didn't like that"; "This opens up an idea I could do another way," etc. Also, this approach has aspects of competition in a *positive* sense—not as competing against known standards, but as building on another's experiences.

The leaders had a feeling that space had not been made for minority differences to emerge and be used in resourceful ways. A political issue then current in the San Francisco neighborhood of the workshop afforded the opportunity to get feedback from the third-world participants. A leader made an announcement in front of the whole group just before the lunch ritual asking that the third-world people meet with the leaders apart from the others. From past experiences, I knew that this announcement would create a stir, and it did. The cry went up, "Who constitutes third world? I'm Jewish, I'm minority also!" "I don't like being left out—I want to listen in!" However, the lunch score went on and the third-world group of blacks, Asians, and Chicanos met alone. "How does it feel to be singled out and now be here as a third-world minority?" They laughed a lot. They liked it, and at this point a flow of feelings and talk came out that for the first time revealed differences in backgrounds and the satisfaction in being reinforced by one another.

Then it was time to reenter with the lunch score, and both groups found the reentrance difficult. As one group was planning a score to ritualize the reentrance the other group had already planned one. The food group made a procession with the good-smelling food and as they hummed and carried the food they wove into the other group's space. Smoothly and effortlessly all joined the food procession.

In the next day's score this separation of the third-world people became a valuable resource that fed into the process. It made a breakthrough into differences which had remained submerged and would have either festered or caused apathy. Now it could become a positive force, although there could also be explosions based on a tentative release of this energy.

2:00 TO 5:00

Learning about Scoring

The large group was divided into six smaller groups. Each of the six groups was given the same activity elements to score with. For example, carry and be carried, move low, separate male/female. Each group was given a different environment. The environment was the variable and the activity ideas were the fixed elements. Each group had thirty minutes to develop a score to present to the rest of the group. The purpose was to gain more and more scoring and performance experience and to develop a sensitivity to uses of environmental differences. One group used cars and a driveway, while another group used a redwood grove. There were four other environments, and although the basic activities were the same, the six environments created vast differences. What emerged during performance was a tremendous richness of ideas and variety of material. Performances ranged from a serious jail scene, to an automobile happening, a hilarious waterhose event, and an animal fantasy.

This process of collective creativity allows for many unexpected combinations of elements that when brought together result in incredibly imaginative performances; no one person in thirty minutes could possibly create so many dances. Each one of the six "miniproductions" could, under more conventional circumstances, have taken forever to emerge. This reinforces the notion that collective creativity achieves results that individual creativity cannot.

Group Valuaction

The issue of criteria for a performance was important in this valuaction session. What criteria do we use to valuact success in terms of the score itself? Do we consider performance skill in implementing the score?

In the valuaction discussion, absolute standards were not applicable. A great deal of discussion centered on how to measure success and failure and how to grow from both. Questions of accountability arose; some performances weren't as compelling as others, and we discussed whether the problem was in the score itself or in the performance of the score. Some performances triggered violent reactions among the viewers that surprised the performers. Although these questions were not resolved completely, the valuaction session brought to light conflicting points of view, disagreements, and certain questions to be followed up in later sessions on the questions of standards and criteria for success in scoring and performing.

Staff Meeting—Valuaction

At the staff valuaction meeting there was general agreement that signals of discontent and tension were evident. These were reflected within the staff itself. It was clear that something had to change. What was unclear was what the problem was and how to deal with it.

Even though the day had been interesting and we had worked with valuable material, still there was an undercurrent of unrest. In attempting to discover what was wrong we asked each staff member to identify the problem, stating his input or opinion on what was "wrong" in such terms as too regimented, not enough variety in movement session, not enough attention to personal problems, and so forth. We concluded that the problem basically was one of scheduling and quick pace. A score was therefore developed which we hoped would deal with this problem. The score in essence was to offer a variety of activities simultaneously so people would have a choice and also loosen up greatly on the time factor.

Second Day

I will describe this day quite broadly simply to give a sense of what happened rather than analyze methods as I did for the first day.

In the morning a movement session and a period devoted to listening to unresolved situations were offered at the same time. People who were dissatisfied in ways that blocked them from full participation shared in valuaction discussions and listened to each other's input. The movement session which was going on simultaneously went through some alteration in direct response to the needs expressed at valuaction the day before. The minority Third World group asked to prepare the lunch this day as a follow-up of yesterday. They wanted to be a separate group to prepare lunch. The staff had an active-listening session for two of its own members.

That afternoon, three media were offered from which to choose:

1. Chanting and drumming

2. Clay modeling as scores for movement

3. Learning a massage technique

Everyone complained about having to make the choice. The participants then decided we'd repeat the score tomorrow so that they could do then what they missed today.

Toward the end of the day the entire group joined together to perform a score which two of the participants had prepared for the rest of the group. The objective was to reveal and appreciate all types of differences: age, size, color, sex, handicaps and physical ailments, and so on. The score turned out to be terribly funny and outrageously bold as body parts were compared and old, young, fat, and skinny all found their rightful acceptance in the group.

During the valuaction, a Chicano woman from Albuquerque began to talk about her experience in preparing lunch with the minority Third World people. She commented that she didn't understand why someone who was not in the workshop had invaded their territory by bringing in a birthday cake and arranging to present it. No one had been aware of this at the time, but it made a big impact on her. She was asked to confront the person who invaded her space directly, rather than generalizing to the group. What came out was her deep sense of not being respected, her hurt and anger. As she touched into these feelings, a flood of tears came, and she shared with the group her life-long experience of being treated disrespectfully and of being unappreciated—and how she had suppressed her anger and hurt all of her life. As she let us into her world of being and feeling, we all loved her more and became closer to each other. Without the need to intellectualize and analyze we were able to discover the benefit of recognizing differences and letting them be available for our enrichment: a little more humanity in each of us.

MY EXPERIENCE OF CANCER

In 1972, I was diagnosed with cancer. While it's not unusual to be stricken with cancer these days, the circumstance of my diagnosis *was* unusual. As a dancer working from a holistic approach, I have always been concerned with the relation-ship between the mind and the body. Understanding the connection of movements with feelings is easy enough, but understanding how the mind works in relation to the body isn't as simple. At the time of my diagnosis, I was exploring the use of imagery as a way of making that link. I found it wasn't enough to create images in the mind's eye; I wanted people to draw their own images, reflect upon them, and begin to learn physically the language of these images. This process of connecting with our internal imagery involved "dancing" the images that welled up from the unconscious as another way of connecting the mind and the body. In learning this imagistic language, it became clear I was receiving messages from an intelligence within the body, an intelligence deeper and more unpredictable than anything I could understand through rational thought.

While I was participating in this PsychoKinetic Visualization Process, I drew an image of myself I was unable to dance. This was a signal to me. Why couldn't I dance it? What was blocking me? I had drawn a round ball in my pelvic area, and I intellectualized that it was a symbol of an embryo and romanticized that it was pointing the way to new beginnings. But some part of me was sure that this approach to my drawing was nonsense, because I wouldn't put the drawing into motion. That night, when my mind was quiet, I had intimations that the image I had drawn had something to tell me, and that I was not listening.

The next day I made an appointment with my doctor. I asked him to examine me precisely where I had drawn this round ball. He diagnosed cancer.

I went through the traditional operation procedures, and radical ones at that, which altered my body for life, leaving me with a colostomy and feelings of real uncertainty about my future. Would I ever dance again? The doctor assured me I was just fine, which was funny because I didn't feel fine! He also added that if I didn't have a recurrence within five years, I would be totally out of the woods. Three years after my operation, I had a recurrence. I knew then that I was going to have to make some very drastic changes in my life.

After my recovery from the operation, I began intensive research. I wanted to understand how it was possible to receive an unconscious message about something in the body through a drawing. For a period of three years, I collected slides of drawings done by students in my classes, and I studied them, trying to find a coherent visual language I could understand. I thought perhaps certain colors and shapes meant something, or that certain symbols had a particular meaning. But if there was a system in this, I could not find it. What I did find was that none of these questions could be answered in a rational, logical or systematic manner. It just didn't work that way. What seemed to work was the *process*: when people danced their images and moved back and forth between dancing and drawing, the messages would be made clear through the movement and drawings. The visual images couldn't be codified in rigid terms because each person had their own unique story, expressed in their own personal way.

At the same time, certain symbols and principles seemed to repeat themselves. For example, in a whole classroom of self-portraits, you might notice that almost everyone had a snake or a tree or a water image in their drawing. Or that the drawings indicated polarities and opposites—a dark and a light side. In conjunction with the intense individuality of the drawings, I saw certain common themes repeated over and over again. I also learned that until these images were personally experienced through dance and movement, their messages remained mysterious. I began to suspect that some of the repeating images and polarities had to do with the ways we are all connected to our common environment, the natural world, and the elements that make all of our lives similar to one another.

Let me describe an example of how I was able to learn something about my life story, the mystery of my own personal imagery and my connection to the natural world by dancing a self-portrait I did at the time of my illness. When I first drew myself, I made myself look "perfect." I was young and brightly colored. My hair was blowing in the wind. I was the picture of health and vitality. When I looked at the picture after drawing it, I knew I couldn't even begin to dance it; it just didn't feel like me. I turned the paper over and furiously began to draw another image of myself. It was black and angular and angry and violent. I knew that this back-side image of me was the dance I had to do. When I did it, I was overwhelmed by the release of rage and anger. I kept stabbing at myself and howling like a wounded animal. Witnesses said it sounded like I spoke in tongues. I had to have witnesses because I knew that unless I did, I would never be able to go through this ordeal. My witnesses were my family, my colleagues and my students, and they kept me honest, urging me to go deeper, reinforcing my sounds, calling out parts of the picture I was to dance. I danced until I was spent, and I collapsed and began to sob with great relief. Now I was ready to turn the picture over and dance the healing image of myself.

As I danced this image, I imagined my breath was water and that my movements flowed through my body just as water would flow. I imagined the water was cleansing me. I had an image of water cascading over the mountains near my home, and that the water flowed through me and out to the endless vastness of the sea, taking with it my illness. I believe I was experiencing the forces of nature as they are imprinted onto my body, which gave me a deep sense of the real connection between my body and the world around me. The movements of this dance started soft and small and as I continued to dance, I added sound. My witnesses again reinforced these sounds, as the movements grew and grew, until my whole body was engaged in the image of cascading water. When I finished, I invited the witnesses to join me in a circle; I felt ready to return to my friends and family.

Something happened in this dance that I can't explain. I felt I had been on a mysterious journey to an ancient world. Time and place were suspended and I was in a timeless blue void. The experience left me trembling and purified. Later, as I gained distance from the experience of my dance, I began to notice a pattern within it that seemed relevant to other healing processes. I have mapped out the touchstones of that journey.

The first was simply to look and see and *identify* the issue, the polarity between the dark side and the light side. The second point in my journey was the actual *confrontation*, which was followed by a *release*. After the *release*, the third task was finding some way to *integrate* the new changes in my body. That's what I did when I did the water dance. The last step in my journey was an *assimilation*, a coming back to my community and my family and my life.

Much later, when I was developing theory and methods to apply to my teaching, I saw how this experience was the source of a healing process I had begun to identify. This experience gave me a new way of looking at healing, which I have used ever since as a guide to working with others. I call this process the Five Stages of Healing, and I have adapted it to working with other people with life-threatening conditions, and in larger community contexts, in the form of ritual and group healings.[1] In 1981, I began to apply this process to a whole community of people. I

NOTE

1. Daria Halprin-Khalighi has deepened and developed the Five Stages of Healing in her work with groups and individuals. Her book *Coming Alive! The Creative Expression Method* further details this process and offers a more comprehensive method. This method is used extensively in the Tamalpa Institute training programs, and is one of the central components of our use of dance as a healing art.

began to create large-scale rituals that addressed the different needs of the communities with which I worked, and I always applied this process of drawing and dancing as a way to generate what I call resources. By 1989, one of the largest experiments using this process had evolved into *Circle the Earth: Dancing with Life on the Line*, a large group dance for and by people challenging AIDS. The Five Stages of Healing were the guiding choreographic structure for this dance.

I am so captivated by the discoveries that happen in the visualization process and in this road map for the healing journey that I often forget to tell my friends and readers that after this dance my cancer went into spontaneous remission. It is the healing process implicit in this journey that interests me as much as the cure, because healing is a whole process available to all of us, all the time. A cure is an event, neither predictable nor always available. The process of healing rests within dance, an ancient practice with wonderful possibilities for us today.

I imagined the water flowed through me and out to the endless vastness of the sea, taking with it my illness.

Photo by
Lawrence Halprin, 1974.

THE WORK IN COMMUNITY

―――――――――――――――――

Audience interaction,
Exposizione, *1963. Left to*
right: Daria Halprin and John
Graham (in gold helmet).

Photographer
Unknown.

INTRODUCTION

Janice Ross

In the 1960s, spurred by a confluence of personal, artistic and social concerns, Anna Halprin intensified the communal and process-oriented nature of her work. This concern with community was not an invention, departure, or discovery for Halprin so much as it was an amplification of processes that already deeply concerned her.

From the start Halprin had always made work reflecting a broad view of what the artist does and how the work of art mediates the distance between audience and performer. Halprin had an inherent faith that interest would follow sincerity and that if her passion for her subject were real, audiences would know it and respond. Since the Bay Area in the 1960s was just developing an audience for modern dance, Halprin was free to reimagine that invisible social body, the audience, for whom her works were destined. Equally important was the fact that her performers felt invested in what they were doing. For them neither salary nor glory was the payoff; personal satisfaction was the biggest reward as a dancer in San Francisco in the 1960s could hope for, and Halprin's work addressed this readily.

Midsized proscenium theaters suitable for intimate modern dance works were equally rare, and so an ancillary aspect of community for Halprin became the environmental community, the physical context in which the dance happened. Situating a dance in the physical spaces in which people lived their lives, as happened in *Citydance*, while perhaps a pragmatic solution to the lack of a suitable theater, served to heighten profoundly the immediacy and authenticity of Halprin's work, and also its links to the larger community in whose playgrounds, streets, and parks the dance unfolded.

The setting in which a dance happened also constituted a spatial community for Halprin, an environment that could be as much a determining force in the dance as the participants themselves. For Halprin this means of generating work then alternated equally between a focus on the external context of the dance as well as on the internal context of the performers.

In a series of summer workshops she gave on the dance deck, alone or with her husband and the psychologist Paul Baum, Halprin began to explore the outdoor environment as a vital element in her and her dancers' work. The performer too became a central focus of the work as Halprin then turned her quest for veracity to the dancers, drawing out of them candid and immediate responses to stimulus and each other as a means of generating material with unfabricated meaning. The physical environment was now a force and a presence to be acknowledged, incorporated, or reacted to as one might a silent but steady partner.

Always as much a teacher as she was a choreographer, Halprin also began to use new methods to heighten the performers' presence and their involvement in these dance works. As she states in *Mutual Creation*, she intended the work as a public catalyst—a means of releasing people's buried creativity. "I'm coming to see the artist as a guide who works to evoke the artist in us all," she said. In time the performer's identity would come to be inscribed on the work as vividly as Halprin's own. The result was an emotionally and physically engaged dancer, which for Halprin was an important first step toward creating a fully engaged audience, and ultimately, and most idealistically, an attentive society.

As a result, in works like the *Myths* series, *Ceremony of Us* or *Citydance*, the design of the dance becomes a porous score, a template for real-life actions discovered by the performers and guided by Halprin. As Halprin's own writings reveal, the nature of this process remained fairly constant throughout her work of the 1960s and 1970s, although the process might be variously described as improvisation, mutual creation, or open scoring or transformation.

The effect, however, was basically the same. The meanings and ramifications of these three works were that art inheres in the ordinary and that it can be reinvested in the community and in life. As Marcel Duchamp and John Cage had shown, if one shifted the context around mundane sounds, objects or actions, if one reframed the unnoticed, then this focusing of our perception could render the familiar strange, and the strange was art.

Also constant was the challenge and intimacy many of these works invited. As the *Ceremony of Us* writings make clear, the workshop process of this piece unleashed risky sensual intimacies between the black and white male and female performers. While Halprin didn't court this confrontation directly, neither did she deny it. During this period there was a dogged intensity about Halprin's persistence in shaping works out of behavior rather than the other way around. The artifice of performance was one of the things Halprin had deliberately left behind in New York. For her the task as a West Coast artist was to define a new territory of immediacy.

What was most radical about all this work was that it went so far in erasing boundaries. Others such as Merce Cunningham had looked at the simultaneity of different actions, non-narrative movement, task performance, and other concerns that Halprin too was interested in, but she differed significantly by *defining* far more loosely the degree of technical training one needed to be a performer. For Halprin the notion of training was viewed as more of an internal affair—the physical equivalent of candor. Literally any body could do it, and movement exercises were a means toward greater personal expressivity. This is one of the reasons why Halprin's works of this sort often effected their transformation more fully on the performers than the audience.

All of the works described in this section reveal an emphasis on immediacy as a means toward more authentic theater. Almost intuitively Halprin had begun working in the same arenas that not just political activists but particularly West Coast personal growth therapists were exploring. In this decade of turning on and dropping out, Halprin had found a new passion in disengagement, a passion where the reality of the moment could transcend theatrical conventions and artifice.

Accordingly there were times when the tensions and sentiments Halprin unleashed in workshops were more than she anticipated. But harnessed into theatrical moments they became compelling art, art that gained by its hairbreadth proximity to life.

One of the single biggest ideas to emerge from this whole era for Halprin was that of collective creativity. In those summer workshops Halprin saw firsthand the originality that could be unleashed when one abandoned the notion of creativity as a private act. Instead it was replaced with an alternative model of individual solutions merged into lush complexity. What Halprin had found was that for her the most meaningful art was more a consequence of discovery than a planned product of invention. She had found new ways to connect art with life. In the process she was making art relevant to individuals and groups the American avant-garde had yet to address.

YVONNE RAINER INTERVIEWS ANN HALPRIN

HALPRIN: I was trained as a traditional modern dancer. The big break came for me about fifteen years ago when I left the scene. I didn't know what I wanted to do except to leave . . . and that's when we built our outdoor platform.

RAINER: *Had you been doing solo work before that, or collaborating?*

HALPRIN: Solo work. I also had a group.

RAINER: *And you choreographed for the group?*

HALPRIN: Yes. I had a studio with Welland Lathrop (1948–56) and was part of that tradition of modern dance. But, in 1955, I was at New York Dance Festival, an American National Theatre Academy (ANTA) event, and I was the only dancer from the West Coast, and I hadn't seen what was really going on in dance on the East Coast. When I came back I wasn't excited about anything. That's when the big break came. The workshop idea started when I left San Francisco and moved to Marin County. Some of the students who worked with me in San Francisco followed me. Because I didn't know what I wanted to do, or what I wanted to teach, we set up a workshop situation in which I gave myself permission to explore. Even though I was the catalyst of the group and somehow or other the teacher, I still made it very clear that I wasn't teaching in the usual sense. I didn't feel that I had to have an answer and teach it to somebody.

NOTE

After my operation for cancer, I had an occasion to look at my birth certificate and noticed, to my surprise, that my name was Hannah Deborah, after my mother's mother. I was working with the multiracial company at the time, and reclaiming our heritage was a big part of our philosophy. Many people in the group were changing their names, and it was an important time for me to change mine. I changed my name from the Anglo-Saxon "Ann" to the much more Jewish "Anna." I was Ann Halprin until 1972.

Yvonne Rainer, one of Anna Halprin's most illustrious students, was a prominent member of Judson Church and the Grand Union.

The dance deck,
designed by Lawrence
Halprin and Arch
Lauterer.

Photo by
Lawrence Halprin.

RAINER: *What was the role of the people you brought?*

HALPRIN: They simply wanted to have the opportunity to stay in contact with the activities I was interested in. They also wanted to explore and work together. I wanted to explore in a particular way, breaking down any preconceived notions I had about what dance, or movement, or composition was. I began setting up situations where we could rely only on our improvisational skills. Everything was done, for quite a few years, with improvisation. The purpose of the improvisation was not self-expression. I was trying to get at subconscious areas, so things would happen in an unpredictable way. I was trying to eliminate stereotyped ways of reacting. Improvisation was used to release things that were blocked because we were traditional modern dancers.

RAINER: *Was the focus physical? Did you start out with the body?*

HALPRIN: Sometimes it would be purely physical; we worked on technique this way. My training is in anatomy, so it was easy for me to go into the bone and muscle structure and to work like a kinesiologist. We would isolate the body as an instrument in an anatomical and objective way. We would improvise with rotation or flexion or other anatomical structures. We began to work with how you can articulate this part of the body, and isolate it from another part of the body. What is the efficient way to do that movement? Do we really need to do this or is it just habit? When we improvised we were finding out what our bodies could do, not learning somebody else's pattern or technique.

As the teacher or director of the group, I never told anybody what a movement should be or how it should look. In that sense, too, they had to build their own technique. Even now in our company, there is no unified look. There's a unified approach but everybody is different in movement style. And we used improvisation to explore space and certain kinds of dynamics. We would set up a situation where two people had a focus that concerned the amount of space between them. They would improvise to get a feeling of what could happen, and what one person did would elicit a reaction from the other. We got involved in cause and effect. After a while, we noticed that this was restrictive. But that period gave us a certain technique which is still one of our resources. All of us began to feel the need for another step.

RAINER: *When was this?*

HALPRIN: I think we worked together for four years using improvisation. Out of that period we evolved compositions with a particular improvisational focus. We began to allow the voice to become an integral part of movement, where breathing

We incorporated actions that had never been used in dance before. Four Square, *1959. Simone Forti and A. A. Leath.*

Photo by
Warner Jepson.

Trunk Dance, *1959. Simone Forti (on trunk), John Graham, A. A. Leath.*

Photo by
Warner Jepson.

became sound, or some heightened feeling stimulated certain associative responses and a word came, or a sound, or a shout. Free-association became an important part of the work. This would very often manifest itself in dialogue. We began to deal with ourselves as people, not dancers. We incorporated actions that had never been used in dance before. Works that came out of this period include *Trunk Dance* and *Four Square* (1959).

RAINER: *Were the dances improvised for performance?*

HALPRIN: No. They were improvised in order to get the result; once that was there, it was fixed. You can see how that would wear itself out. The next step was a system in which we would be forced to adapt ourselves to some outside direction.

RAINER: *In performance?*

HALPRIN: No. Now we go back to work. Each performance represents several years' investigation. Each new work represents a new concept, and a new system of composition. We have never been a repertory company; we may repeat a piece within the year we're doing it, but once we have felt the need to explore another area, we drop what we're doing.

We began to explore systems that would knock out cause and effect.

RAINER: *You mean between people?*

HALPRIN: Between everything. Anything that had to do with cause and effect got you back into your own habits again. I wanted to find out things I'd never thought of, that would never come out of my personal responses.

RAINER: *Did you find you moved in patterns?*

HALPRIN: Yes. It wasn't so much repeating patterns, it was a repetition of similar attitudes that didn't lead to any further growth. Improvisation is still a basic part of our technique. Everything we do keeps growing. It's not that we don't do something anymore, it's that the skill is there but it's not used in the same way.

The next step was to find a way to separate the elements we were using. We had gotten enormously involved in a lot of complex and diverse materials. We were using vocal materials and words, and musicians were improvising with us: LaMonte Young, Terry Riley, Warner Jepson, Bill Spencer. We were using objects and props and space in a deterministic way. I wanted to isolate these elements. I began to work with a system where all these things became independent of cause and effect. In order for the music to do THIS you didn't have to do THAT.

RAINER: *The musicians worked out their things in a different place, or what?*

*The first full-length
work. I put a bamboo
pole in everyone's hands,
and we had to do the
dance we'd always done,
holding these poles.*
Birds of America, *Anna
Halprin and A. A.
Leath, 1960.*

Photo by
Chester Kestler.

HALPRIN: We separated from the musicians for a while. I began to chart movement. I put everything on charts. Everything became arbitrary.

RAINER: *Movement patterns, space patterns?*

HALPRIN: Anything I was dealing with, I could do with a movement. I have a great chart on which I've taken every possible anatomical combination of movements, put them all on sheets of paper and given them numbers. One sheet had to do with flexion and different joints; another sheet had to do with extension. I would pick some elements and make a pattern. I tried to do them and I got into the wildest combinations of movements, things I never could have conceived myself. All of a sudden, my body began to experience new ways of moving. We applied this in bigger compositional ways. We would experiment with all the elements we worked with, even combinations of people.

Even though I got the composition system formalized, we still worked it out with improvisation.

RAINER: *So you invented new movement.*

HALPRIN: We invented new movement possibilities, new ways of combining the elements. But when the dance was finished, it was fixed.

Birds of America (1960) was our first long work, about fifty minutes. We spent two years doing exercises, exploring things that led to this system; then it took us about three months to compose the work. We performed it once. By that time we had gotten into doing something else. With that system, we could have composed other works, but I wasn't interested. Something else was happening.

By chance, I happened to become very aware of the space in the theatre, the stage. I just didn't like it, it bothered me and I didn't know what to do. I got this flash: just before the performance, I put a bamboo pole in everybody's hands, including mine, and we had to do the dance we'd always done, holding these bamboo poles.

RAINER: *For fifty minutes?*

HALPRIN: Yes. The poles were very long and they created their own spatial environment. This was the beginning of our next jump. I became preoccupied with movement in relation to environment. I began to feel that we had paid such strict attention to self-awareness, kinesthetic response, and each other, that we developed a stifling introspection. So we began to extend our focus to adaptive responses in the environment. We worked with musicians, painters, all kinds of artists.

RAINER: *Could you go into some detail about that?*

I had the task of taking wine bottles and putting them overhead, getting them to disappear into the ceiling. Five-Legged Stool, *1962.*

Photo by
Ralph Hampton.

There was an enormous amount of juxtaposition in Five-Legged Stool, *1962. I didn't want anything to look like it had any meaning.*

Photo by
Warner Jepson.

HALPRIN: In *Birds of America*, they [the other artists] came into a situation the dancers had already established. Their influence was not a real cross-fertilization yet. But the music wasn't accompaniment. We'd gotten away from that when we began to work with separate elements. And it wasn't even background. The dance was always first. It was a matter of finding sound, finding costumes, whatever was suitable to the dance. In that sense, the dance was still the focus, but I felt that breaking up the categories would be much more exciting. The people we were working with had many resources and they weren't really using them. By that time, we were interested in finding out about what there was on the outside that could affect our ideas for movement.

The next big thing was *Five-Legged Stool* (1962). This was a full-length evening, in two acts. This work further developed the cross-fertilization idea. Up until then, we had been content with using the space we had. But I got discouraged with having to be up there in that relationship to an audience. I began to look at the lobby, the aisles, the ceilings, the floor. Suddenly I thought: "Who says we have to stay on that stage? This is a whole building." In *Five-Legged Stool* what happened was that all these independent elements were developed: the use of sound; vocal material; the word and its content; the painter and the way in which a painter became, very often, the choreographer. For example, in Act II, I wanted to keep bringing objects out and putting them down and going back, taking objects out and putting them down. Jo Landor, the painter we were working with, kept watching this and one day she came in with forty wine bottles and said, "I want you to bring these in." She almost set the kind of movement I did. It's pretty hard for me to know who choreographed that work, me or Jo Landor. It was a true collaboration.

RAINER: *Supposing you had not wanted to do what you had to do with those wine bottles?*

HALPRIN: It worked out fine, because I had also gotten attached to the idea that I wanted people to have tasks to do. Doing a task created an attitude that would bring the movement quality into another kind of reality. It was devoid of a certain kind of introspection.

RAINER: *I remember that the summer I was here with you, you assigned tasks. But as I understood it, the tasks were to make you become aware of your body. It wasn't necessary to retain the task but to do the movement or the kinesthetic thing that the task brought about.*

HALPRIN: Afterwards, we became much more concerned with doing the task itself. Then, we set up tasks that would be so challenging that the choice of a task would be the idea of the movement.

RAINER: *Rather than it being transformed?*

HALPRIN: That's right. The wine bottle task that Jo gave me was so challenging and difficult that I was quite content to do it. I couldn't get up and down; I had to stay in a stooped-over position or I'd break my back. Then I had the task of taking these wine bottles, and putting them overhead, getting them to disappear in the ceiling. I had to balance on a stool. The task was sufficiently compelling in itself that I was able to turn my full attention to it. It took me forty minutes.

RAINER: *Did all the movements in* Five-Legged Stool *have to do with tasks?*

HALPRIN: Yes, and all the tasks were chosen for different reasons. For example, John Graham had a plank that was on a diagonal resting on a ceiling beam and the floor. He crawled up to the ceiling and his task was to slide down that beam head first. It was a complete fantasy; it had nothing to do with anything functional. It wasn't the kind of task that had to do with something as recognizable as carrying a bottle and placing it somewhere.

RAINER: *Did he do it?*

HALPRIN: Yes. By achieving the impossible, he arrived at an incredible bit of fantasy.

RAINER: *In that particular piece did being yourself, not having a character, carry through?*

HALPRIN: Yes, quite automatically. Actually, I was very pleased by it. In doing these tasks, we were not playing roles or creating moods; we simply did something. By the choice of the objects and tasks, we could determine the overall quality. For example, in the first act of *Five-Legged Stool*, each person had several gambits that could be done the same way. Things like pouring water. I had a big box of colorful material and tin cans, and other things I had chosen, and just throwing them as high as I could would be another task. There was a task like changing clothes. There would be another task that had to do with falling, a movement task. Even though these things were repeated exactly the same way in every performance, their sequence changed so that the composition would be different for the audience and the performer. This was the first composition where we had a different performance every night.

RAINER: *In looking at the photographs, a lot of the visual impact has to do with the decor and costumes, which were not essential to the carrying out of the tasks.*

HALPRIN: True. There was a enormous amount of juxtaposition in *Five-Legged Stool* and it was done deliberately. There was an attempt to really break down cause and effect. I wanted everything to have such a sensory impact that an audience would not question why. I didn't want anything to look as if it had meaning, or continuity. What we wore had nothing to do with the tasks. We went down to McAllister Street and everybody was asked to collect things that interested them for their costume. I loved those dresses from the 1920s, those spangly things, with beautiful, luminous colors. I'd go down and collect as many of those as I could. Other times we used everyday clothing.

It was a big thing for us—the first time we hadn't used tights and leotards. They were taboo. We danced with shoes on. I felt like a naughty little girl that first day, because a modern dancer used bare feet, and I was wearing high-heels. A. A. Leath was wearing tennis shoes. This was a very important breakthrough for us, and it helped us have completely new images of how we were. It was the last time we ever really thought of ourselves as dancers.

The other thing about *Five-Legged Stool* was that we began to use the space; we explored the entire theatre—the outside, the corridors, the ceilings, the basement, the aisles, everything. What happened was that the audience was in the center, and the performance went on all around them, above them and below them and in front of them, and outside, sometimes they would hear things from the street.

Something happened in that performance that we never experienced before, and which began to establish a next step. We got a violent audience reaction. That's when people started throwing things at us. People wouldn't whisper to each other, they would talk so everyone could hear.

RAINER: *During the performance?*

HALPRIN: They talked all during the performance; they talked to the person next to them as if that person were ten miles away, as if everything they said to each other was a public announcement. There was a definite kind of involvement we had never experienced before, nor did we know what to do with it, or why it was there.

RAINER: *They didn't actually interfere?*

HALPRIN: Sometimes they did. One time during the bottle dance, when Leath and I balance on a stool and shout at each other, people in the audience started shouting and throwing shoes at us. We were completely naive about what we were doing. We didn't know this would affect anyone else. Everything made complete sense to us because, after all, we spent two years investigating these techniques. We'd worked with juxtapositions, with this kind of unrelatedness. We couldn't figure out what was wrong, or why everybody was getting so excited. People would walk out in a rage. We gave sixteen performances of this and always got this kind of

We used all the space available in the theater, which brought us into direct contact with the audience. Lynne Palmer in Exposizione, Venice Opera House, 1963.

Photographer **Unknown**.

Practicing on the cargo net from Exposizione, *Marin County, 1962.*

Photo by **Paul Ryan**.

reaction. When we did it in Rome, it was ten times worse. Absolutely violent. When we came back we were concerned about what we were doing to the audience.

RAINER: *This was after Rome. What else did you bring to Europe?*

HALPRIN: *Exposizione* (1963), a commission. Lucianio Berio saw *Five-Legged Stool* and felt that he wanted to work with us. He had been asked to write a small opera for the Venice Biennial. We started out with the architecture of the Venice Opera House. The first thing that occurred to me was that the stage looked like a fireplace in somebody's living room—if we tried to dance on the floor, we'd look like little ants. There were only six of us in the company; we'd be drowned by that space. It's built like a horseshoe, with five tiers of seats and only two hundred people on the bottom floor. The first problem was how to integrate ourselves into that space. I felt we needed something vertical, and we evolved the idea of suspending a cargo net across the proscenium, forty feet in the air. The bottoms were stretched out like wings over the orchestra pit and way back into the stage. That is the way in which we were able to alter the proscenium and allow the dancers to be able to move vertically.

RAINER: *Was one cargo net enough?*

HALPRIN: Yes, it was very big. We also built a big ramp on the floor, so that we really had no floor. The floor itself was a slant.[1]

RAINER: *You built the ramp out of boards?*

HALPRIN: Out of fiberglass. We cut down eucalyptus trees in Marin and shipped them all the way over to Italy because we had worked with this cargo net on those trees and it was scary forty feet up in the air. We weren't about to take any chances, so we shipped our own trees! That dance evolved out of a spatial idea, an environmental idea. We said the theatre was our environment and we were going to move through the theatre. And we took a single task: burdening ourselves with enormous amounts of luggage. The whole group had this one task, to be burdened with things.

We chose objects for their texture and form, everyday objects: automobile tires, gunny sacks filled with things. At one point we had a big hassock filled with tennis balls. There were bundles of rags, parachutes stuck into containers, newspapers rolled up and stuck into things that could come out and explode. Each person had to carry these things and allow his movements to be conditioned to speeds that had been set for him. Some started in the plaza, some started in the prompter's pit.

NOTE

1. Jerry Walters was the sculptor for this piece.

We started all over the place, so that it was like an invasion. The music started at a different time; dancers started at different times. You just didn't have any idea when anything would start. The cargo net started going up during intermission, and people couldn't tell if things were starting or if this was preparation. The whole dance—it took forty minutes—was a series of false beginnings. Nothing ever got anywhere. As soon as something got started, something else would be introduced. The dancers' task was to carry things and to penetrate the entire auditorium. This meant we had to go through that stage area which included the cargo net. One of the most compelling parts of the dance was the effort of carrying those things up that cargo net, because the stuff would fall.

RAINER: *It actually did fall?*

HALPRIN: Yes. We had a hassock filled with 200 tennis balls and one dancer's task was to take that hassock up there and when she got it up there, to overturn it. When we reached the high point, there were an enormous amount of objects by that time: automobile tires rolling down, and tennis balls flying. It was a great crash of things. Tennis balls bounced all over so that the whole space exploded. People's bodies dropped down through the net and were caught by ropes. We would hang on; we turned into acrobats. We worked on that cargo net for a year. We got so we could fall from one point to another, catch ourselves on a rope, hang upside down. We developed a whole technique to operate that cargo net. The nine-year-old child [Rana Halprin] who was in the piece started off at the top of the cargo net, jumped onto a perpendicular rope, and swung. She got a big momentum going and swung clear across the heads of the audience in the first few rows and all the way back into the stage. *Exposizione* was a very bold use of the architectonic concept of space. It also was a continual repetition and variation of one task.

RAINER: *Did people have set speeds that were constant throughout?*

HALPRIN: Yes, we had time scores. Everything was done according to seconds. We never heard the music until the night of the performance and the time score

When we reached the high point, there were enormous amounts of objects: automobile tires, bundles of rags, parachutes, newspapers. Exposizione, *1962.*

Photographer **Unknown.**

helped us correlate with the music. We had so much time to get from here to here. This is what determined the effort of our movements. Sometimes it was almost impossible to cover a certain terrain in a certain length of time, because of the burdens we carried. We would stumble. It was like a life and death situation.

RAINER: *You had cues in the music.*

HALPRIN: We never heard the music.

RAINER: *How did you keep time?*

HALPRIN: We had five people stationed all over the place who were giving us cues.

RAINER: *Vocally?*

HALPRIN: We would keep track of them. We would look and they would give us hand signals. Each person in the dance had his own conductor who managed to get to various spots and just like musicians, we looked to our conductor from time to time and found out where we were. We just had to be where we had to be when the time came.

RAINER: *The conductor would be where you were supposed to be?*

HALPRIN: No, he would be in a place where we could see him. We had it worked out.

RAINER: *So they moved around?*

HALPRIN: Yes. It was so important for us to do that; if necessary, we had to drop one of our bundles in order to get somewhere. We left a trail of litter everywhere—in the balconies, in the aisles.

RAINER: *Did you take all this stuff over with you?*

HALPRIN: Yes, we did, which was really stupid. We got very possessive about the things we collected. And our costumes were designed in such a way that we could only wear them for one performance. The cargo net ripped them to shreds. The task, the effort in doing it, the amount of stumbling, and having to get through certain environments would just rip us to shreds. We would start out absolutely beautifully attired.

RAINER: *What kind of costumes?*

HALPRIN: The costumes were designed as extensions of our props. Each person was different. John Graham had a tuxedo and a gold helmet, and it was all black and white. Daria [Halprin] was just full of different transparent, thin things. She was very bulky but also very soft and transparent. Each person was really designed as an object. We also had a musical score in three different languages and we had to sing and speak in Italian, English, and Greek.

RAINER: *How was this established?*

HALPRIN: Berio simply gave us the score. At certain times, according to its elements, we said the score, or sang it.

RAINER: *You learned it?*

HALPRIN: Yes. The parts were sent to us. John Graham did an amazing thing on the cargo net. I was giving him one task and Berio was giving him another. They were both very difficult. He had to be going as fast as he could up that cargo net carrying this baggage, and at the same time, Berio gave him a score which took seven minutes to read, in which he was constantly talking and shouting. He had to alternate speaking in Italian and English. He didn't understand a word of the Italian, so he memorized it. It was just this continual stream of words and every one had to be memorized because it had a particular sound value to Berio. It was considered a small opera because we had that much vocal activity. Then he had vocal people—two young boys and a woman. The only trouble with the vocal material was that we never heard it in performance because the audience shouted so much and responded so excitedly to all the vocal material you couldn't hear ours as separate from theirs.

RAINER: *Do you know what the vocal material was in Italian?*

HALPRIN: Yes, we knew. Rana [Halprin] had a passage in which she was sitting in one of the tiers, blowing soap bubbles and wearing a yellow raincoat, telling a biblical story in Latin. We were trying to get up to the top of that cargo net with all of our baggage falling. We were scrambling and being torn apart and she was sitting out there and telling this story. Those are things Berio had planned that became very interesting juxtapositions.

RAINER: *You never did* Exposizione *here?*

HALPRIN: We never did it anywhere else. It was a difficult work because of the musical score and the eighteen-piece orchestra. It was a very complicated thing.

RAINER: *What are you doing now?*

HALPRIN: When we came back, we took a long rest. Then we began to explore the audience. We wanted to find out what an audience was, to understand a little bit more of what we were doing to the audience.

*We had strange juxta-
positions of realities
going on at the same
time.* Parades and
Changes, *1965.*

Photo by
Hank Kranzler.

RAINER: *I'd like to know. Was it mostly outrage you experienced in Europe?*

HALPRIN: Not with *Exposizione*. They were very excited; they'd never seen anything like that. They had never been so overwhelmed with performers all around them, and so forth. I felt hostility only one time: when the music became very repetitious and monotonous, they started yelling, "Basta! Basta!" The press was interested in it as a new form and there was no hostility. They responded to it for what it was, not because it was or wasn't dance. They were appreciating the fact that it was new; what Stuchenschmitt called "sur-naturalism," a new use for dance and movement. There was hostility to *Five-Legged Stool*. It was very controversial in Zagreb, and was almost canceled after the first performance.

RAINER: *Why?*

HALPRIN: "Decadent Western art." The audience didn't say a word. They just sat absolutely still. Apparently there was enormous hostility. In Italy, when we did *Five-Legged Stool* they threw things at us, but asked us to come back. They said they'd never had such a gorgeous scandal. That's apparently what they enjoyed. They didn't care whether they liked the dance; they had permission to misbehave.

RAINER: *The response affected you?*

HALPRIN: I was concerned not that it offended me, but that we had this kind of power to stir people up. If we have this kind of power, how should we use it? I was concerned with our own naiveté. In Rome, the audience was very hostile and they really knew how to be effective with their hostility. When they threw a shoe, it hit.

For the first time, I realized there was a real encounter going on between audience and performers. This is what we were interested in exploring next. We invited fifty people to join a series. It was announced as a "Series of Compositions for an Audience." We explored this power: Where is it? Who has it? How can we use it? We set up situations where the audience could investigate its role as an audience and learn how to use its power and then we could measure what it did to us.

RAINER: *Do you feel that it's a moral issue? Can this power be misused? Do people have to be educated?*

HALPRIN: No, it's not a moral issue. It's about throwing something away. I never realized we were stirring people so deeply. I now know why. It gets at their preconscious and kinesthetic responses. It's very sensory and primitive. The more we know about this power, the stronger we can be using it. The audience has a power too, and if they can be given an opportunity to use it, we could have an encounter that would really send sparks. At Cal, we did a performance that upset a woman so much that she started shrieking, ran up on stage, snatched our one and only light,

Let's use each other as material. A. A. Leath and Anna Halprin, Apartment 6, *1965.*

Photo by
Hank Kramzier.

Putting clothes on, instead of taking them off, creating a series of juxtaposed images. Rana Halprin and John Graham, Parades and Changes, *Poland, 1965.*

Photographer
Unknown.

The performers are working with real-life themes in the creation of this piece. John Graham (on top), A. A. Leath (crouching); Apartment 6, *1965.*

Photo by
Hank Kranzler.

bashed it up against a scaffold, injuring a dancer and putting the whole auditorium into total darkness, ran up the aisle, smashed herself into a door, and then disappeared into the night. When that woman got up and smashed the lantern, she was using her power as an audience member, but because we didn't appreciate that fact, we threw it away. Had we responded and allowed the audience to realize that her act was a spontaneous, unplanned, vicious attack—WOW! would they have had an experience! Instead, we just threw it away, by pretending we weren't really reacting to it. . . .

We learned that summer that we and the audience had power. But we didn't appreciate their power, and we didn't use ours. What we didn't have was the experience to deal with it when the encounter happened.

RAINER: *Can you really prepare for this kind of thing?*

HALPRIN: We did. We had a week of therapy on it. We became completely brainwashed; we analyzed it from beginning to end. Now, we're just waiting for the opportunity to see how we'll use the power, and not throw it away.

RAINER: *Are you going to deliberately provoke an audience?*

HALPRIN: No, never. Now we know that because of the things we do and the way we do them, we will stir people up. We've accepted that; we're not naive about it anymore. Now we have to take the consequences when we stir up an audience, and we have to have an attitude for dealing with it.

RAINER: *Tell me about* Parades and Changes *(1965).*

HALPRIN: It is compositionally a most satisfying fulfillment of an idea that was started with *Birds of America*. A very complicated score was worked out by Mort Subotnik and me, which permitted us complete and total flexibility. When we go to Stockholm in August (1965), we will take absolutely nothing but the score. We will use only the materials we have in the theatre and that we collect when we get there. *Parades and Changes* has a set of cell blocks. Each person is in his own medium: the lighting person, the musician, the dancers. Everyone has his own series of blocks.

RAINER: *Which are not coordinated?*

HALPRIN: They're not coordinated at all. They can last five to twenty minutes. The selection of blocks was made on the basis of their contrast—there are eight completely different uses of sound. One might be magnetic tape, one might be lute, one might be live sounds, one might be vocal sounds, another might be a Bach cantata, for example. Each block has been chosen on the basis of the difference.

RAINER: *Different lengths?*

HALPRIN: No, that is the one thing that can't change. That's a "set piece." It's exactly four minutes, and can be coordinated with any number of things. Sometimes the dancers work as musicians, and sometimes the musicians use our material. We are conducted by a conductor. The dancers become musicians and sometimes they're also environmentalists. We work as a crew.

RAINER: *What determines when things take place?*

HALPRIN: With all these little cell blocks, it's like you arrive with a trunk full of different clothes, and then, depending upon the weather, you decide what you're going to wear that day. This is exactly what we do. We come into a theatre and look and study it. What is it? What will work here? We say: "I'm going to pick out five of my blocks. I'm not going to do two of them because they just won't work here." The musician picks out what he wants, and so forth.

RAINER: *No one depends on anybody else?*

HALPRIN: That's right. Then we get together and decide which ones will work together in sequence, based on practical matters. Very often a whole new section is invented during the performance in order to make a link between one block and another. Sometimes blocks overlap in a way that they never have before, in order to fill the space.

This has been a delightful composition to work with because so far we have given three performances and they are so completely different that people who have seen them all don't even know it's the same dance. It's been a culminating point for us in developing a system of collaboration we started five years ago.

This is completely different from another work, *Apartment 6* (1965), that we're not taking to Europe because of the language barrier. It's done with a lot of dialogue. It's more of a play than *Parades and Changes*.

RAINER: *How long is* Parades and Changes?

HALPRIN: It can be anywhere from five minutes to five hours—it's completely fluid in its duration.

RAINER: *And* Apartment 6?

HALPRIN: We've done it as a full-length work, a two-hour piece in three acts. This is new for us, and it's very hard for me to talk about because I don't quite know where it came from except that A. A. Leath and John Graham and I, the three people in it, have been working together for fourteen years. We know each other so well that our relationships are terribly complicated. We set up a problem for ourselves: Let's use each other as material. Let's see what will happen if we don't use any props, music or anything. Let's just use each other. Let's explore who you really are in terms of me.

RAINER: *Are you talking about feelings?*

HALPRIN: Yes, what we really feel about each other. We were in therapy together, the three of us, to explore what our feelings for one another are. We worked on the piece for about two years, and we had outside supervision. A psychologist helped us explore our feelings.

RAINER: *Why did you think this was important? Artists can work without knowing their feelings, or analyzing them.*

HALPRIN: Partly by chance, and partly by intuition. We felt that unless we began to work this way, we wouldn't be able to work together any more. We wouldn't be able to get any feedback from each other anymore. We had to go further, otherwise we were finished with each other. Everything we had evolved, we evolved together with Patric Hickey, Jo Landor, Morton Subotnik, Terry Riley and LaMonte Young. But the three of us, John, Leath and I, were the nucleus.

Also, it was something that we were beginning to feel about everybody. The person who is the performer is working with his body as an instrument. He's making sounds and he's doing everything as if he were an object, when actually he's more than an object. He's full of the most fantastic psychological phenomena, but he's completely cutting these off and blocking them. These are the most unique parts of the performer. The musician can't do this because he's got an instrument between him and the thing he's doing; and the painter has his material. But the dancer and the actor are their own instruments. They can find out why they are different from chairs or flutes or tape recorders.

There was also a desire to find out more about the human interior. To tell you the truth, I was scared to death about this whole thing. I don't know if I'm the only one, I don't know how you feel about it, but when you start exposing your unconscious behavior, when you start exposing your feelings about other people or yourself, you're opening up a lot of areas that are very uncomfortable. It would be much easier if you just left them alone. It was uncomfortable and torturous. I approached it as a technical problem. I said, "OK, this is just new material that's been buried for a long time. I'm going to expose it, and try to find the skill to use it." There were times when I was upset and depressed because I was beginning to find out things about myself from the point of view of using it as an artist. That's how *Apartment 6* grew. We set it up as a domestic scene, so that the audience would have definite things to deal with. We cooked. I fixed a breakfast for John on stage. We read newspapers. We played the radio. We talked.

RAINER: *Your roles in relation to each other, were they what they really are, so you were not acting?*

HALPRIN: I was myself. John was himself. I pretty much knew by then what some of our relationships were all about. We spent three years developing the skill to deal with this. We would set up a focus. I would set a task for myself to do. John would set a task for himself. Each person had something to do, so that we had a very formal structure. The process of trying to do this task would always be encountered and interfered with by the other person. This is what we couldn't help. We were so aware of how we were using each other.

RAINER: *Was it always interference?*

HALPRIN: It was either interference or reinforcement. Both altered the work. Also we developed a technique called "three realities." When those three realities went on at different times, there would be a fourth reality. One was the simple act of doing something, which could be cooking. I made pancakes, and I just made them. I followed the directions on the box. People would come to the theatre and they would see John really reading what was in the newspaper that day. It was absolute, complete realism. Then there would be another kind of realism—Leath reading the newspaper, John playing the radio. The radio starts annoying Leath, so he wants to turn it off. Now we're dealing with another reality at this point. He's beginning to get feelings about that radio which put him in contact with John. All of Leath's hostility against John is stirred up by the radio. So he puts the newspaper down, and does the most violent movement you have ever seen. He might explode in mid-air. That's how he's feeling about John at that particular moment.

RAINER: *It's not what he would do in reality, necessarily.*

HALPRIN: No. We had great limitations. John was allowed to express these kinds of feelings in words. Leath was not; he had to express them in movement.

RAINER: *Why did you restrict them?*

HALPRIN: It's very complicated. We wanted to guarantee that Leath would be able to make very sudden shifts. If he talked about his feelings, the audience would lose direct touch with what he was feeling because his verbal material came out so sarcastically. But when he used movement, he was direct. John uses words, and they come out in a way that transfers.

RAINER: *You're making aesthetic judgments on the basis of . . . ?*

HALPRIN: On the basis of our particular skills and development at that moment. We were able to bring certain formalized controls to these things.

RAINER: *It had to do with effectiveness?*

HALPRIN: It had to do with our skills at that particular moment. At that time, Leath couldn't handle words, so he used movement. In certain areas of fantasy, he would start using words which would come through fine.

We got strange juxtapositions of realities going on at the same time. I might be in an absolute tizzy about my pancakes and go into a terrific fantasy about those pancakes and Leath would be just sitting at the table eating his grapefruit and reading the paper, while John was listening to the radio. Do you see what I mean?

RAINER: *Yes. Sometimes people were using different realities at different times. What was the third one?*

HALPRIN: A fantasy. Leath would simply turn into a dog, or a dart board, and John would throw darts at him. But he really fantasized these things, like daydreaming. So he could do it in action.

The fourth reality is when the other three [realities] come together in their peculiar ways. We had it divided up: Leath and John first, then John and me, then Leath and me. There were three completely different relationships, which became the three acts. The performances were completely different each night. It was the here and now, you couldn't do any pretending. Everything was completely real at that moment—what came out of the radio, what you read in the papers, your feelings about the other person. They all might change a little bit from one day to another. It was very, very exhausting to use your skill at a consistent level for all that time. It wasn't until the last, the sixteenth, performance that I felt we had captured what we wanted to do, which was to simply have two hours on the stage of a real-life situation, in which you as a performer and you as a person were completely the same thing. That finally happened. It worked for us and it worked for the audience.

RAINER: *The Stanislavsky Method, as it's taught in New York acting schools, seems close to what you were doing.*

HALPRIN: I don't know anything about it. I tried to read Stanislavsky but I don't understand it. It doesn't appeal to me.

RAINER: *You don't see any connection?*

HALPRIN: None at all. In our situation, there's absolutely nothing pretended. We don't play any roles. We just are who we are. I don't know where it's going to lead to. We use our skills as artists to respond to the material. We use certain structures to guarantee a possibility for the audience to be in on it. We avoid personalizing.

RAINER: *What was the response of the audience? How did the power thing relate to this situation?*

HALPRIN: There wasn't any of that. It affected them very differently than *Parades and Changes*. They laughed a lot and they cried a lot. Some people were crying and some people were laughing at the same time. I don't know why. It was a very curious thing. You may not know why you cry; something hits you and you cry. The audience does the same thing. I never experienced anybody crying before in an audience. I don't really know very much about this yet, but there was none of that power bit.

What I heard from people is that they identified with us closely. There were people who walked out, too, who thought they came to see a dance concert. One person had an interesting reaction. She said, "I enjoyed myself thoroughly while I was there but I'll never come again." Patric asked why. She said, "It just isn't art."

RAINER: *Do you feel a necessity to relate what you're doing to dance any more?*

HALPRIN: No. I don't even identify with dance.

RAINER: *Do you have another name for what you're doing?*

HALPRIN: No. It's as much dance as anything—if you can think of dance as the rhythmic phenomena of the human being reacting to the environment. Essentially, this is what dance is. If the audience accepted this definition, then I'd say, yes, it's dance.

WHAT AND HOW I BELIEVE:

STORIES AND SCORES FROM THE '60s

I am interested in a theatre where everything is experienced as if for the first time, a theatre of risk, spontaneity, exposure and intensity.

I want a partnership of the audience and the performer.

I have stripped away all ties with conventional dance forms: the lives of the individual performers, the training, rehearsals and performances for a process which is, in itself, the experience.

I have gone back to the ritualistic beginnings of art as a sharpened expression of life.

I wish to extend every kind of perception.

I want to participate in events of supreme authenticity, to involve people with their environment, so that life is lived whole.

"The final episode of the piece wherein, to the sound of silence, feathers drop from the ceiling to the floor of the stage, is worth the price of admission itself. Each one of those feathers has a personality all its own. This, I suspect, we should not see if our sensibilities had not been sharpened by watching the rest of the *Five-Legged Stool*."
    —from a review by Alfred Frankenstein (1962)

I went to the Cathedral in San Marco Square in Venice and saw a Mass for the first time. People in costumes of rich brocade, lace, tall hats, jewels, and long gowns sat in formalized rows, and in the center, the priest, flanked by assistants and a boy swinging incense. There were sounds from high above and hidden voices chanted. Drab crowds of people knelt, heads bowed, genuflecting, lips moving silently. Military-looking men with large staffs cleared pathways in the crowd, and the long-robed priest and his followers marched from the big altar to the smaller one.

Everyone seems to know what to do. As I am writing, I feel blanked out, nothing comes into focus, too many images flood my mind, and I want to stop writing and go sit in the sun. I think I will. I'm scratching my head.

Allen Ginsberg was chanting his poetry on a platform at one end of the Fillmore Auditorium. Members of the Dancers' Workshop were all around the audience on balconies, painting one another's bodies in intricate, fluorescent patterns. Allen finished chanting and the Grateful Dead began to play. The dancers climbed down from the balcony on ladders and in pairs, one on the shoulder of another, walking into the center of the space. They spread out, holding poles with plastic sheets between them, and the rock and roll audience danced, under and around the plastic, which was now covered with film projections. It was impossible to separate the dancers from the painted pole carriers from the film images.

3 SCORES FOR PERFORMERS FROM *PARADES AND CHANGES:*

Embrace. *(Dictionary definition: A close encircling with arms and pressure to the bosom, esp. in the intimacies of love;*
i. to clasp in the arms, as with affection;
ii. to take in hand; to take to heart, to receive readily; to welcome; to accept;
iii. to include as parts of a whole.)
Go as far as you can (and get away with).[1] Maintain this focus and relax it only when your action is interrupted.

Paper dance. Make ten single sounds on the paper. Crumple the paper for sixty counts, then tear continuously, listening to your sounds. When you have had enough, collect as large a bundle of paper as you can, and exit.

Dress and undress. Focus on the audience and begin slowly and steadily to take off your clothes. When you are naked, notice your breathing, then put on your clothes. Focus on someone in the group and repeat the action. Repeat a third time.

As part of a score from *Exposizione* (1963), carry your litter from the plaza, through the audience to the balconies, over the cargo net, onto the ramp and into the pit. Use only whatever movements you need in order to accomplish this task. Get help when you need it.

NOTE

1. At the time, I felt this kind of physical contact was a radical notion, a revolutionary step, something "to get away with." Looking at this score today, I can hardly understand this perspective; due to the work we did in the '60s, the charged meanings of physical contact have been largely diffused.

On a given signal from the conductor, everybody and everything falls into the cargo net. Exposizione, 1963.

Photographer
Unknown.

Dress and undress: Focus on the audience and begin slowly and steadily to take off your clothes. From left to right: Norma Leistiko, Morris Kelley, Nancy Peterson, Daria Halprin, Peter Weiss, Paul Goldsmith. Dancers' Workshop Studio rehearsal, 1965.

Photo by
Coni Beeson.

A large group of us marched down Market Street in San Francisco carrying blank placards. Someone was interviewing the bystanders, and taping their comments. Each person had decided what the march was all about, and everyone had a different interpretation.

At the Atheneum Museum, we had two performances going on at the same time. I had been in the Fountain Room watching *The Bath* (1967) and decided to see what was happening in the Medieval Room where the costume parade was going on. The night before, we had planned an event in a way that defined a pathway with flash-lights and separated the dancers from the audience. When I came into the room, the first thing I noticed was people adorning themselves in scraps of materials and everyone in the room joining the parade.

In Rome, during the performance of *Five-Legged Stool*, I placed bottles on the stage, and then handed them up to a hand coming from the ceiling. The audience was hostile, and eventually a man threw something at me. My movements became angry and intense, and I picked up a bottle and threatened to throw it at him. The audience became quiet and afterwards, cheered.

The Wadsworth Museum in Connecticut had a court with a large fountain in the center. It was this room and this fountain which precipitated the idea of *The Bath* as a production for a program there. Preparation for this performance began during a training session on a hot day in July 1966 on my outdoor dance deck. The first direction given to the group was simply to give one another a bath. Bowls of water, soap and towels were the props. The next time we worked, the directions were for each person to give himself a bath. For ten sessions, new directions were given, each developing from the first. By this time, we had moved the rehearsals indoors and the dancers had begun to find recurring themes which were meaningful to them. The bath-taking was becoming continuously more personal in its individual state-ments, with more ramifications evolving from the original bath-taking. In September 1966, a production was given at our studio in San Francisco in which the form of the production was a recapitulation of the process of its development. It started with a very simple group taking and giving a bath, went on to individual statements, and ended with a communal third section, using candle light and becoming more ritualistic. The production was dropped for several months, and we returned to it after the material had become integrated in our systems and was part of our familiar world. In returning to it, we all came with ideas, and kept adding more and more. At the Wadsworth Museum, the group had one afternoon to become attuned with the environment which was to be our theatre. Within that

Touring company,
Exposizione, *from left to right: A. A. Leath, Cady West, Patric Hickey, Jerry Walters, Lari Goldsmith, Jo Landor, John Graham, Melinda West, Daria Halprin, Rana Halprin, Betsy Ford, Susie Gilbert, Lynne Palmer, Jerry Mander, Anna Halprin, Italian publicist (name unknown), Ken Dewey, 1963.*

Photo by **Venecia Fotografica Industriale.**

A large group of us marched down Market Street in San Francisco carrying blank placards, 1967.

Photo by **Lawrence Halprin.**

time, with extreme concentration, we created a spontaneous theatre piece. Morris put his head in a bowl of water and kept it there until he began to drown. His body responded with a violent series of contractions. Then he lifted his face ceremoniously from the water and with red eyes, searched each member of the audience. Afterwards someone said, "I was watching the boy with his head in the water. How did he breathe?"

Daria was lying still along the edge of the fountain. Daria was lying in the water in the fountain. Daria was lying still on the feet of a statue in the fountain. Later, Daria gave a bath to the statues in the fountain. A girl from the audience came into the fountain and pressed her body against the statue.[2]

Morris had seven bowls in the water. As he walked into the water, the bowls hit and made music that filled the room.

Jim took a bath with a bowl of bolts and nails.

Nancy balanced a bowl of water on her head and dipped a wash rag into it and continued to balance the bowl and bathe at the same time.

Michael gave Daria a bath and washed her face and hair, her arms, breasts, back, belly, thighs, feet. She bathed him at the same time.

Everybody bathed and washed one another and beat one another with branches of bay leaves.

Michael emptied his bowl of water from a balcony overhead and into the fountain. Everybody got a little wet.

Our group went to a wild beach in Mendocino County which had piles of driftwood. I put a pole in the sand and asked everyone to make a structure either alone or with others, using only the materials at hand. Within a few hours, an archetypal

Daria was lying still along the edge of the fountain.
The Bath, *1967.*

Photo by
Peter Moore.

NOTE

2. That girl was Deborah Hay.

village had emerged. There was a place for music and theatre, a public meeting house, a series of individual dwellings on a cliff, a tower, a bulkhead bracing the surf, a chief's palace and sacred grounds.

Dear Ann Halprin:

Last night I saw in the TV your dance with the paper and I wish to express the DEEP impression it did on me.

I am a Swedish farmer living rather isolated on a [illegible] farm with my family. (Unfortunately the rest of the family had gone to bed at the time of your program.) Perhaps may I also mention that I am a member of the Society of Friends.

You started the program saying that a good deal of the "action" should happen inside the onlooker. Perhaps this (rather impulsive??) words should be MORE emphasized?? The dance impressed me very deeply indeed. At first, I was very skeptical (even if I am interested in classic dance) because a lot of modern art seems to me to be too much egocentric and without all-human [illegible]. A lack of humility.

But so the dance became slower and taking off the clothes started. The rolling out of the paper, the light-setting took in a certain degree away the growing feeling of striptease. Very soon I [illegible] in a human drama. I saw the naked Human Animal slowly and afraid and shy and clean just like one of my own newborn cattle or lambs approaching, going near to hear something unknown. I saw the innocent Being of Ours touching a new subject. Was it newspapers, or culture itself? I don't care. In the dance, you and I together the always unknown Life itself.

The mystical experience of God or the Inner Light which is the rest of the Quakers' silent meeting for worship is not DIRECTLY touched at in the fragment of the Holy Life which you and the dancers hold up in your hands but it was so much of deep [illegible] and humbleness that I felt cleansed and washed and shakened [sic].

With warm greetings and thanks to you and all dancers in your troupe of seekers,

Sven Kyberg
Sourtbacken, Rimbo

Patric Hickey turned all the lights off during the paper dance and nothing could be seen. It made me nervous until I noticed the sounds of the tearing paper.

Morton Subotnik makes electronic music which stretches sound beyond familiar expectations. Human bodies have not been able to extend movement possibilities. I have tried climbing forty-foot cargo nets, scaffolds, slanting floor surfaces, swinging

Our group went to a wild beach in Mendocino which had piles of driftwood. I asked everyone to make a structure to move in, using only the materials at hand. Experiments in the Environment, *1968.*

Photo by
Paul Ryan.

Paper dance: make ten single sounds on the paper, crumple the paper for sixty counts. When you have had enough, collect as large a bundle as you can carry and exit. Parades and Changes, *1965.*

Photographer
Unknown.

from ropes, springing from elasticized ropes, using film projections, blinding lights, distorted movement images. In a theatre in outer space, we could float free.

Patric Hickey used a movie projector for light and moved it all around. A fish swam over a dancer's body, a blimp exploded on a wall and motorcycles got stuck in the mud while a brass band of performers marched through the theatre. We went to Union Square to experience a theatre of everyday objects, things, and people. My young daughter had just been saved by a Navajo Indian who once was deaf and dumb. His faith in Jesus had restored his speech. Now she was sitting next to a very old and very black man. They were both looking straight ahead. Without changing, she asked him what he was thinking. For a long time, he did not answer. Then he said, "I'll tell you later." The 3:00 chimes sounded. It was time to stand and face the sun.

Thirty of us spent an entire day together in *Silence* (1967). We did whatever we chose in the morning. Some people exercised, some wrestled, others did spontaneous dances, some sun-bathed, others sat quietly and listened or looked. I took a massage. We all ate together silently and after lunch, we put costumes on, linked hands and took a silent walk into the hills and to a creek. We all did what we wanted at the creek and then when it felt right we left and came back to the deck. We bathed each other and everyone was very noisy with the water and their squeals. After that it became quiet again and people dried off in the sun, looking and listening. Eventually, one by one, or in small groups, everyone put their costumes back on and drifted off. I guess they went home.

COMMUNITY ART AS LIFE PROCESS:

THE STORY OF THE SAN FRANCISCO DANCERS' WORKSHOP

How can I compress into a few printed pages the vitality, the excitement, the heart-break, the frustration, the wonder, joy, sadness, miracle and ecstasy that have characterized the journey into body consciousness that the members of Dancers' Workshop have experienced together? Some people have gone on to pursue their own journeys, a few of us have remained to deepen and clarify the work, and new people have come in to reinforce and add their own intensities and lifestyles. One thread along the way has been an ongoing aspect of this journey: an attempt to find a process that unites personal and artistic growth, life and art, with one aspect continuously feeding off the other and coming together in new ways. We have an urgent passion to come closer and more clearly to becoming a humanistic society, a humanistic person, and to reflect this in our theater pieces.

We are still in need of exorcising those societal and interpersonal blocks interfering with the celebration and spirituality of the life force. Within this ongoing process we have had many great people bring new information and knowledge which has had enormous impact on us: Fritz Perls in Gestalt therapy, Lawrence Halprin in the creative process, Ida Rolf, Moshe Feldenkrais and Dr. Randolph Stone in body work, and many, many others. It is in this area that I will put my attention for this essay: the impact of psychology, social sciences and the new technologies we have evolved as a result of these influences, and how our theatre pieces and workshops reflect this influence. I will, in describing this journey, strike only some of the highlights and describe some of the theatre pieces and workshops that are the manifestations of this process.

A significant piece along our journey to body consciousness is *Parades and Changes*. The whole nudity section of the piece came from an experience I had in one of Fritz Perls' workshops. I was looking at a man sitting across from me. He had on a neat, tailored businessman's suit with a white shirt and tie. He was wearing black silk socks and very conservative shoes. All of a sudden, everything he represented to me pushed my buttons, and I got up from my chair, walked over to him, and in a very brazen way, began to pull my clothes off piece by piece, until I was standing right in front of him, stark naked. He was appalled, and I was gloating. Fritz, in the meantime, had been standing in the doorway watching this little melodrama, and from behind a cloud of cigarette smoke, he calmly walked in, took his seat, looked over at me sitting naked on a chair, and nonchalantly said, "And why do you have your legs crossed?" In *Parades and Changes*, I kept experimenting with dressing and undressing, trying to shift my feelings of hostility to a more natural openness. The result was a score that required we pay attention to our breathing and to one another as we undressed and dressed again. During performance, the selection of partners would be random, and the distances would vary from very distant to very close. At different times, the distance would vary with the same partners.

Fritz Perls based his experimental approach on staying in the NOW. We learned in our work together through many, many workshops with Fritz, and other Gestalt practitioners, to get in touch with our feelings so we could be in the NOW in our performances. We wanted to live an authentic situation, not play-act with being authentic. Fritz used role playing and acting out parts of our dreams, like being the top dog and the underdog. A favorite game was a dialog in which you sat in one spot and took on a set of postures and attitudes as you acted out your top dog (moralizes, specializes in "shoulds," generally bosses and condemns), then moved to the opposite side so you could completely change your body and take on the underdog (passively resistant, makes excuses, and finds reasons to delay). Fritz developed and invented exercises in movement to help us act out our polarities. In this way, we avoided "head trips" and interpretations and could experience ourselves nonverbally. All of these approaches reaffirmed my own vision of linking the theatrical experience and the life experience.

I became convinced that each performer could only essentially perform him or herself. Each of us is our own art and whatever was being suppressed in the individual would become a severe limitation to the artist. Furthermore, the individual, in order to realize his or her potential, needed the reality of a group situation where more life-like experiences and diversity could be confronted and checked out. About this time in our journey, Dr. John Rinn, with whom I had worked in Fritz's workshop, began to collaborate with me. Together we began to invent exercises in body work. John introduced me to bio-energetics and I was impressed with how the body could go past self-imposed limits in order to break through preconceived modes of physical behavior. Just as someone who has never seen the color yellow has no way of conceiving what the color is like, people bound into specific body controls cannot experience the vivacity of physical freedom until they break those controls.

We worked on aggression first, to release anger and tears. After that, we worked on sensuality and sexuality. We used the techniques of pounding the mattress until we manufactured rage; we kicked our legs frantically and energetically, evoking hysteria and tantrums. We hollered and screamed our long buried hurts and hates. We put our bodies into positions of stress and we shook and trembled and released tension blocks. Then we went on and broke through our controls by making up our own exercises to link movement with feelings.

BREAKTHROUGH MOVEMENTS

The Struggle

Objective:	Release energy in the arms and chest, check out response to struggle, aggression, applying resistance to another person.
Description:	**Person 1:** Lie on back with fingers laced and behind back of head, elbows on floor. Let out a sound as you bring your elbows together.
	Questions: What image was evoked as you listened to your sound? How did you feel doing that movement?
	Person 2: Straddle your partner, and place your hands on his/her elbows and apply strong resistance as your partner struggles to bring elbows together.
	Questions: What did you feel forcing your partner to struggle? What images were evoked by your partner's sound?

The Drawbridge

Objective:	Break tension in the inner leg and pelvic region. Evoke flow of energy.
Description:	**Person 1:** Kneel in front of partner placing hands on inside of knees and *slowly* opening legs, drawing knees toward floor. Hold when your partner says "Stop." Apply resistance as partner pulls legs together. Observe your partner's face and breathing.
	Questions: How do you feel about applying pressure and resistance? What did you observe? What did the voice sound like? How do you feel about your partner now?
	Person 2: Lie on back, legs bent, soles of feet together. As partner slowly opens legs, sense when you reach an uncomfortable range. Breathe, let out the sounds, let go. Say "Stop" when you reach your limit. Pause, relax, breathe. Go past your limit and say "Stop" when you need to. Hold. Pull legs together against the resistance and let out sounds. Listen.

Animal Ritual, *American Dance Festival, 1971.*
Performed by multiracial group.

Photo by
Raymond Macrino.

Breaking the taboo surrounding sexuality and
the body, Initiations and Transformations,
City Center, New York, 1971.

Photo by
Bruce Davidson.

Questions: What did you experience? Were you frightened? What did you do? What is your response to the genital area? What did your voice sound like? How did your breathing change? Did you have any fantasies? Are you holding back any feelings?

Back to Back

Objective: Release tension in the whole body from head to feet. Stimulate energy flow.

Description: Stand back to back and do movement slowly and evenly.

Person 1: Place legs apart in wide position, lower body until partner's butt is pressed against your lower back. Wrap your arms around hips and upper leg and hold firmly. Bend forward and hold partner on back.

Questions: Do your legs feel solid and grounded? Are they trembling? Did your partner give over and feel released on your back?

Person 2: Let your body sink into your partner's back as you are lifted. Let your legs hang, your head hang, arms overhead. Breathe and open in midriff. Let out sounds.

Questions: How does your body feel? Did you feel any strain? Where? What can you do for the strain?

Spiral

Objective: To release tension in the lower back and chest (pectoral muscle). To experience from this release a new image of the lower back; letting go and strengthening.

Description: **Person 1:** Lie flat on back. Cross bent leg over body, knee resting on floor. Shoulder stays hanging back into floor.

Person 2: Place one hand on partner's hip and the other hand on partner's shoulder. Push and stretch diagonally from these two points. Release. Let the sounds out and give the person stretching feedback on how far to go.

These exercises help us to move into the body in bolder and more effective ways than those relying totally on self-initiated movement. We were able to release more energy, and had more feelings to work with.

I recall working with the all-black group in Watts when we were creating *Ceremony of Us* (1969). I introduced the bio-energetic movement of hitting in

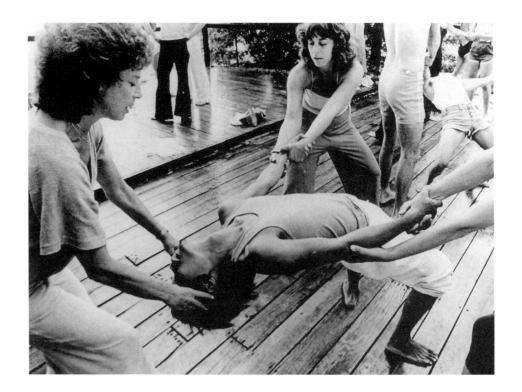

*Breakthrough movements
on the dance deck, 1971.*

Photo by
Peter Land.

order to try to release rage. A black man in the group said to me, "I'm not ready to do that movement. If I let go, my rage will be so destructive I will tear this whole room apart and everyone in it." Two years later, after much more work, this same man performed with us in *Initiations and Transformations* (1971).[1] He was doing a violent scene with me and I came back to the hitting exercise. "Johnny, can you do this now?" and he said "Yes, I will." He did it and was able to direct his rage into the movement. "Good," I said, "Now I'll work with you on this scene. I trust you and know we will not hurt each other." We did a scene in which I related to him using repulsion and he related to me using sexual frustration. The combination led to gross name calling, lewd gestures, and simulated rape. The performance was at the razor's edge each time we did it, but never once did John or I lose perspective of directing the feelings into the movement with total sensitivity and awareness. These new techniques of the body permitted us to go past built patterns and freed us in movement. This freed us to utilize a larger, and more effective, range of feelings.

About the same time, I was being Rolfed to correct my back alignment. Dr. Ida Rolf calls her work structural integration. She says we "may choose the satisfying experience of voluntarily organizing our physical body in the patterns of balance demanded by earth. In doing so we can find our goals reinforced, and their fulfillment brought nearer." In her process, the deep alteration of the fascia muscles structurally integrates the body. The principle is based on the idea that, either because of an injury caused by accident, or illness, or by some psychological incident, these experiences lodge themselves in the muscles, which in turn create tension and block the natural capacity for centering and alignment in relation to gravity. Rolfing alters the body drastically, but in so doing, also alters your capacity to feel and increase energy. Obviously, such increased capacities are invaluable to the performer. We utilize Rolfing as part of our training program.[2]

Sometimes it is necessary to go to the physical body to repattern, and sometimes we go to the emotional body to do this work. For example, a young man in our company could not stand on his head although he had both the strength and the balance. One day, in a workshop, he was working on standing on his head and flashed on this moment when he crumbled. "I'm five years old, my sister and I are

NOTES

1. *Initiations and Transformations* was originally *Animal Ritual* and was performed at the American Dance Festival, 1971.

2. Of all the body work that I have experienced, the one I have been able to apply most specifically to my work has been the work of Moshe Feldenkrais, who I met in Israel in 1948. What I find congruent in our approaches is the way he directs people to experience their own movement rather than imposing a dogmatic system upon the body. For many years, Norma Leistiko, a Feldenkrais practitioner, taught this material as part of the Tamalpa training program.

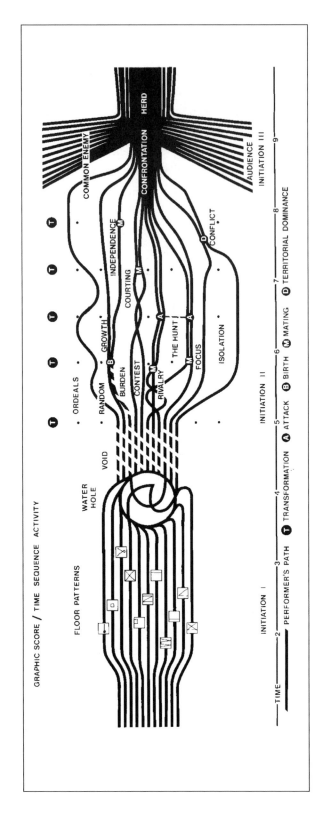

Graphic Score/Time Sequence Activity as part of Animal Ritual, *1971.*

Initiations and Transformations,
City Center, New York, 1971.

Photo by
Raymond Macrino.

Animal Ritual, *American Dance
Festival, 1971. East Coast performers confronting West Coast
performers.*

Photo by
Peter Moore.

INITIATIONS AND TRANSFORMATIONS

INITIATION
TRANCE DANCE
CEREMONY OF SIGNALS
ANIMAL RITUAL

A dance event in four parts.

As performed by Ann Halprin and the San Francisco Dancers' Workshop at Williams College, Williamstown, Massachusetts; the Museum of Art, Richmond, Virginia; George Washington University, Washington, D.C.; and New York City Center; during October and November, 1971.

INITIATION

OBJECTIVE
To take possession of performance space and make it home. To establish relationships with each other and the audience. The intersection of performer/space/audience will form the environmental Gestalt for the event.

SCORE
Everyone create a kinetic/graphic with the rest of the group. Call this image loudly and precisely to the rest so that they can do it. Group support calle in making the image visible. If the audience perceives the score and calls out images, perform them also.

CEREMONY OF SIGNALS

OBJECTIVE
To survive an ordeal of physical and emotional exhaustion. Individual/ group involvement in sustaining attitudes of rhythmic movements until limits of energy are reached. Initiation-catharsis ritual.

SCORE
Each member develop a precise rhythmic movement and repeat it over and over with high energy until there is a slight alteration in pattern or tempo. Then stop.

Group provide support and attention to each Initiation, using movement or sound if they are appropriate.

Score from Initiations and
Transformations, *1971.*
Graphic score by John Muto.

This is a graphic score. Its purpose is to record, describe, and document the event. It takes its graphic form from the content of the dance experience. The photos were taken from the above performances. The verbal instructions below are those from which the performing group evolved each individual performance.

Graphics and photography © 1974 by John Muto.

Graphic Music Score / Joy Muto

TRANCE DANCE

OBJECTIVE
To create a communal rhythm to flow between everyone — performers and audience. Abolition of resistance through moving into trancelike state — dissociating the 'mind' from the 'body.'

SCORE
Adopt and repeat a basic step with up-down rhythm. Flow with other movement ... vocalize breathing ... merge with other sounds ... allow and reinforce "Myth" to happen, when audience enters and claims Trance Dance as its own group creation as a moving community.

RITUAL   *Time Total of 30 minutes.*

People: Relate to any people in performing group or audience.

Perform individual animal score as pre-planned. For safety purposes and survival improvise a 'human' score when 2 or more scores come together with dangerous risks.

Rules of the game: Performers can change to other animals, human, male or female, any age. Transformation should come when you are in an impulse of survival.

ANIMAL   OBJECTIVE
To enter our individual and group atavistic fantasies and liberate feelings and bodily impulses without censorship.

SCORE
Each person decides on his or her bush-soul animal. Perform it in own micro-scores without Master score.

Activity: Perform rules and task within own fantasy animal.

Space: Define your 'turf' in the performance area.

playing, she pushes me and I'm falling down the stairs." He started to holler and cry and held his hands over his head. He recalled that experience, relived it, released his anger, his hurt, his need for comfort. The next day he was able to stand on his head.

Recently, we have worked with Polarity therapy. This therapy is based on the concept that tension fields in the five elements of the body (air, ether, earth, water, fire) must be balanced in action and function and united to the inner conscious center of being. Dr. Randolph Stone, the founder of Polarity therapy, uses pressure points in the polarity zones to release the flow of energy. He says, "The body is a part of nature and must be tuned to nature's rhythm of fine, subtle energy flow, as cells breathe air in and out." Dr. Stone worked on my body for twenty minutes and released so much energy I didn't need to sleep for two nights. Convinced that here, too, is another dynamic way to reach into the body for renewed energy, I pursued the study of Polarity therapy and use simple aspects of it in relationship to movement and the body. All combinations of these techniques—Gestalt, Rolfing, bio-energetics, our own inventions, and Polarity therapy—are used in new combinations and have proved to be essential for bringing out potential human resources.

ARCHITECTS, DANCERS, AND A PSYCHOLOGIST

My husband and I, along with psychologist Dr. Paul Baum, a former student of Dancers' Workshop, gave a joint workshop for dancers and architects called "Experiments in the Environment" (1968). My husband was concerned with how this workshop could relate communities to their environments. I was concerned that we did not have a perspective that reflected community diversity. The next summer we led another workshop because we wanted to work with a multi-racial group. The twenty-three participants were black, Asian, Chicano, WASP, Jewish, rich, poor, educated at Harvard, or educated on the streets. We were diversity of the first order. We had absolutely nothing in common other than the commitment to go to the sea coast and explore the ways we could live together. We lost all our black women after the first three days, even before we got to Sea Ranch. We almost lost two of our white men. We survived on the energy of everyone, the strength and discipline of some, the support of others, the humor and wisdom of a few. We did not intend to set up a commune. We instinctually and simply became one for that brief time, and the dance rituals, rites, ceremonies and initiations of that time came about naturally. Four years later, the nucleus of that group is still together.

Animal Ritual, *Anna Halprin*
and Company, American
Dance Festival, 1971.

Photo by
Raymond Macrino.

The experience left us with the need to find a technique for our community to develop a set of values. Lawrence Halprin began to develop the RSVP cycles. There was an urgent need to clarify a process of creativity that would allow many different people with different lifestyles to come together and create collectively. The RSVP Cycles has provided us with a workable solution. In Lawrence's words, it is essentially this:

I found that what I had really been working towards, what I really wanted to explore, was nothing less than the creative process—what energizes it—how it functions—and how its universal aspects have implications for all our fields. Scores alone were not doing this. I was not interested exclusively in what the score-performance relation was—how the particular event, the building, or piece of music, or piece of legislation, was beautiful—but how the process of arriving at it came about. I found I had to understand the context in which it all happened and to see if, by understanding what had been required to make it happen, I could apply the principle across many fields, multidimensionally, to a life process. Perhaps most importantly, I found that by themselves scores could not deal with the humanistic aspects of life situations, including individual passions, wills and values. And it seemed necessary to round out the scheme so that human communications—including values and decisions as well as performance, could be accounted for in the process.

When that became clear, I found the procedures I needed to get all these inputs into some context had four parts and they were all interrelated. Each part had its own internal significance, but got really cracking only when it related to the others. They have similarities to Jung's cycle, which he called the compass of the psyche.

R   *Resources are what you have to work with. These include human and physical resources and their motivation and aims.*

S   *Scores describe the process leading to the performance.*

V   *Valuaction analyzes the results of action and possible collectivity and decisions. The term "valuaction" is coined to suggest the action-oriented as well as the decision-oriented aspects of V in the cycle.*

P   *Performance is the result of scores and is the "style" of the process.*

Together, I feel that these describe all the procedures inherent in the creative process. They must feedback all along the way, each to the other, and thus make communication possible. In a process-oriented society, they must all be visible continuously, in order to work and to avoid secrecy and manipulation.

Together they form what I have called the RSVP Cycles.

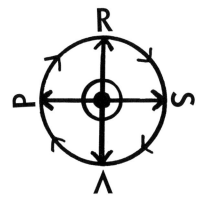

The above diagram describes the multi-dimensional and moving interconnectedness between all the elements of the cycle. It can as correctly read P, R, S, V or any other combination. It is important to emphasize this point. The cycle operates in any direction and by overlapping. It can start at any point and move in any direction. The sequence is completely variable, depending on the situation, score, and intent. By chance, when I finally put the headings together, they spelled RSVP, which is a communications idea meaning "respond."

This is, obviously, an essential ingredient of the cycle. As I and others have worked with this cycle it has become increasingly clear that the cycle must work at two levels. The first of these is the personal, private level of the self, which I use with a lower case "s" according to Gestalt psychology. This cycle is an inner one, and refers to one's own personal Gestalt: the people who are close to you, your personal environment, attitudes, interests, even hangups; one's motivational inner world as distinct from one's outer-oriented world. This self RSVP cycle appears graphically at the center of the community or group RSVP cycle, which is in effect composed of all the individual self-cycles engaged in the activity of scoring.

The private, self-oriented inner cycle and the community group-oriented outer cycle together make up the RSVP Cycles necessary to encompass all human creative processes. Thus, we deal with two RSVP Cycles. The inner cycle as the separate self and the outer cycle as the collective self: individual and community.[3]

Another creative communications process that has aided us in working out conflict together is called "active listening." It is a system originated by Carl Rogers and applied by Thomas Gordon in which the needs and feelings of both sides of a conflict solution are solved through mutual participation. In it, one person "owns" the problem, and the other listens without judgment, feeding back feelings and content. This often allows the person who is speaking to resolve the conflict in an effective manner. We began to apply the principles of active listening as part of our partner work in

NOTE

3. The *RSVP Cycles: Creative Processes in the Human Environment*, 2–3.

movement as a way of training ourselves to become witnesses. Together, the RSVP Cycles and active listening provide creative means by which the social transactions of creativity have a chance of working over a long time span. Living, working and sharing collectively can lead to a remarkable sense of involvement and participation. Interpersonal problems can be demanding and overwhelming and often lead to chaos and group destruction. These techniques have become necessary for our creative art process to function, as well as for the survival of our community.

In the past few years, we have made use of two techniques that have uncovered profound discoveries, personally and as a creative community. They are "Totem" and *Trance Dance*.

"Totem" refers to a life-size self-portrait which a workshop participant is asked to make as one of his first initiations. The person begins by making an outline of his body, and then after each session, the portrait is gradually and cumulatively filled in until it is complete. During the overall period of working on the portrait, the participant has a dialog with himself about what he sees in it. At the end, each person performs this portrait which becomes, in and of itself, the score. In the art of performing the portrait score, several things seem to happen. The person never knows in advance what will happen, yet when the time comes, the material often spills out in an extremely heightened manner. People will shake or cry as if tremendously relieved, and in the movement and sound there seems to be a struggle to bring all the body parts together: the polarities, the parts that are appreciated, the parts that are unclaimed. The self-portrait work exists in a realm of consciousness that can only be explained by the following anecdote.

At the end of the Christmas workshop in 1970, Lawrence Washington drew a portrait with a large helmet on his head with arrows crashing into it; an arrow through his throat with dripping blood; one half of his body as a dead tree; the other half as a live tree; one arm and one leg chained to the side of the page; a sunset across his chest; and a shotgun on one side of the page. His words were NO NO KILL KILL. That night, we had a New Year's Eve party and a fight broke out between our black brothers and some strangers off the street. Lawrence Washington was hit over the head, rushed to the hospital, and after a five-hour operation, was left paralyzed in his arm and leg. He couldn't talk, had no use of his voice, and was in the hospital on the critical list for a long time.

One day, I took his portrait to him and asked him to tell me what to do. He told me to cut the chains. I did and after that, he began to improve. A year later he was dancing with the company in Connecticut and New York City. The last night in New York, he had a seizure on stage. As he lay there, I hovered over him as his animal mother giving birth. I stayed with him for a long time, and slowly he came

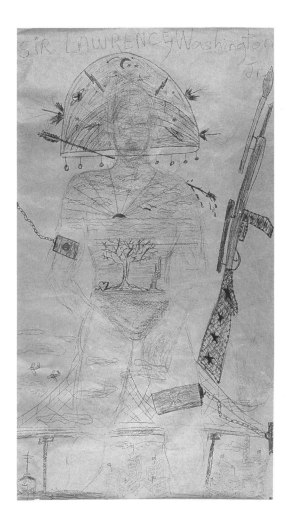

Lawrence Washington's self-portrait, Christmas 1970.

Photo by **Anna Halprin**.

Closure of a Trance Dance. *Anna Halprin, center, standing, 1970.*

Photo by **William Vorpe**.

out of his state, and became my baby deer. We danced this role until he was able to walk by himself, and gradually continued until the end.

Trance dancing is to be found in many ethnic cultures throughout the world, and dates back in time to biblical prophets who, we are told, whirled in dance until reaching a state in which they had visions which were then proclaimed as prophecies to the people. The Balinese, the American Indians, the early American Shakers, various African tribes, and many other groups have all devised trance dance forms that serve important and vital functions in the community. The purpose of all the various trance dances is similar: to tap inner riches that lead to an altered state of consciousness and transformations that will overcome evil spirits; cause the earth to yield nourishment; heal the sick; see other worlds; integrate with nature and become one with the universe; get in touch with the divine essence of the self-universe. The motivation in this trance dance is to experience the process of the journey from the self to the many and back to the self again; to move with collective energies and flow with them, discovering where they will take us without knowing anything before it happens. Through trance dancing, I have been allowed to experience a deep centering, which allows me to enter into the eternal, ongoing questions of life and death.

Trance Dance

Objective: To create a communal rhythm to flow between everyone, performers and audience. Abolition of resistance through moving into trance-like state. Separating the "mind" (intellect, attention) from the "body" (feelings, awareness).

Score: Adopt and repeat basic step with up-down rhythm. Use drumming as unifying element. Flow with other movements . . . vocalize breath . . . merge with other sounds . . . allow "myth" to happen through the creation of this moving community.

As we do this dance, outside stimulus fades out, the drum correlates and unifies the dancing, the collective energy and group consciousness gather, and a *Myth* (tribal happening) emerges. A *Myth* is a formalized event that emerges spontaneously from the group. The *Myth* is unique to that moment in time and space. It is a tribal event that has never happened before, with only one life. This *Myth* symbolized the spirit of the collective psyche of the group. It is a configuration that grows out of something else and takes on its own character. It could be anything, and whatever the event is, it is unpredictable. As you read this, you may wonder, what is a *Myth*? It will happen, and when it does, you will know.

VISION FOR THE DANCERS' WORKSHOP

At Dancers' Workshop, we believe that each person is his own art, and each community is its own art. We believe that art happens through a creative process of growth, in which performance provides closure, which facilitates creativity, which facilitates . . . We believe art becomes more valuable as more diversity and energy is unified and incorporated within it. The Dancers' Workshop has undertaken research into the nature of art and the creative process and it has formulated that research into a unique approach, which it uses as its working process. The Dancers' Workshop presents the results of this research in classes, workshops, performances and through documentation in order to get more resources, which it uses to continue and deepen the research. The goal of the research is to learn how to be valuable individuals in a valuable community, surviving and having a useful impact on the natural, social and spiritual worlds.

MUTUAL CREATION

"*Myths* are experimental. The performers, members of the Dancers' Workshop Co. and participants in Ann Halprin's Advanced Dance seminar, are unrehearsed. What unfolds is a spontaneous exploration of theatre ideas. *Myths* are meant to evoke our long buried and half forgotten selves. Each evening will explore a different relationship between the audience and performers, and between our awareness, our bodies, and our environments. The audience should not be bound by accustomed passivity, by static self-images, or by restricted clothing. *Myths* are your myths. They are an experiment in mutual creation."

For 10 consecutive Thursdays, starting in October 1967, groups of about 50 people came to the Dancers' Workshop studios in San Francisco. Most of them expected a "performance," and instead found themselves "performers." The Workshop had attempted to prepare the public by mailing the above announcement, but people were too pre-conditioned to understand what the release meant, and could only be convinced by the actual experience.

The "audiences" were, by and large, neither homogeneous nor an in-group. They were a mixture of hippies, student groups from the San Francisco Institute of Art, all types of businessmen, dance students and professionals, architects, city planners, psychotherapists, tourists, and those lured by our reputation for nude performances. In short: no pattern.

Although each *Myth* was different, the central idea of every evening was to release people's buried creativity by answering one of their basic needs through ritual.

The experience, of course, was not like that of a frightened nightclub patron pressured by a performer or friend to get up on stage and make a fool of himself. Certain general conditions were suggested to the group in the briefing room. Thereafter, anyone was free to participate or observe. A few people left. But the vast majority stayed, participated, even participated ecstatically. For some it was simply fun, for some a bore, for some extraordinarily sensual, for some a Happening, for some a kind of atavistic tribal reawakening. For me, it was all these things—and a new exploration.

People sought individual freedom, found it, and found community as well. Order through freedom: freed from the constraints of a normal "performance," the whole group found its own social and artistic structures. At times the birth of this new and more natural order seemed chaotic—the public would alter the instructions, the sound, or the physical environment, and there were periods of great destruction and reformation. During these phases a few people became disturbed and left the building. However, most of those who were not in the midst of the action just withdrew to some quiet spot on the side, and eventually rejoined the group after a new period of order had been established—an order completely real in that it reflected deeply rooted intuitive drives.

One aspect of the original idea was to explore different relationships between audience and performer. I, and the audiences, assumed that total audience involvement would be either chaotic or impossible. During the first few *Myths*, the company members were used as a core group: catalysts, demonstrators, guides. But soon the audience transcended this, the company members began to merge with them, and by the third *Myth* we were mutually creating art.

Perhaps in the future my role will need to be redefined. I am coming to see the artist in another light. She is no longer a solitary hero figure, but rather a guide who works to evoke the art within us all. This is the true meaning of a seminal theatre.

MYTHS

Myths was a collaboration between myself and Patric Hickey. Patric created the environments that are represented on these pages. The use of the environment was an integral and vital aspect of the total experience. Our intuition was to allow the environment to elicit actions and responses from the participants, and in this sense, to be part of a self-directing score.

Myth One: Creation

Hanging from the walls at 8 and 12 foot elevations were 60 opened folding chairs, unoccupied, over platforms at different levels. Lights were attached to the platforms, lighting the central area and the platforms. Audience seated themselves in the area of light and on the platforms, thus becoming a visual part of the performance.

No briefing was given either to performers or audience. The performers entered next and sat in a circle on the floor, recalling some primitive place of worship. A performer was asked to come forward, stand in the center, close his eyes

Atonement. Myths,
1967–68.

Photo by
Bob Klein.

and wait. Someone from the circle of performers was asked to stand behind this person and slap him up and down the spine, gradually passing over shoulders, arms, hips, legs, the entire body.

Drum beats were introduced and the slapping merged into a highly stimulating rhythmic action leading directly into movement responses. A chain of people extending into the audience was established. As one still person began to move, another person was called up to partner the one who was slapping, and this continued until more and more people were brought into the main line of action.

A dance began with audience becoming performers, the original performers acting as catalysts. The physical environment, originally meant for seating, became the stage. The director began to work with responses in movement, guiding them, shaping them, and adding new ideas until everyone actively participated in a mutual creation. As the energies spread through the studio, the idea of the original circle with its unconsciously perceived powers kept reappearing.

This first *Myth* was passionate, exuberant, strong, and drew its life from the circle and the beat.

Myth Two: Atonement

After being briefed on the floor of a small room, and deciding whether to participate in this "ordeal," the audience entered the studio one at a time. They stood facing the wall, looking into a blinding spotlight. They selected a position, altered their clothing, and remained still and silent for one hour. A loud continuous roll on a snare drum was played in the center of the room.

The participants maintained their roles without a hitch. When the snare drum stopped everyone remained in position and did not leave for quite a few minutes. They then returned to the briefing room and were asked to think of two words that best described their experience. They formed small groups and, using these two words, shared their experiences.

The walls and floors of the studio were entirely covered with newspapers from one day's edition. Only one selected page was used, in complete repetition.

Myth Three: Trails

The audience was ushered onto a small platform at one end of the studio, with chairs arranged in an intimate setting. Everyone was asked to relax in his chair, and let out whatever sounds he could from his breathing. This eventually led into a shout, and then subsided into long sustained hums. Each was then blindfolded; they held hands and formed a line. The person at the end of the line was to move forward and find his place at the head of the line. He had to feel his way through space by touching.

The audience was then divided into several trails (lines) and the same directions were followed. This action continued silently for one and a half hours, after which people took their blindfolds off and looked at each other for a long time.

The experience of being cut off from sight awakened people to new ways of perceiving.

Myth Four: Totem

Performers and audience were both put in the same space and in chairs. The performers, however, were in the room ahead of time, had chairs which they had altered, and were in costumes they had chosen. Each performer was in an area of his own with empty chairs all around.

The audience first met in the briefing room and were told that they had the choice of sitting next to any performer, they were free to change places at any time, and free to respond—if they wished—to questions I would use as the focus for the performers. Or they could simply observe. However, the audience did not particularly want to be observers and took over and became performers. I added new elements on the spot and let the rest of the evening go where the audience wanted to take it. It ended with all the chairs being constructed into a gigantic totem pole in the center of the room, and the audience doing a very formalized stepping dance around it, as suggested by a member of the audience.

Afterwards, coffee was served and James Broughton, poet and film-maker, talked about myths as related to totems, the idea of the chairs, and different ways that people at different periods and in different cultures had specific sitting styles.

Myth Five: Maze

A maze was constructed from a grid of wire, suspended 12 feet above the floor; heavy cord was attached to eyelets in the floor for verticals and walls made of clear plastic, black and white opaque plastic, wrapping paper, and newspaper. Five Dancers' Workshop members were in the maze in a series of confrontations planned for the audience as they came through.

The audience were told to go through the maze, come out whenever they wanted to and pass into the briefing room, which was filled with paper and writing crayons. They were to write whatever words came to mind and go back through the maze again.

Trails. Myths, *1967–68.*

Photo by
Coni Beeson.

Maze. Myths, *1967–68.*

Photo by
Bob Klein.

People went through the maze and wrote on the paper. Very soon, however, this rhythm broke down and they destroyed the maze, creating great momentary disorder. They reconstructed a totally new maze and stayed in it for the rest of the evening. People drifted out of this maze at different times and left to go home while others stayed for hours.

Myth Six: Dreams

The audience was brought into a room which was filled with an assortment of junk, including ladders, ropes, boxes, risers, etc. Half the group was told to go into the briefing room, and the other half was told that they had 15 minutes to alter the environment into which the others would return.

Without hesitation they went to work and in the exact time allotted they created, each by himself, a fantastically complex ritualistic place with all kinds of things happening for the others to do.

The first group then left the room and the other group prepared the environment for them. The second group tended to be more formal and the entire event was more ordered.

The first group was led into a definite pathway, which included going through dark tunnels, climbing high levels, passing couples making love, or being pelted by balls of paper.

The evening was most provocative and generated a great deal of discussion about the differences between group one and group two.

Myth Seven: Carry

People—not, for this performance, defined as audience—entered the performance area and sat on high levels. Drums were playing and they sat facing each other and looked at one another for a long time.

The director then asked, "Would anyone volunteer to choose a person and carry him through this passage?" After a pause, a man jumped down, selected a girl, and very simply carried her, and the drumming rhythm, the lights, and the carrying action began to work together. This kind of activity continued very simply, and began to include "Will two people carry one person?" "Will five people carry two people?" etc.

New direction was added on the spot as a result of what was happening. "Will those of you who want to be carried stand in the passage and wait?" After much waiting: "Will those who volunteer carry those who want to be carried?" People realized the primitive, archetypal connotations of this act (carried in the womb, bride carried across the threshold, pope carried to altar, corpse carried to grave, etc.)

and the scene, especially when it seemed to resemble a Bacchanalia, was suffused with a ritualistic quality. The event concluded with an action that involved everyone either carrying or being carried.

This evening was the most movement oriented of all, and at the same time, extremely controlled by the instructions.

Myth Eight: Masks

After a briefing, everyone was given an apple. The audience sat in pairs opposite each other eating their apples, and were told to look at each other's faces while eating. They were asked, in partners, to mold each other's faces. They began to respond to their own faces and the way the altered face made them feel and behave, to react to people around them with their faces. Groups moved their chairs to the center space facing the platform and we took photographs of groups of people reacting to each other with their altered faces frozen. Small groups performed, supposedly for the camera, but actually for the rest of the people who were watching. There was rapt attention given to the performers, and much humor, laughing and tremendous enjoyment with one another.

Myth Nine: Story Telling

This *Myth* was devoted to storytelling, and placed great stress on an individual statement to the group. Each person walked around the interior of a large circle of people. He was asked to tell a story he had never told to anyone before, something that happened when he was a child. A lighted candle was given to him, illuminating his features, and he was told to pass it to another person when he completed his story. As it was passed, the musicians improvised and the mover and the musicians were doing something together. The story telling was woven into the moving and passing of the candle.

Each person revealed the intimacy of himself, his deepest feelings, in a story that had been so personal that he had never told it before. His use of the candle, the place he chose to tell his story, and the gestures he used, all contributed to the inner qualities of his story. The audience then broke into smaller groups and those who had not had a chance to tell stories began to tell theirs to a person sitting next to them. The evening concluded with everyone moving and dancing a very soft and ceremonious dance with his own candle lighted.

Myth Ten: Ome

In the briefing room we had a rehearsal in which everyone practiced breathing and letting the voice come freely. People were in a solemn state and in this state they walked very quietly into the performance area. They did their breathing and let the

MYTH ONE — CREATION
321 DIVISADERO STREET
SAN FRANCISCO, CALIF.
FALL 1967

D/WSF
ANN HALPRIN, DIRECTOR
PATRIC HICKEY,
    ENVIRONMENTALIST

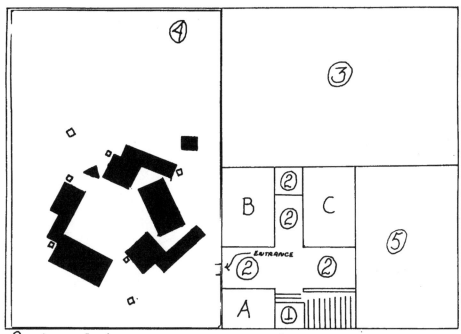

SCALE: 1"=8'

CODE:

— Platform elevation 2 feet
— Platform elevation 4 feet
— Platform elevation 8 feet

○ Audience-performer
▲ Percussionist
□ Lighting instrument
■ Lighting control

①- Stairwell from street
②- Corridor
③- Small studio
④- Large studio
⑤- Lounge
A- Rest room
B- Office
C- Storage

NOTE:
    Hanging from walls
at 8 foot and 12 foot
elevations, 60 opened
folding chairs, silently
unoccupied.

Myth 1—Creation.

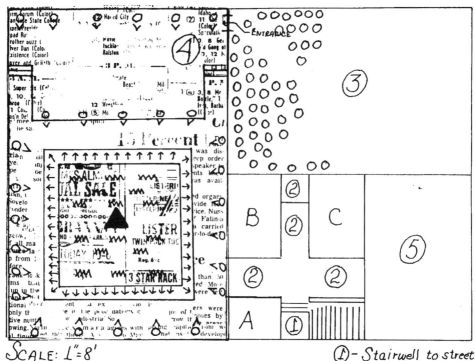

SCALE: 1"=8'

CODE:

→   Audience standing facing in direction arrow indicates.

O>   Spotlight, 150 wt. white focused direction indicated at 6 feet elevation

∧∧∧   Columns of newspaper 12 feet elevation

▲   Percussionist

O   Position for aud. briefing.

① - Stairwell to street
② - Corridor
③ - Small studio
④ - Large studio
⑤ - Lounge
A - Rest room
B - Office
C - Storage

NOTE:

Entire room (walls and floor) covered in newspaper from one day's edition. Only one selected page used, in complete repetition.

Myth 2—Atonement.

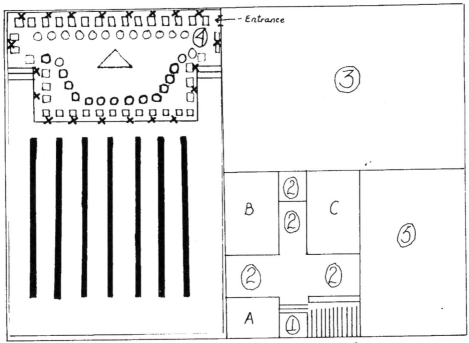

SCALE: 1″=8′

CODE:

☐ - Chairs
◯ - Sponge discs

✕   60 wt. colored bulbs
      suspended 8′ from floor

△   Blindfolds

▮   Starting line-up of
     blindfolded audience
     (no light in this area.)

① - Stairwell from street
② - Corridor
③ - Small studio
④ - Large studio
⑤ - Lounge
A - Rest room
B - Office
C - Storage

Myth 3—Trails.

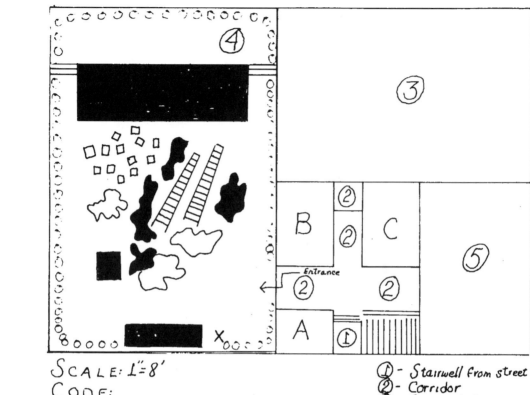

SCALE: 1"=8'
CODE:

○   Sponge disks for audience. (Later, used as building material.)

▢   Empty folding chairs.

■   Movable platforms.

    Piles of huge plastic sheets - black and white.

⊞   Ladder.

■   Very large box of assorted materials (i.e., wire, string, paper.)

■   Boxes lighting equipment.

X   Lighting attendant.

① - Stairwell from street
② - Corridor
③ - Small studio
④ - Large studio
⑤ - Lounge
A - Restroom
B - Office
C - Storage

NOTE:

When audience is divided into two groups, one group exits to room 3.

Myth 4—Totem.

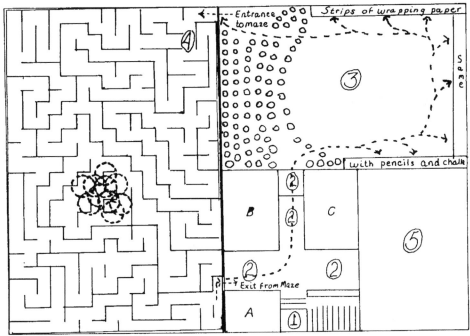

Myth 5—Maze.

SCALE: 1"=8'

CODE:

O — Sponge discs on floor for audience briefing. (Discs are removed when audience has started entrance to maze.

- - -→ Travel route between maze exit and re-entrance.

◯ Suspended, free-form chandelier w/12 60wt. colored flashing bulbs.

①—Stairwell from street
②—Corridor
③—Small studio
④—Large studio
⑤—Lounge
A—Rest room
B—Office
C—Storage

NOTE:
Materials used constructing maze: Grid of wire, suspended 12 feet in elevation; heavy cord, attached to eyelets in floor for verticals; walls made of clear, black and white opaque plastic, wrapping paper, newspaper.

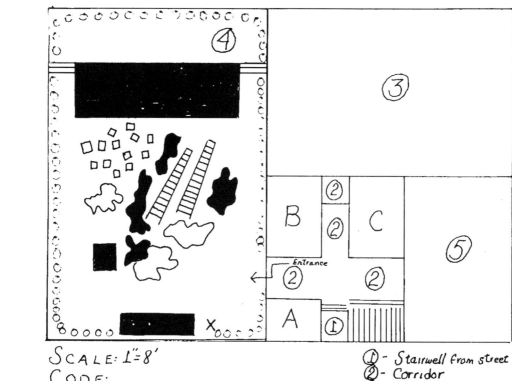

SCALE: 1"=8'

CODE:

○ Sponge disks for audience. (Later, used as building material.)

□ Empty folding chairs.

▬ Movable platforms.

🗨 Piles of huge plastic sheets - black and white.

▭▭▭ Ladder.

■ Very large box of assorted materials (i.e., wire, string, paper.)

▬ Boxes lighting equipment.

X Lighting attendant.

①- Stairwell from street
②- Corridor
③- Small studio
④- Large studio
⑤- Lounge
A- Restroom
B- Office
C- Storage

NOTE:

When audience is divided into two groups, one group exits to room 3.

Myth 6—Dreams.

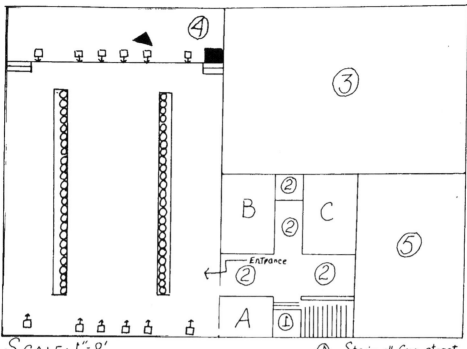

SCALE: 1"=8'

CODE:

[platform symbol] Platforms, 8 feet elevation; audience seated facing across from one another.

▲ Percussionist

[lighting unit symbol] Lighting units, focused direction indicated.

■ Lighting control.

① - Stairwell from street
② - Corridor
③ - Small studio
④ - Large studio
⑤ - Lounge
A - Rest room
B - Office
C - Storage

Myth 7—Carry.

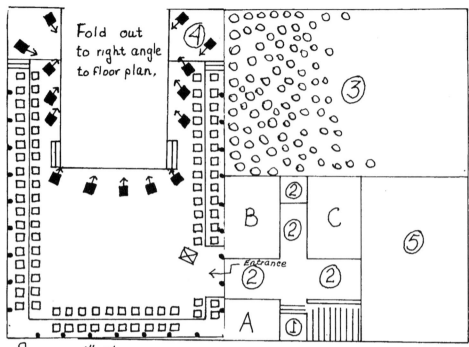

Fold out to right angle to floor plan,

SCALE: 1"=8'

CODE:

☐→←☐ Chair, audience face to face.

● 60 wt. frosted, large decorator lamp.

◼→ Spotlight, 150 wt. white, focused direction indicated. Instrument suspended 12 feet elev.

⊠ Box of apples.

O Position for aud. briefing.

① - Stairwell from street
② - Corridor
③ - Small studio
④ - Large studio
⑤ - Lounge
A - Rest room
B - Office
C - Storage

NOTE:
Audience moves chairs to center space facing platform during picture taking.

Myth 8—Masks.

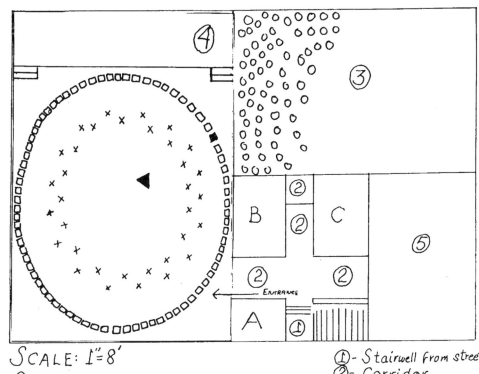

SCALE: 1"=8'

CODE:

□ Audience seated
   in folding chairs.

× Candles

▲ Percussionist

⊠ Candle attendant.

○ Position for audience
   briefing.

①- Stairwell from street
②- Corridor
③- Small studio
④- Large studio
⑤- Lounge
A- Rest room
B- Office
C- Storage

Myth 9—Story Telling.

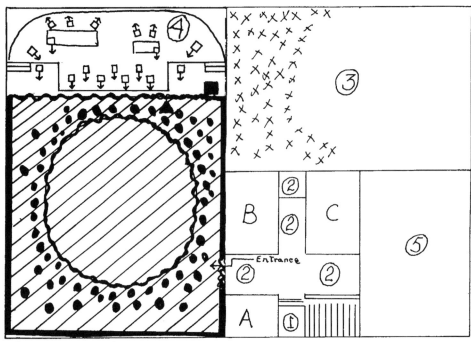

SCALE: 1" = 8'

CODE:

●	Audience position on floor
∿∿∿	Clear plastic sheets, 16 feet elevation
▬	Black plastic sheets 16 feet elevation
///	Black plastic sheet
⬡	Clear plastic sheet 16 feet elevation completely closed
⌒	Cyclorama
▢→	Lighting unit
■	Light control
▲	Percussionist
X	Audience pre-briefing

① - Stairwell from street
② - Corridor
③ - Small studio
④ - Large studio
⑤ - Lounge
A - Rest room
B - Office
C - Storage

NOTE:

At a certain time, attendants cut openings in center circular plastic sheet.

Myth 10—Ome.

sound OME come out easy and effortlessly, creating a mysterious effect. They did this for 30 minutes and then the drummer began to play. Attendants cut openings in the center circular plastic sheet, and one at a time people went into the center area and did a movement: roll across the floor, or stand and stretch the arms high, or sit and rock. It was done by themselves, and meditative in spirit.

Then a new, unexpected energy was felt and the studio seemed to explode. This subsided into meditation and a new quiet was restored with nothing but the quiet sound of OME coming from relaxed bodies. These people were no longer an audience but were by now a community. They had built up common understandings together and there was a bond between them.

AN INTERVIEW WITH ANN HALPRIN BY DOUGLAS ROSS

ROSS: *How did you participate in* Myths?

HALPRIN: Some *Myths* required me to give directions, to guide the results as the events unfolded. But when the material was self-generating once it got started, I was able to enter in like anyone else.

ROSS: *Did your reaction match the audience's?*

HALPRIN: I'm always studying the process, looking for ways in which the individual experience turns into a collective one, while most members of the audience react in terms of what a *Myth* did to them personally. No *Myth* is a failure to me because I always learn from it—but it might be a terrible failure to a participant.

ROSS: *What about non-participating observers?*

HALPRIN: I would say one *must* participate. But there are some who enjoy it on a sociological or anthropological level, and there are always two or three who sidle up to me and give me their interpretations. Sometimes there are unique circumstances; once, for example, we were involved in going up and down the platforms and around the room very actively, throwing balls back and forth. These two older women were in the audience, and of course they couldn't engage in the action, so

NOTE

The following interview by Douglas Ross contextualizes Halprin's participation in, and understanding of, the Myths process that is scored and described in the previous article. Like much of Halprin's work at that time, participation was the key to understanding and interpreting the work. In addition, issues central to the development of Myths—the exploration of conflict, sensuality, sexuality, aggression, game playing, etc.—are discussed in this brief interview. In its original form, these two articles were published simultaneously by the *Tulane Drama Review* and thus have been reproduced in their entirety here. *Editor*

they sat on a riser in one area and observed, and then moved to another part of the room and watched while the balls were being thrown around them. Later the musicians said that the most provocative thing in the whole evening was the marvelous juxtaposition of these two old women and the environment, in whose context the very fact that they were so thoroughly spectators made them into performers.

ROSS: *Of what value was the preparation room?*

HALPRIN: This is a developing thing. The way people—especially the regulars—come into that room and start their own warm-ups is becoming a free improvisation. They know they won't be told what to do, they are going to do what they want, or make or allow it to happen. People really like to have this kind of responsibility. It gives them a feeling of self-esteem, a chance to use their full capacities. I hope that before long this so-called preparation period will *become* the myth.

ROSS: *And the de-briefing coffee klatches?*

HALPRIN: Through group contemplation and discussion, the evening can be transformed from a passing turn-on into art, a part of a person's being.

ROSS: *How did your response to a* Myth *already performed affect your plans for a future one?*

HALPRIN: We learned how things worked, and then we based our next *Myth* on something that didn't work but could have. Audience questionnaires were used, and they had some influence. We quickly noticed that we had to evolve structures that were free enough to allow everyone to become involved in his own way, avoiding any feeling of manipulation, but simultaneously we had to set up boundaries, so that the inclusion of so many people wouldn't lead to complete chaos. It was touchy, balancing these polarities. It meant avoiding the use of words and relying on the materials to create stimuli and multiple choices—verbal explanations are either interpreted a hundred different ways or simply forgotten. The controls brought people together, so that they reinforced rather than worked against each other. I don't mean that we were avoiding tensions or conflicts. But they had to be aware that they were a collective, not just 50 individuals on private trips.

ROSS: *Why did you hang unoccupied chairs from the ceiling, or newspapers on the walls?*

HALPRIN: The chairs were a statement to the audience that there would be no way to sit down, to be apart from the experience. We are all in this together, we are all actively involved in this. They also became an irrational note, to stir the imagination, to ask the question . . . The newspapers were used primarily because they had a very good texture and turned the room into a marvellous light experience, a particular void.

ROSS: *Was there a unique philosophical core behind each evening?*

HALPRIN: There was an idea behind each evening but I doubt it was unique. I try to avoid that. I try to deal with ideas that are very common, basic, and ordinary. Sensuality, sexuality, conflict, aggression, game structure, play, confrontations, celebration, bewilderment, the sharing of tragedy.

ROSS: *Why have you said that the public urgently wants to determine its own artistic environment?*

HALPRIN: We can no longer depend on our masterminds. There is too much for one mind to master. It's more enjoyable and more unpredictable to let things happen that just let everybody be, and it's wonderful to see what comes about when you release people's resources. You can allow yourself to find out what is possible and not just what you think *should* be. One person determining everything for everybody: it just isn't like that any more. It doesn't have to be like that.

CEREMONY OF US

INTERVIEW BY ERIKA MUNK

HALPRIN: When James Woods, director of Studio Watts Workshop, invited me to perform in Los Angeles last summer, he had recently seen a Dancers' Workshop performance and felt something of the participation, freedom, and involvement between performers and audience which we create. He wanted such a theatre event for the Los Angeles Festival of the Performing Arts in February. It was part of his plan that people from the Watts community would come to the Mark Taper Forum, most of them for the first time, and mingle with the affluent whites who attend the Mark Taper regularly. That theater itself, a status symbol of "let me in," was to be, as he said, "a tool for social change."

MUNK: *The piece involved two groups, one black, from Los Angeles, and one white, from San Francisco. How did you get the two together?*

HALPRIN: I wanted to do a production *with* a community instead of *for* a community. My plan was to give a workshop at Studio Watts School for the Arts open to anyone regardless of training or experience. Out of this workshop a group of performers representing Watts would be developed. We started in September, meeting once a week. I began to conduct a similar workshop for a white group of the same size in San Francisco. The two developed separately until ten days before the performance. During those days, working and living together, they collectively created their performance around the experience of becoming one group. My role was to see what the group was most ready for and what materials turned them on, then to guide them in choreographing their own responses. Charles Amirkhanian, the composer, recorded their singing, shouting, laughing, crying, music-making, and

NOTE

Erika Munk worked in an editorial capacity for the Tulane Drama Review *at the time of this interview.*

I wanted to do a production with a community instead of for a community. Ceremony of Us, *1969.*

Photo by
Susan Landor.

During rehearsal, working through a disagreement. Ceremony of Us, *1969.*

Photographer
Unknown.

made a tape score of this natural but juxtaposed material. Patric Hickey used his medium, light—he respected the nature of the Forum and treated the environment directly and openly, strengthening our total attitude: authenticity. We didn't try or want to convey explicitly political messages, but these meanings emerged from the process and the material itself.

MUNK: *How did the kids' reactions—to the rehearsals and to each other—change during the time they were together?*

HALPRIN: The first weekend they were together each group performed for the other group. They were using the same format, the same improvisational focus. Body exercises, massages, psychic-stress movement, improvisations to break through an individual or group impasse, drawings, self-portraits, and group portraits. We modeled ourselves in clay, we wrote about the ways we identified with our workshop experience, we spent time breathing in and out of each other with our bodies; vocalizing, singing, touching, looking, leading and following with eyes closed, acting out dreams, fantasizing with dress-up costumes, acting out roles on street corners with pedestrians as audience. When things got too heavy, we'd play tag, have horse races, do red light–green light, construct pyramids with our bodies, etc. Out of these games we built the second half of our program. So the Watts group watched the SF group first, and then the SF group watched the Watts group. And what came out of that very first encounter was the highest-pitched kind of nervous expectation and excitement I've ever seen between people. Before the nature of what was happening became clear I noticed a major difference between the San Francisco group and the Watts group: the Watts people seemed to have a built-in loyalty. I had the feeling that they would really help each other, they really were together, they really had a sense of unity—perhaps because they *were* unified by the Watts riot. Our members said that before the Watts riot there were a lot of gangfights and a lot of robberies and killings among themselves, but afterward people suddenly became brothers and sisters. The streets were safe for black men. And it's the same thing I felt in the group. Tremendous concern for each other, no matter how much they argue. We in the white group knew we didn't have this yet.

MUNK: *Weren't the Studio Watts students already a group before you started to work with them?*

HALPRIN: Four were, out of eleven. With the white group, about half knew each other from having worked together before. The big difference was that the whites were very diverse, independent, self-sufficient. Perhaps in white society we don't have the need to support each other. My fantasy is that if a black man were found lying on the street, the blacks would all come and pick him up. If a white man's lying on a street?

MUNK: *That's a reality. We mostly don't.*

HALPRIN: The thing that was so wonderful was how fast the whites saw their own weaknesses—though they only recognized them by being put in that position, realizing how the blacks were together. They said, "We're not strong as a group, and we'll have to be. Let's work on it."

MUNK: *Given this structure, what created the excitement you started to tell about in the first encounter?*

HALPRIN: Powerful sexual tensions. This became the unifying theme—it was as if sexual attraction and repulsion was *the* force that either brought them together or split them apart. It was the pivotal dance element. On Friday night it was on a level of unbelievable sexual potency. The white women were so liberated by the black men that I've never seen such dancing in all my life. It was completely beautiful, but, well, one white man's first reaction was that the women were being raped. My impression, as a white woman watching it, was wow! those white women are really seducing those guys and they're really going right to it.

MUNK: *How did the black women react?*

HALPRIN: They were abandoned. The white fellows were so engrossed in this thing that was going on between the white women and the black men, it put them in a state of shock—they weren't free to relate to the black women that weekend. It was very hard on black women and white men.

MUNK: *It's a miniature of a certain social scene.*

HALPRIN: OK. But what I found so exciting was that changes took place. If it had remained that way it would have been very trite—one would have had the feeling of so what? What's the use of the dance experience? But the next week, when they came back, everybody had had a chance to absorb the experience and the white men were in a very different place. They had a great deal of trust and openness and sexuality for the black women.

MUNK: *And by the time it got to the actual performance?*

HALPRIN: There had been very real comings-together between particular people. The relationships between white men and black women were just as strong by performance time as black men to white women, and it evened off. They did see it the way you read about it, in *Black Rage* and so on—but it didn't stay like that—and that's what threw some of the audience. They expected to come and see the familiar configurations—and there had been too many changes already. Barriers were breaking down fast.

MUNK: *In ten days.*

HALPRIN: That's what's been very difficult to convey to some of my friends who found the performance too loving. There *were* some very sad things that happened—but it didn't stay like that. What those white men went through in one week would ordinarily take men years to overcome, that feeling that they had been emasculated by black men who came in with a sexual ease that they were able to express so fluently in their hips, just a gorgeous flow. And the white fellows overcame this.

MUNK: *How?*

HALPRIN: Working it out in their heads and then working it out in movement situations. The women asked more of the men, they became almost taunting. One girl started pushing this guy all over the floor, just pushing him, and he wouldn't react. And she set up almost a fight situation and she said, "Well, push me! Push me against the wall." He finally pushed her very hard. And she said "More" until he became much more aggressive. And the women did a lot of screaming and hollering and crying and shouting and demanding that the men do something. At the same time the white women realized that they had made it hard on their men, and the men realized that they just had to get out there and do their thing, there was no time to moralize. They began to challenge the black men physically, though the black men were very strong and the white men had been afraid. They began tug-of-war type movements with them. All of these real-life things came out as rituals in the dance.

MUNK: *If everyone got over the cliché part of the whole black-white, male-female thing and back down to reality, what were the real-life tensions and how did they come out in performance?*

HALPRIN: Would you like a specific example? After the first part of the dance, "When I look at you I see," we separated the two groups. They went back to the first part with all the blacks separated from the whites and they made a line and they started this movement that's like two snake forms and the black group moved along their orbit and the white group moved along theirs. There was expectation and tension: what's going on over there? First thing that happened, I interpreted as a subtle hostility, done in a very curious way. The white group was not allowed to come together. The structure was: you start one by one falling in behind each other.

"At the beginning, I didn't know how to relate to a black woman." Wanda Coleman and Paul Pera, Ceremony of Us, *1969.*

Photo by
Laurie Grunberg.

"One man, one woman, one family, one joy, one sorrow." Pepe and Nancy Peterson, Ceremony of Us, *1969.*

Photo by
Laurie Grunberg.

The black group cut off four people from the white group and circled around them and entrapped the four white kids. And they said, "We cut them off." So the black group got going and was unified, but the white group was just standing around waiting for those four people to get out so that they could get on with their thing. Cut 'em right off—now, what do you think that was?

MUNK: *Guerrilla warfare and sex games.*

HALPRIN: Well, it was something. This had never happened before. They were cut off. They did a very interesting thing. They didn't try to fight it, but just waited it out, really cool. You see, cutting them off wasn't an outright mean thing to do. It was almost amusing. If the white group hadn't already developed esteem and affection for the black group, they might have really gotten annoyed. But they just accepted it as, "Okay, you're going to do that? Okay, we'll do this." Apparently some of the black members said, "Let them out!" and they wouldn't be let out, so they had a little thing going among themselves. That was one of the first things I noticed. The other was that the white kids had to compete. These kids aren't inclined to compete, but they had to. If they didn't really compete in the true sense of the word they would be wiped out. Dancing to drums seemed so unnatural to many of the whites—not the ones from my teenage group, but some of the older members. Both men and women. The blacks would get something in their shoulder and something in their head, and the whites seemed so clumsy by comparison, particularly the men, because they had no movement in their hips, and so the movement would just stop midway in the body. The white group, for the first time, stood their own ground. They used their space magnificently, they were together for the first time, they were very intense, very concentrating, they didn't try to be black dancers—they were what they were. One reason was that they were so challenged at the beginning when their group was divided. You could just see the expression on their faces, it was a life and death matter. There they were, and they were going to make it. And they did. Okay, now did the audience see it or not? They *must* have felt the tension.

MUNK: *Did the women ever act as one group?*

HALPRIN: It happened after that weekend when the black women felt abandoned, the white men crushed. Later, the white men were coming on strong to the black men, diverting their attention from the white women. It threw the women together, and it threw the men together. Until I saw this pattern emerging, everything was deteriorating, because each group had destroyed its familiar configuration, nobody was working, they weren't even arguing, just passive resistance. So we changed the rehearsal conditions. The women had prepared a magnificent meal for the men and said, "We won't serve this to you until you do something for us." And the men wrote this beautiful song and serenaded each of the women. And this did it. They went on walks together, they played. The next day the men went in one room and the women in another, and they worked out the men's dance and women's dance—that was the second structure of the performance, while the first one was black and white. The women's was a birth dance; people in the audience were so shook up by it that they giggled. Here was a black woman giving birth to a white baby. Then there was another kind of a sexual dance.

The dances were no longer of novelty, conquest, pure physical sexuality—the men had had a chance for ten minutes to watch those women giving birth and when they came to them they really looked at them with wonder and caution. After that the sexual conflict was no longer prevalent, sensual things seemed to operate on a different dimension.

MUNK: *I meant to ask you what's "red light-green light"?*

HALPRIN: That's a beautiful power structure game. If the person controlling the game board points to red light–green light, the first person who sees it in the group—while they're doing something else—immediately stands out with his back to the group. Then everybody has to line up, and they say "green light," and everybody tries to move to get his place, and then he turns and says "red light"—"stop!"—and if you move he says "back." This person has complete control. But he might tell somebody to go back and then they'll start arguing. "I didn't move." "Yes you did, you motherfucker, you're just doing it arrarrghhh." A real power structure game, and once they got playing you could hardly stop them. They would practically kill themselves to get up there. One guy did a leap in the air from this position and he just landed WHAM! I just thought he'd be a bloody mess when he got up. They risk their lives to have control. All the things in the second half were done as games, but they were really revealing. Not one white person got up there, ever! Until the performance.

MUNK: *Did they try hard?*

HALPRIN: You're damn right they did.

MUNK: *I'd think that the particular kind of white people you get in your group are those who have deliberately rejected this competitiveness.*

HALPRIN: Exactly.

MUNK: *They want to be nice.*

HALPRIN: Not exactly. Sometimes we wanted so much to become a loving community that we weakened the real conflict in the material. Or maybe it was lack of experience. But working in movement has strengthened all of us. The day after the performance we met to confront the issue of dissolving or continuing as a group. Suddenly we crashed head-on with suppressed problems: angry complaints about personal recognition, money, policy-making, decisions coming from the top affecting each person's life, control versus self-determination, desire for inclusion, fear of losing black identity—screaming, fighting, crying, comforting, walking out, and coming back. As people and artists, blacks and whites, we had to face these conflicts which opened up like a whole shocking new beginning.

MUNK: *Are the two groups still functioning together?*

HALPRIN: Yes. There's a whole new format now. The material is the same in that they're still using the same process, but now they're so strong as one group that they're able to go out and direct *Ceremony of Us*. They can infiltrate a group of two or three hundred people and create the structure of the piece out of the things that are happening.

MUNK: *In the Taper Forum I assume the audience was outside the dance until the end. Do you want the audience to become the dance?*

HALPRIN: That's right. Exactly.

INSTRUCTIONS TO PERFORMERS:

CEREMONY OF US

In the lobby report, "When I look at you I see . . ." Comment objectively on precisely what you see, no more. As the audience goes into the auditorium, follow them in and continue reporting, allowing for the incorporation of their responses. Your prerecorded tapes have been playing during this activity. On the shouted word "Paul," leave the auditorium space, go to the edge of the platform, and remove your outer clothing. Take places on the platform, either sitting, standing, or lying down. Remain silent, be looked at. Your prerecorded "confessions" ("When I look at you I don't see . . ." "When I look at you I imagine I see . . ." "I want to see . . .") will be played during this time.

When you hear your voices on tape calling each other's names, begin the action of *looking* and *touching* each other, responding to your immediate feelings about the person you are looking at and reacting to.

When the name calling on tape fades out, the drummers will decide when to start sounds for the snake dance. Begin your separation into two groups. Allow a leader to emerge naturally in each group, and begin to follow his movements. Keep the focus in your own group, not paying attention to the other group. When the leader's movement statement has been made, the group should move over him as he is replaced by a new leader. This is repeated as long as new leaders continue to emerge.

When everyone has been a group leader, crouch and stare at the other group. Wait. Come together, staying low. Wait—drummers, dancers—wait. All find the moment when group feeling builds toward culmination in one instant YELL. DO IT! Find ways to merge the two groups and improvise, using the snake form and exploring the periphery of the performance space. Incorporate any audience members who join in either sound or movement.

When you feel repressed by group action, break out into center space and begin your own thing. Group members continually try to reinforce each other's actions.

From within group, men separate from women. Women draw aside, but respond openly to the actions of the men up on the platform.

Men draw aside. Women mount the platform and do your ritual.

Men join women. You have received a quote by the woman you are to join, which you now read for the first time. Let this be the basis of your actions with her.

After you have washed each other, move out and wash a member of the audience. Then pour your water into the common receptacle, take your candle, and move off the platform.

RED LIGHT-GREEN LIGHT

LINEUP

MONOLOGUE
(improvise)

TUG OF WAR

CAMEL

BRIDGE & SING YOUR FAVORITE SONG

MOUNDS

COSTUMES

LEVITATION

DISAPPEAR

PYRAMID

ANIMALS

HORSE RACE

SILENCE

LOTUS

STIRRUP

CARRY

TUNNEL

FALLING

PROCESSION

*After you have washed
each other, move out and
wash a member of the
audience.* Ceremony of
Us, *1969.*

Photo by
Tylon Barea.

The Attendant will decide which activity the group is to do and point to it on the wall chart. The first person who sees her change an action will start it immediately. The Procession will be last. Involve the audience strongly and eventually lead it up the aisles, through the lobby, and out into the plaza.

Left to right: John Hopkins, dancer; Casey Sonabend, drummer. Ceremony of Us, *1969.*

Photo by **Tylon Barea**.

MICROCOSM IN MOVEMENT

James T. Burns

The audience enters a shallow circular lobby and is immediately confronted with the decision: black or white, which way to go? Lined against the curving walls are: left side young blacks, right side young whites. In the auditorium, before the beginning of the event, participants approach viewers and gaze intently into their eyes saying, "When I look at you I see . . . pink skin, brown skin, black hair, groovy earrings, a soul sister, yellow mustache, love, trust, uneasiness, a smile." Tapes play words and sounds made earlier by the group itself. Participants move to the apron of the stage, strip to leotards and shorts, gather on stage, let themselves be seen as performers by the audience, and begin. To one member of the audience it looked and felt like this:

A ceremony of coming together, of forming as a group performing together before an audience, of discovering each other and beginning to work as a group. They shout, call each other's names, move toward each other, kiss, touch, embrace. Louder cries, laughter, drums.

The discovery of differences, of separation and conflict, of racial competition, identity, strength, soul. Two group lines form, black and white. Breathing noise. Lights out, shadows moving, lights up. Jumping behind screens, in front, blacks penetrate white line, separate, lie down, dance over, lie on, hump and dance over, clap, stretch legs, run, jump. Whites in a silent dance, whites yell and crawl around steps, blacks attack white line. Stomping karate motions. Around and around each other's lines, changing leaders often, the groups bounce off each other, blacks bugging whites. They subside onto steps, blacks on right, whites on left.

A coming together again for celebration after conflict. Humming, they swim into center stage together, intermingle at floor level, over and under each other, rest, moan. Group humming. They rise—lights up—jump, scream, run around—

NOTE

James T. Burns has watched and written about a great deal of Anna Halprin's work.

The discovery of differences,
of separation, conflict, racial
competition, identity,
strength, soul. Ceremony of
Us, *1969.*

Photo by
Tylon Barea.

Ceremony of Us, *1969.*

Photo by
Tylon Barea.

colored lights—play tag, yell—all together hey hey hey—snake dance. Drums again. Clapping. Group dances, singles, doubles, little groups, everybody.

Sexual differences arise. The men feel their maleness and need to prove it against other males, black against white. The women feel their womanness and identity as givers of life. The two come together to re-create love, then share that discovery with the audience. Male competition. Screens part. Black guys jump against white guys—one by one, two by two, back and forth across the stage, higher and higher, shadows against light wall at back, growling and threatening from the two groups. A fight, women egging them on from the steps: men struggle, fall, suffer, edge toward women who reach out and drag them down off stage. Women move onto stage carrying each other, abandoning guys on steps. Heavy breathing, swaying, a moan, birth movements, a scream, belly held: girl is born between legs. Babies inch forward, mothers catch up and fondle them. Earth mother rear center: all draw toward her. She, black, has a white child who cries like a baby. Earth mother surrounded. She croons, they all hum. Men come back on stage to get women. Colored lights up and down, moving, loving, holding, fucking. Attendant woman places a water tub, cloths, bowls and candles around, all wash each other, move down to wash hands in audience. Move off slowly.

(End of "Starting Point." Interval.)

A celebration of the group's existence as a creative community performing a festive event. An outpouring of gaiety, emotion, movement, sound, light, color in a series of episodes fashioned by the participants themselves. The coming together is here complete, and the audience is asked to join in. Wall graphics name activities and movements to be done, pointed to randomly and in spontaneous combination by woman attendant. Men on drums, women out yelling. They assemble together for playdancing, celebration. Construction dance—build with bodies. Lotus—contemplative, decorative. Red light, green light—humping, carrying. Silence. Drilled into a straight line, they drop one by one as boy sings "Ave Maria." Attendant is last to drop after it is all over. Horse race—up on backs. Monologue—man from Watts: "Watch love grow tall as trees." Bridge—walk across crouching bodies and sing own songs. Levitation—rise and fall into group's arms: trust. Circle, pyramid, and fall. Tug of war—big competition. Dressing each other in costumes to monologue about a man who drilled a great hole to the center of the earth: process thing by Nick Peckham of San Francisco. Noises—group animal score. Carrying, lights, colors, water sounds. Up and down aisles, taking more and more members of the audience along: humming, chanting, everyone up and moving, on stage, in aisles, on outside into Music Center Plaza, stomp and clap, drums, dance, colored plastic billowing overhead. People coming out of symphony across way get involved to their own amazement; hippie kids appear from nowhere; dancing, drumming, moving together, back into theater. To end.

*Anna Halprin and John
Graham,* Apartment 6, *1964.*

Photo by
Hank Kranzler

A REPORT ON *CITYDANCE* 1977

───────────────────────────────────

INTRODUCTION

The performance of *Citydance* was the most unique style of performing I've ever experienced. The simultaneous combination of highly trained "professional" dancers performing prepared dances, with dances guided by workshop leaders for people of all ages and backgrounds, plus spontaneous dances, music, and poetry created and performed by members of the public, made the performance aspects of *Citydance* unusual, interesting and exciting. Above all, it was authentic in its diversity. Children play-performed at South Park; a healer enacted a ritual at Twin Peaks; a poet created a thread throughout—reading at every episode; bums and crazies joined in at Market Street; dancers from the Mobilus group gave performances at the cemetery; and individual dancers and actors appeared in masks and costumes, contributing their individual pieces of theatre unexpectedly and effectively.

PERFORMANCE ASPECTS OF *CITYDANCE*

One element which characterized the entire performance of *Citydance* was the spontaneity that was displayed throughout, combined with the remarkable amount of individual input by the participants. This input was highly sensitive and fit in so well with the whole. In the case of the members of the Dancers' Workshop Training Program, *Citydance* was an opportunity to prepare performances at chosen locations, combining their personal dances with the process of leading the public in a participatory activity. These dances were being seen for the first time and in themselves were wonderful surprises. Present also were people who had read the score in the newspaper and had come with their own dances to perform. And finally, as the dance moved through the city, people in neighborhoods and on the streets joined and added their artistic gifts.

There were three layers of performances taking place simultaneously during the *Citydance*. One was the overall performance of the *journey* through the city,

*Dancing in the Museum of
Modern Art,* Citydance.

Photo by
Buck O'Kelly.

Dancing at dawn,
Citydance.

Photo by
Buck O'Kelly.

starting with the sunrise ceremony at Twin Peaks and culminating in the later afternoon at Embarcadero Plaza. The second layer was composed of the *activities* or *episodes* at the nine different locations, and the third was composed of the *individual dances* within the activities.

Citydance Introduction: S.F. Museum of Modern Art

Score your dance for Saturday. Explore the use of space and how you interact with people and objects within a space. Recycle your performance back into your written or drawn score. Use the entire experience as a resource for your performance in the city on Saturday.

THE DANCES

Sunrise: Twin Peaks (5:35 A.M.)

Score: Welcome the sun. Incantation. Welcome the new dawn. Strangers becoming friends by acknowledging and honoring the sun.

 The arrival at Twin Peaks at 5:30 in the morning was greeted by everyone with tremendous excitement and anticipation. Everyone had wondered if they would be the only ones to get there and were delighted to find 75 other brave people had joined them. We instantly felt like a special clan and there was much comradeship as a result. When we walked up the hill, a poet (Kush) was already up there bellowing out Gary Snyder's "Prayer for the Great Family." The poem was very appropriate as it brought our attention to an acknowledgment of nature. Kush walked majestically to all four corners of the peak, saluting the city, and chalking words from the poem onto the rocks. People brought all kinds of artistic and ceremonial gifts. Some danced, some played music. We meditated, and we huddled together to keep warm, for the wind was chilly and it was dark. The most outstanding performance was the sun's. The fog was like a curtain between us and the sun. As we chanted the traditional Native American sunrise song, the fog would teasingly part and let the sun peek through and the chant would soar out with exuberance and laughter, then the sun would retreat again behind the fog. A great red glow on the distant bay, then an orange flash in the sky, then just gray again. Finally the fog curtain thinned just enough so that we could look at the sharp round spot of brilliant light with our naked eyes. At that point we witnessed a healing of the whole city by Dolores Kreiger who had come to join us that morning.[1] Hugs and cheers, then down the hill we went for hot tea and coffee. The performance of this first ceremony/initia-

NOTE

1. Dolores Kreiger is a nurse who developed a healing technique called Therapeutic Touch.

tion had variety, spontaneity, sensitivity, originality, creativity, imagination, and coherence. It was deep, yet joyous in its spirit.

Woodswalk: Buena Vista Park

Score: Follow the banners. Listen to the music. Pay attention to your senses. Leave an impression.

The next performance was in Buena Vista Park—the Woodswalk. A young man called Rainbow magically appeared with twelve hand-dyed, rainbow-colored silk banners mounted on poles. He gave us a delightful dancing demonstration with the banners and then passed them out to people who wanted to dance with them, leading the group through the woods. All along the way the poet would stop and write words with chalk on trees and stones. Musicians, whistling and playing flutes, were nestled among trees and rocks throughout the woods, guiding us with their sounds. All was silent except for the sounds of birds, musicians and our own laughter and enjoyment. When the group reached the open space there was a spontaneous series of game-like dances. The heralds balanced on tree stumps and waved banners in various formations and patterns, while others sang and did circle dances under them. There was tumbling and acrobatics of all sorts. I had the impression of a morning stroll and morning exercises. It was still early, between 7 and 8 in the morning, with not too many cars or stray people around, although windows were opening in houses across the street with an array of yawning faces peering out at this living color dream. Break for breakfast in the neighborhood and get ready for the CITY!

Icon: Dolores and Market Streets

Score: Discover the sculpture. Teddy Roosevelt in Cuba. Transform the image into something else with sketches, music and 3-D movement.

The third site was a statue in the Mission District. We had planned to sit down, rest, and draw the Icon. People did this and more. After a while the energetic ones began to become more involved with the sculpture by climbing up on it and relating to the figure in various poses. It was very enjoyable to watch and some of the neighbors came out of their shops and homes to join the gathering. They were a friendly group of people, and one even offered to buy us all some beer (it *was* getting hot). In the meantime another participant, who I'd been traveling with in her VW bus, brought out her mask-making materials and decided to help people make extra faces. There had been a month of preparation for mask-making for the *Citydance* by a volunteer called Jericho, who appeared every week at our studio and taught people how to make their own. Now, one of his students helped others do the same.

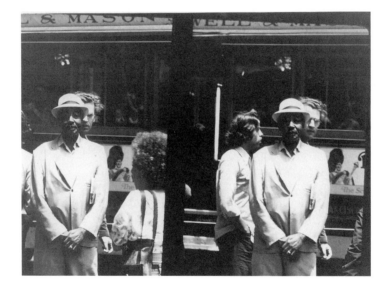

Dancing in the park,
Citydance.

Photo by
JoAnn Vincent.

Making and breaking
contact with strangers,
Citydance.

Photo by
Charlene Koonce.

Long Ago: Graveyard of Mission Dolores

Score: S.F. started here more than 200 years ago. Here are: our first mayor, three victims of the explosion of the steamboat *Jenny Lind*, Louise Dotter—six days old, an Irish fireman . . .

From the statue we all walked along the grass boulevard in this Spanish-speaking neighborhood and arrived at Mission Dolores. We entered into a cemetery that was laden with history and memories. There we were treated to a spectacular performance by Mobilus dressed in black robes and stark white masks, evoking a mysterious mood of ghosts. I was interested in the resident priest, who was also in the garden, and what his reaction to all of this would be. He was astonished and also accepting. He was dressed in black robes, and his smooth gliding walk through the garden cemetery added to the performance as a whole. People were very quiet, walked softly, and when they exchanged they whispered.

Roleplay: Civic Center

Score: Individual and collective transformation of this formal space. Feasts, circle dances, people become birds, beasts, politicians, ballet stars. Play out your fantasies.

The formal space between the Opera House and Museum was the next stop. Mobilus and other members of Dancers' Workshop had planned fantasy dances. One was a lunch in which the performers dressed in formal black and white and ate their food in slow motion, right in the center of the sidewalk with traffic whizzing by. Jason Serinus whistled classical music through a bullhorn while different people acted out their secret fantasy dances. Everyone who had a mask was wearing it. I had a bird mask and enjoyed being incognito while performing a bird dance to Jason's whistling. Jericho came soaring around the corner in his extravagant mask, with his silk robes billowing, and performed a glorious dance on the spot. There were all kinds of dances going on simultaneously so that the place took on the quality of a Brueghel painting and a definite surrealistic mode. It was fun and full of merriment.

Rap: Powell and Market Streets

Score: Cable car turnaround and rapid transit plaza. Making and breaking contact with strangers. Ask them to join you at Embarcadero. Enjoy the drama of this space.

From the Civic Center we proceeded to the Market Street site and the same surrealistic mode continued, except the setting was in the heart of the city and in a place where all kinds of people accumulate and hang out. Here the surrealism became bizarre—now like a Bosch painting. A group of participants had an old

parachute with many openings, so that as they played inside it you could see only pieces of their bodies with the rest enclosed in mounds. It was such a weird juxtaposition in that setting. However, the people got into the spirit of things, and the "bums" who hang out there began to take on various roles. One created some lively music via sticks and lightpoles. A little old lady making grimaces danced her dance and soon a circle of bystanders was formed, gawking and not protesting. A religious fanatic used the opportunity to do his "Jesus Saves" dance, and I noticed a certain kind of somber tension building up even though the outer aspects of the performance seemed jolly.

Playtime: South Park

Score: A ghetto park in an industrial neighborhood. Play with the kids. Rap with the neighbors. Merge. Appreciate what they're doing at their playground. Bring them along to the celebration.

A playground in an all black neighborhood was next. I was stunned at the isolation of this neighborhood from the rest of the city. The playground was totally surrounded by buildings, so that a person could feel completely enclosed and cut off from everything else. Although Jim Burns had advised us to notify the neighborhood that we would be coming, there was a sense of suspicion and a pulling back of the people as they watched us arrive. The sight of neighbors standing and leaning on cars, or in groups on the stoop of their houses, or leaning on door frames and out of windows, brought a growing sense of our entrance into some "foreign territory" and of not being sure if it was "all right." This entrance for me was a powerful dance in itself. The first of us who arrived simply went to a nearby bench and sat there taking in the atmosphere, not feeling comfortable to do more than just be there and let ourselves be seen. More of the *Citydance* people began to trickle in. What finally broke the ice and brought about release was that the children in the neighborhood, out of curiosity, began to come over to us, and before long an enthusiastic baseball game was in full swing. Others were swinging on swings, going down slides, climbing, etc. Drummers assembled and began to beat out rhythms which became an accompaniment for the games, lending rhythm to the movement so that it was experienced as dance. One tired group

Audience? Performer?
Everyone dances.
Citydance, *1977.*

Photo by
Charlene Koonce.

went to a grassy space and began to massage each other around the shoulders and feet. One of the young persons who had been staring from a doorway came over to me and wanted to know what the people were doing. Face painting began in another corner, and a young fellow from the neighborhood joined; then people began to paint each other's faces. Children wanted to join this too. A mother came onto the scene, saw her child's face painted, gave him a smack, and ordered him into the house! This was definitely the most challenging location, and in retrospect I feel the time element limited the fruition of this performance. When we were leaving for the next site, a picnic-like quality had begun to emerge and the whole neighborhood was just beginning to get involved in a fun-loving manner. When it was time to go, some local people did join and continued with us to the next place.

Totem: Sacramento and Drumm Streets

Score: Louise Nevelson's three-story sculpture rising in a courtyard of Portman's new skyscraper. Move up and down stairs and escalators and around balconies . . . Sketch impressions of change as you rise to the top and look out toward the final stop.

The next stop was Louise Nevelson's three-story totem. I had to hustle over to Embarcadero and do some "guardian-of-the-score" dances in preparation for the Celebration. Cachelle Cummings, who scored the Totem Dance, will report on what took place there: "Many costumed dancers and many passing-by dancers— who don't know they're dancing—are here. We perceive the totem and depict our individual impressions on a long piece of paper—tall and stretched out like the totem. The late lazy afternoon is catching. Slowly and languidly, low-keyed people move quietly up to the second level and begin their dances. Miscellaneous instruments are invented as we create our own accompaniment. A single triangle is heard below on the first level. We are aware of movement above, below and next to us. My own awareness of vertical space is magnified. Involvement on each level is deep, and it is difficult to leave what we are doing and progress to the top—to the sun. Those of us on the third level begin chanting to those on the second level, pulling them up to the sun with our voices and our bodies. A linear feeling of space is strong as a long line forms around the square upper balcony. Hand in hand, we move carefully along the square together, aware of our brotherhood and unity, chanting our goodbyes to the totem, to each other, and chanting our gratitude to Louise Nevelson."

Playing at the
Embarcadero Plaza.
Citydance, *1977.*

Photo by
Buck O'Kelly.

Celebration: Embarcadero Plaza

Score: Culmination of scores and performances in the vast brick plaza at the foot of Market Street. Share the day's experience with each other. Build a totem with our bodies and with objects we've collected during the day. Conga dance. Processional with banners and sunset ritual.

The final performance was now happening. Close to a thousand people were gathering in the vast brick plaza. Musicians were on the platform—a group of drummers, horn players and singers. Here were musicians who had played at all the Museum events, plus new ones from the crowd who augmented our own band. At the moment of gathering, and synchronized with the lifting of 50 brightly colored 18-foot banners, a bagpiper dressed in traditional costume began to play and march. The space became a magnificent play of color, movement and sound. From this burst of display, people glided into various formations and then into a procession. They followed the piper all around the Villaincourt Fountain, going around and through (!) the waterfalls. It was a very grand and joyous sight with fathers holding children aloft, the banners marking the way, and people in fantastic masks and costumes. I was startled at the ease in which all these people took directions when offered; the cooperation and group commitment was remarkable. The final dance was a series of circles—one growing out of the other—with the bagpiper in the center and the banners forming an outer circle to define the whole series. We ended this by singing and facing the sun, holding our palms up to receive the sun's energy. The poet once again offered the poem of Gary Snyder, moving to all four corners of the gathering, and the musicians on the platform beat the rhythm, mingling it with a single penetrating tone from a large Tibetan horn. The final formal celebrative act was unifying, inspiring and very well supported by all the participants.

No one wanted to leave. The musicians continued to play and people who wanted to kept right on dancing into the later afternoon. I left while the celebration was still going on. It still goes on, in some way, in the lives of everyone who was there.

*Ending the day at the
Embarcadero,* Citydance.

Photo by
Charlene Koonce.

LEANING INTO RITUAL

---

*Working in the natural environ-
ment often evokes archetypal
forms. Sea Ranch, 1983.*

Photo by
Coni Beeson.

INTRODUCTION

Rachel Kaplan

When Anna was very ill and recovering from cancer, she had a vision. When she came home from the hospital, she was very vulnerable, weak, and frail. She was lying in her bed, facing the trees, and a black raven flew in and sat on her bed. She was terrified because the black bird, according to Jewish legend, is the Angel of Death, and when the black bird comes, it comes to take you to Zion. She was sure that this was what was happening and that she was actually dying. The bird began to talk to her in bird language and said, "It's time to go now." She began to negotiate with the bird, and said, "I don't feel I have finished my work here yet." And so the bird said to her that she could stay if she committed herself to using dance to create love and peace between people, and between people and the earth. And she promised. The bird said, "I will circle around you from time to time to see that you are living up to your commitment." Then the bird hopped around three times on the bed and flew away. The black birds periodically visit Anna, sending their call out overhead, and making large, lazy circles in the sky.

For the artist whose life becomes her art, all experience is grist for the mill. Anna Halprin's experience of cancer is no exception to this rule, and the changes this confrontation wrought on her life and her work are far-reaching and consequential, both personally and socially. Upon discovering her illness, Halprin convened her many formidable resources—her indomitable spirit, her endless curiosity, her fierce will and her wide-ranging experience as a performing artist—and devised a strategy that not only helped her come to grips with her experience, but catapulted her work into an entirely new realm. During this process, her art reformed itself around global social issues and the complex processes of healing, and began to edge farther away from the theater and closer into the realm of ritual activity.

Now fully discontent to work within the context of "art" and with specific art-making communities, Halprin's instinct drove her to create events and processes which speak directly to what is human in each of us: the experiences of birth and aging; the tandem processes of union and separation; the balancing acts of illness and health: in short, life and death in the fullness of its many cycles. As her art had once circled around themes of community and the breaking down of the fourth wall, it now pushed even farther beyond the boundaries of the traditional Western theater, leaning closer and closer to ritual, closer and closer to what Halprin has come to believe is the ancient root of dance: a dance of meaning, which we dance with our spirits and the spirits of those we worship—the earth, the community, the ancestors.

Halprin's confrontation with her own cancer set her to study in depth the connections between body, mind, and emotion. What evolved was a deeper understanding of the inner structure of healing, and a working practice called the Five Stages of Healing. She has since applied these ideas and processes not only to her own body but to her work with large community groups, and it is an integral part of the training programs conducted at the Tamalpa Institute. On this leg of her journey, Halprin in her art instinctively broadened the uses of dance to include healing, and kept crossing and re-crossing the boundary betwen these forms, seeking a synthesis between the two. As part of the California culture which has nurtured and been nurtured by Halprin's work, this cross-over would seem to be inevitable. Halprin's career is the epitome of the New Age mentality *in action,* and her work has hovered for years in that liminal zone between "art" and "therapy."

Both her art and the practice of therapy are often concerned with the reclamation of stories (what Halprin calls "myths") and the integration of the past, the present and the future (what Halprin calls "ritual"), and the line between the two has grown more and more indistinct in her work. As someone who has sought continuously for ways to integrate life and art, Halprin's experimental union of art and therapy is a happy by-product of this larger quest. Yet Halprin is committed to being an "artist," refuses the label "therapist," and resists interpretations of her "successful cure" as the direct effect of the processes she has evolved. Rather, she cultivates a stance of curiosity and has not fallen into the role of "guru" or "healer" which her position might afford her. Richard Schechner queries in "A Life in Ritual," "Can your dance change the world?" Halprin replies, "I don't know. Maybe it will and maybe it won't, but in this threatening world, it's worth a try!"

The Five Stages of Healing detail the processes of identification, confrontation, and acceptance of a wound or loss associated with grief, injury, or illness and can be applied not only to personal illness, but to the distress confronting families or communities. It is a process fully conscious of the interactive matrix of the body, mind and spirit, and its central drive is toward integration within the individual, the community, and the larger world. In this process, healing affects not only the personal body but the social body, the public body, and in its largest extension, the planetary body. It is a direct manifestation of a belief in the connection of all living beings to one another, and as a theory and a practice, implies a paradigmatic shift of belief and action away from the cultural norms of dualism and division.

Following this trajectory of integrating self, community and environment, the evolution of *Circle the Earth* is reflective of this paradigmatic shift. The Halprins' workshop "The Searth for Myth and Ritual in Dance and the Environment" began with the intention of discovering a community "myth." Functioning experimentally and gathering resources applicable to the community involved, this project evolved into *Circle the Earth*. This community ritual has been the physical manifestation of Halprin's search for a dance that has a use and a function in contemporary culture and consolidates not only her earlier quest for a total theater, but her research into collective creativity, community, illness, and recovery. Of great consequence to *Circle the Earth* is the collective way in which the piece is generated, and how the form and content of the piece serve not only the needs of the group, but the needs of individual participants as well. In *Circle the Earth,* Halprin has struck a balance between group consensus and individual need.

The *Planetary Dance* evolved from *Circle the Earth* as its theme expanded from a dance done by a specific community to a peace dance done by many different communities. Halprin's initial impulse to dance with/for her community shifted as she connected with a desire to serve the world community. First performed in 1987, the *Planetary Dance* is now danced around the world at the time of the spring equinox. In 1994, 120 people came to the original site in California to do the *Planetary Dance,* while simultaneously, the dance was performed in New York, New Mexico, Arizona, Australia, Japan, England, Switzerland, and Germany. The *Planetary Dance* is simple and easily adaptable to different groups of people, all of whom dance at the same time and with the same intent. A central intention of the *Planetary Dance* is the possible participation of everyone/anyone, and in its evolutionary cycle, the dance includes and integrates all available resources into its prayer. In its observance of the change of seasons, the reaffirmation of community, and a desire for peace, the *Planetary Dance* is a contemporary ritualistic expression of connection and continuity. "The Earth Run," reprinted in this collection, is a graphic score that will enable you to re-create this dance in your own community. Halprin's largest vision of this work is a dance done by everyone around the globe, an intentional action which generates its own end: peace and peaceful coexistence.

As the millennium approaches and artists search for new ways to express the same fundamental human themes, an art that serves individuals within the context of community is of great relevance. It is no longer sufficient to create an art that exists only in an elite space, a "virtual reality"; we must create an art that extends beyond its former venues and into the world itself, so that art can serve not only to entertain but to create and generate community. The isolation and alienation from which many of us suffer can be alleviated, in part, through the creation of strong, supportive community and a deeper connection to our own authentic experience. It is Halprin's belief that art, and dance in particular, serves this end, as a reflection of the whole person and the whole culture, and as an expression of our needs, emotions, yearnings, and visions.

Halprin's gradual, final, yet inevitable movements away from art as object have led her to art as community expression, to that place where life is experienced as art, and through that expression, art becomes a living form. This trajectory has taken her far from the venues where art usually takes place in this culture and brought her into contact with people we do not necessarily think of as artists (people with cancer and AIDS, the elderly). Her work has become distinctly site and community specific and, in that way, serves the individual and the community by participating in the mutual evolution of both. Halprin's direction is the path art must take if it is to serve us and find a meaningful place in the chaotic world we inhabit.

We need an art that speaks to and about and from the center of our lives, not an art corrupted by the ideology and reality of consumer culture and corporate mentality. We need an art that has an objective, rather than an art content merely to be an object. We need an art that transcends our differences and brings us together in our commonality, our humanity, our constant striving for the truth in our lives and an understanding of the mysteries around us. And we need artists willing to transcend the myth of isolation and suffering shrouding their role, artists who will step into the public sphere and take on community leadership and transmit their knowledge about creativity and the life of the imagination. We need artists who know that creativity is a source from which we may all drink and that everyone's participation enlarges everyone's potential and expands everyone's life.

In the last twenty years of her life, Halprin has taken giant steps toward making an art of this nature by challenging the parameters of art to include personal healing, community building, and world peace. Her vision of the connection between these bodies—personal, social, global—not only serves to bring individuals and communities together, but continues to narrow the gap between art and life. Her leadership justifies and relies upon the creativity of every individual—an interpretive leap that makes whole the fractured pieces of our lives, our spirits, and our communities.

AFTER IMPROV

INTERVIEW BY NANCY STARK SMITH

NANCY: *Let's talk about improvisation.*

ANNA: I could talk a little bit about my experience of that. I started improvising about 40 years ago when I was trying to break away from influences that I'd had when I studied "modern dance" with [Martha] Graham, Humphrey-Weidman, and Hanya Holm where everything was highly stylized. All the movements were so recognizable. For me it was very confining. No matter what I did when I moved, I noticed that I kept coming back to one of those recognizable styles. It was disturbing because I had no originality in what I was creating. It was about that time that I began to try to break away from those styles and I did what I called "improvisation." What I found was that within about a year's time, that particular way of working had its own pattern.

NANCY: *How would you characterize those patterns?*

ANNA: I seemed to get into certain kinds of movements that I kept coming back to, certain *attitudes* of movement, certain *ideas*. Perhaps I was dancing *about* things and my movement was representational. And in a sense it became just as repetitious and I began to feel restricted again. I believe the way I was improvising didn't require that I break through my familiar ways of responding. And so, for the next decade I experimented continuously with different ways of improvising. The late '50s and '60s was a dynamic and exciting era of experimental improvisation for me and the many people I had a chance to interact with.

NANCY: *What was the improvisation about? What were you thinking about, what was the activity?*

ANNA: At the beginning it was mostly *pure* spontaneous movement using space, time and force for the playing elements. Then I went into tasks like carrying logs and passing them to people, fall and stand for 20 minutes, lean on 25 things, etc. By now I was giving workshops and meeting up with some terrific people like John Graham, A. A. Leath, Simone Forti, Trish Brown, LaMonte Young, Terry Riley, Morton Subotnik, Charles Ross, Bob Morris and many others. This interaction opened up for me wonderful new improvisational approaches.

NANCY: *For instance?*

ANNA: Elements like voice, words, sound, and found objects were introduced. Movement wasn't so pure anymore. Musicians became dancers, dancers became poets, actors and dancers were the same. The possibilities were endless now and this new release of materials and people sparked a fresh approach to ways we could improvise. Just improvising by connecting these varied new elements was stimulating. Improvising was taking us out on the streets, in the aisles, on the rafters— completely free of the restrictions of the proscenium arch. Freedom from preconceptions, boundaries, familiar patterns. Improvisations often led to outrageous and sometimes threatening situations.

NANCY: *Like what?*

ANNA: Such as taking our clothes off and dancing naked, interacting with automobiles in a parking lot, including audience members as participants. At one university, the head of the dance department accused us of setting dance backwards 100 years. What she meant was there was a total lack of "form." This era of experimental improvisations was risky but also a lot of fun. Apparently not always for the audience. In Italy, one member of the audience summed up the scene by doing a mini-improvisation of his own as he marched down the aisle, stood on the stage as I was slowly bringing out my 60th wine bottle and placing it on the floor and shouted, "FOR THIS COLUMBUS DISCOVERED AMERICA!"

I don't really know why people were getting so uncomfortable—perhaps the breaking of taboos or maybe feeling left out, not understanding what made us behave that way. But I wanted to find out. In the late sixties, I began a two year series of experimental improvisations for audience participation. These included Trance dances, spontaneous events (Happenings) in the environment that eventually led to a one-week *Citydance* that started at sunrise and ended at sunset. In each neighborhood we journeyed, there was a simple direction of activity that generated an improvisational, unpredictable and delightful response. This piece brought audience and performer together in a resolved way by using game-like situations. Now everyone was included and knew what was going on.

The use of improvisation as an approach peaked in the performance piece called *Apartment 6*. We got to where, in *Apartment 6*, we used *total* improvisation

after we had found our themes from our real-life relationships. We would just go onstage with those themes and whatever happened happened and there would never be two performances alike and it was absolutely nerve-wracking. Before every performance I was just a nervous wreck because I *never* knew what was going to happen. The material was scary—I felt exposed and vulnerable.

NANCY: *How did you prepare for a performance like that?*

ANNA: I used to take a gin and tonic *(both laughing)*. I had it right on my little table on stage with every performance.

NANCY: *What was actually happening in* Apartment 6—*what were you doing?*

ANNA: Well, you could call it a kind of relationship exploration.
   . . . As a result of the many years we [John Graham, A. A. Leath, and I] had collaborated, we built up a complex and rich shared vocabulary together. This common ground was absolutely necessary to meet the challenge of being instantly present and responding in movement, sound, and words to the reality of the situation. The piece was hysterically funny. Yet the humor could not hide the intense, real emotional material that was stirred.

A new dimension emerged and to clarify the emotional scripting we could no longer use the improvisational process as I knew it. There was not enough objective criteria to assess or assimilate this experience that we had created as well as the impact upon both the audience and our own personal lives. What I discovered was that if I stopped doing improvisation, even stopped using the word, that that freed me right away. So I began to substitute the word "exploration."

EXPLORATIONS

NANCY: *How did an "exploration" differ from "improvisation"?*

ANNA: What I called "dance explorations" was different, because we would take a specific idea—you might take space or you might take time, you might take force—and we would work with a *very* specific focus and then we would explore what are all the possibilities around working with space, for example. And in the process of exploration, we would come up with information that then later on I began to call "resources." But "exploring" was much more focused and more controlled than "improvising."

A. A. Leath and John Graham, Apartment *6, 1965.*

Photo by
Hank Kranzler.

NANCY: *What "information" or resources would arise out of working with space?*

ANNA: Well, we might come up with a series of resources—that you could work with space in terms of areas, or density and sparsity, or levels or directions or horizontal space, or outside space or inside space. We'd come up with a lot of terminology that I began to call resources. And then we would begin to modulate our vocabulary around the information that would be available to us from these explorations.

NANCY: *And this gave a person something to address other than their own movement patterns?*

ANNA: Other than coming out of their own, what I called at that time, guts. Coming out of your own emotional pattern, coming out of your own pre-set attitudes, coming out of what was already, in a sense, familiar . . . subjective.

NANCY: *Wouldn't a person automatically approach these explorations from their pre-set attitudes in any case?*

ANNA: Yes, except the difference is that the more limits you set on yourself, the more you are required to objectify. The more you limit yourself, the more you have to push the edges out to get at more material. See, if I were just improvising I'd go up to a certain point and I might just leave it and go to something else. An exploration requires that you stay on that particular path, focused on dealing with a particular element, for a given length of time. And that you can't just run off. Or you can't just move into some more familiar way of doing things.

NANCY: *Was the intention to get at some deeper level of material?*

ANNA: Yes. Not only deeper level but particularly broader range. I still do a lot of what I call "movement exploration." *Now* what I call movement improvisation is . . . if I'm sitting here right now and I were to start to improvise, it might go something like . . . *[sitting in place, Anna spontaneously moves her arms and head and torso].* That might be an improvisation. I have *absolutely* no idea, it just came out of a nervous response to just being totally present. And it's nothing I could possibly be familiar with. It just came out of some physiological response. And I can do improvisations at the drop of a hat but it's a different kind of improvisation than what I see people calling "improvisation" today, or what I used to call improvisation.

NANCY: *So what you're calling "improvisation" is sort of un-directed.*

ANNA: Completely. It almost comes from the automatic system. Absolutely can't be any thought interference. And it has to keep moving so fast that you have no idea what you're gonna do until it happens. And then you don't even have time to develop your response to it because the next thing is already happening. So it's like a cough or a sneeze or something more of that nature.

NANCY: *So if there's any sort of mind participation, then it's not improvisation?*

ANNA: Yes, in the way I would use the term "improvisation" now. And I do it every once in a while, but I do it for a different purpose. I might do it because I want to really challenge my nervous system, want to get *completely* out of my head. Or I might want to get in touch with what my unconscious body is saying to me at that moment. So, for me, when I use that word, it's very different than what I *used* to do. It started out as that perhaps, but it became some form of exploration.

NANCY: *So it's the exploration/improvisation line that you're crossing.*

ANNA: Yeah. Like Contact Improv, I would rename Contact Exploration, because you're exploring around a particular theme. I understand what you mean when you use the word "improvisation," and there's nothing wrong with it, because you can define a word any way that you want to. But *I* would call it "exploration." I think the advantage to calling it "exploration," for me, is that then I have some activity that is different from the word "improvisation" that is also a form.

NANCY: *So you have two words to use.*

ANNA: I have two words, because by having those two words I distinguish between two different ways of moving.

NANCY: *Would you say then that the focus of improvisation is to go into your body and to just turn on your electricity, or whatever, and let it mobilize you, be expressed through movement.*

ANNA: Exactly. Yeah, that's a *very* good way of describing it. Yeah, sure, that has an intention. And it tends to have no development in it. Improvisations have a form, but it's a very different form than an "exploration" which tends to have a lot of developmental aspects to it.

NANCY: *That's interesting. In teaching Contact Improvisation I kept finding that people were, in your terminology, "exploring" Contact, but I didn't feel that they were "improvising" anymore. It became more like carpenters just putting together materials they already had. But what happens if you try to open up to material that you don't have yet? That requires something else. And the kind of state you're referring to as "improvisation" seems like something you can't really stay in for very long. This all leads to the question—do you think it's possible to teach improvisation?*

Early Experiments in the Environment, Airport Hangar, *San Francisco, 1950.*

Photographer **Unknown**.

I became interested in the connection between movement and feelings. Rana Halprin and Norma Leistiko at Sea Ranch, "Experiments in the Environment," 1968.

Photo by **Paul Ryan**.

ANNA: I think it comes with practice. It comes with practice and a guide, trying to discriminate *for* you when you're controlling it or when it's totally spontaneous, or unexpected. It *is* curious; *can* you teach improvisation?

NANCY: *It's like asking if you can teach imagination.*

ANNA: Maybe just put people in situations where they can experience it. But it's true, I don't think you can *teach* it as such. But you sure can set them in situations. That's all I can imagine.

NANCY: *Yeah, environment has a lot to do with it. In teaching improvisation it seems that often you're just creating the environment, and then maybe giving a few materials as examples. But what can happen is that people then use those examples as techniques and try to work only from a technical mind. How do you awaken the appreciation of the unknown?*

ANNA: Perhaps you can teach people how to pay attention, how to listen to their body, to what's going on, to a kind of superlative awareness by carefully slowing people down. Like the Japanese Butoh movement. So I imagine you can teach awareness and that that will lead into being able to improvise very spontaneously, because that's what it's based on—awareness.

I also think Bonnie [Bainbridge Cohen's] work, and other work that looks at the origin of movement, develops an *incredible* sense of internal awareness. Work like that is *totally* unstylized. More like the *nature* of movement.

MOVEMENT, FEELING, IMAGERY

NANCY: *What happened next in your relationship to movement exploration and improvisation?*

ANNA: What happened is that I became interested in the relationship between movement and feeling, and then in the connection between movement, feeling and imagery. And I didn't have a container for dealing with that material. Because I could no longer see how, in moving, I could contract muscles without stimulating nerve impulses which, once you're conscious of that stimulation, goes through the thalamus and swings around into different sections of the brain triggering off associations and feelings. And what do you do with all that material? And that then has to do with intention and theme and you just have a whole set of resources which I hadn't been in any way finding a system for. So they were becoming very undirected, and by being undirected they weren't being used.

NANCY: *"They," meaning . . .*

ANNA: The feelings. The feelings, the images, the content that was coming up. That's when I began to develop the idea of "myths." I began to realize that movement in many ways was a symbol. And that out of the symbol came a whole series of responses. And that those responses became the content and then the movement could be used in a way that enacted what it was that you were responding to in relationship to that symbol. And I realized that there was a big picture out there that I was getting into that had no . . . boundaries. I was feeling victimized by all this material and I didn't know how to handle it.

NANCY: *Your own material or other people's?*

ANNA: Both. Images and emotions were overwhelming the movement. People were getting hysterical with it.

NANCY: *What was the focus of the exploration that was bringing up this material?*

ANNA: You mean what would start it?

NANCY: *Yes.*

ANNA: Well, say I would be exploring movement using force. And the force might be in the arms. "What are the polarities in force? What is the most intense force that you can use, what is the weakest? Well, let's just see it in the arms, or just in the legs, or your face." Well, if you start experiencing forceful movements, some feelings get triggered off and all of a sudden someone's crying. And I'm saying to myself, "Wait a minute, I didn't mean to do that." You know, "Take it back." Well, it can't be taken back. And it was that kind of stuff. I didn't realize emotions would be released and have that effect, in that way.

NANCY: *As soon as you started to focus the improvisations into explorations, right away the feeling stuff started happening?*

ANNA: Right away. You know, I am very *physically* based. I was never deliberately evoking emotions. But when they came up I wanted to process this material.

So then I thought, maybe we can understand this link if we start drawing it. We'll *draw* the images that are coming up. If you're crying and yelling, then put it back into movement, draw the image. Well, this was one way of moving that material and keeping it within some sort of a process. But then what resulted from the imagery that came up was just as unexpected, just as surprising.

What was happening was that one thing started triggering off more parts of the body mechanism than I was prepared for. And so exploration, movement exploration, when it became very focused meant that we were going very deeply into those elements. More deeply than I had before, and it was sparking all these various responses.

NANCY: *One time, years ago at Naropa Institute, during a lecture-demonstration you gave, you talked about a particular creative cycle.*

ANNA: I called it the three levels of awareness—the physical, emotional and mental. Then I have a five-part process which develops the material that comes up from integrating the three levels of awareness. It has to do with selecting, zeroing in on a specific item, confronting, expressing, applying and integrating the material back into your dance and your life. It's called emotional scripting. And it's a growth process.

NANCY: *Well, during your lecture you said that at a certain point in your life you met Fritz Perls and that you came to see that there were laws and principles about the way feelings and emotions worked that were just as predictable and understandable as the physical laws. How did you use these principles?*

ANNA: I had found these principles in working with Fritz, but I hadn't gone far enough with it—I hadn't been able to connect the movement and feeling with the content. I could go back and forth between movement and feeling and I would know at a certain point that if you were going to use intensely forced movements with the legs, certain feelings would be evoked that would be different than if you did it with the arms. I could predict certain kinds of general feelings that would be linked to a particular set of movements, but I didn't know what to do with it. I mean, in therapy you work with it in one way, but I didn't think of myself as a therapist. I wanted to channel it back into an art process. *That* information I didn't get from Fritz and that's where I was stuck. So I tried to channel it back by having people draw visualizations, images. But I couldn't understand what those visualizations were saying because it was a whole other language.

NANCY: *The relationship between movement and feeling that you were working with then was a kind of cause and effect of "if I do this movement I'll get this feeling"?*

ANNA: That was one thing. For example, if you're moving inwardly in a certain way and if you're doing it softly, a certain kind of sadness will be evoked. The moment that you hyperextend [arch] the spine, a different kind of feeling will be evoked depending also on its use of space or its intensity. Each person of course has their own particular associations.

NANCY: *Were you also exploring the movement from one feeling to another, the transformation of one feeling to another?*

ANNA: Oh yes, that too. Because eventually through my work with Gestalt therapy and my continuing work, I learned how to *process* that material so that I was no longer afraid of it. So I could help people process their feelings and then once you go *with* the movement and accept feelings, it opens up the channels for something *different* to be there. So you're not just angry and stuck with it. You have the potential of developing and completing the movement that is linked with the anger, and as you complete the movement the feeling changes. That's the nature of the feedback between movement and feeling. The implication is that you have the capacity to change, alter, or transform feelings through movement. Once you've experienced the nature of this feedback process you can tap into this as a powerful motivation and transformative act. This emotional connection, I believe, is a root source in dance. Another aspect is that the transformations of the feelings in movement have a kind of history, a cycling that's pretty much the same individually as it is archetypically.

NANCY: *What do you mean by that?*

ANNA: Well, for example, when I was making the *Circle the Earth Manual*, I was looking for Peace Dances in other cultures and I came across something in which two tribes have a fight, they wage war. Then, the victorious tribe invites the ones that have been defeated to their village. And the defeated ones come and shake each one of the victorious ones. The women come and they do the same thing. And when they're finished *shaking* them up and they've expelled their anger, then they put their foreheads together and they hug each other and the two tribes sit down and cry. And then they hold each other, stand up, and they dance and have a feast, and celebrate.

NANCY: *Wow.*

ANNA: And I experienced this cycle myself when I went through cancer—from anger to sadness, etc. Kübler-Ross's work with cancer patients describes it well. It's a history that's both personal and collective. I find that what the individual will go through in terms of their own personal experiences, if it is at a basic enough level, is also the same on a collective level.

SCORING

NANCY: *Where did you go from there?*

ANNA: At a certain point I realized that I needed some other ways for helping people develop this material fully. It wasn't enough to have a momentary movement image feeling. What do you *do* with it? Where does it go? And that's when scoring came in, which opened a lot of new creative possibilities. That was the most freeing, most liberating experience of my life. And I got a lot of help from my husband

AN ENVIRONMENTAL EVENT:

TIME

	1	2	3	4	5	6	7
PLACE Y	GROUP A GROUP B RESOURCE	GROUP A SCORE 1	GROUP A SCORE 3 GROUP B SCORE 4	GROUP B SCORE 1	GROUP B SCORE 3 GROUP A SCORE 4	GROUP A SCORE 3 GROUP B	
PLACE Z		GROUP B SCORE 2		GROUP A SCORE 3			

- 👁 **RESOURCE** ☞ PASSING OUT & EXPLAINING INSTRUCTIONS
- 👁 **GROUP A** ☞ HALF THE PEOPLE
- 👁 **GROUP B** ☞ THE OTHER HALF
- 👁 **SCORE 1** ☞ CREATE ENVIRONMENT
- 👁 **SCORE 2** ☞ THINKING
- 👁 **SCORE 3** ☞ OBSERVING – EVALUACTION
- 👁 **SCORE 4** ☞ RESPONDING TO ENVIRONMENT

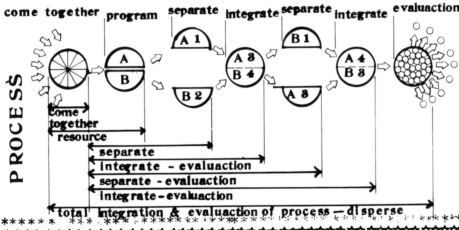

PROCESS

come together · program · separate · integrate · separate · integrate · evaluaction

come together
resource
separate
integrate - evaluaction
separate - evaluaction
integrate - evaluaction
total integration & evaluaction of process – disperse

LOVE LOVE LOVE...

An example of a written score for an environmental event, 1968. Score by Anna Halprin, graphics by Mike Doyle.

Larry because actually he understood about scoring in a way that I just hadn't developed at all. And he began to teach me methods of how you could have closed scores or open scores.

I noticed when I worked with Morton Subotnik, who was among those whom we called in those days the avant-garde musicians—they were working with scores. Like John Cage would work with scores where it would be totally open. He called them "random." No, he called them "*chance.*" I call those, now, open scores. But I didn't have a word for it then. When I worked with Morton, he worked out a system of "cell-block" scores that we did in a dance. But it was like each musician had their own style of scoring. It still hadn't sunk in to me that *I* could use scores until I began working with my husband and he began to evolve this system of open to closed scores. And that just liberated me totally. I realized it didn't have to be always open. Sometimes closed scores were *very* important.

NANCY: *"Closed," meaning "set"?*

ANNA: Very set. I realized that there's so much power in being able to do a closed score, if you're doing it for the proper intention.

NANCY: *So intention started to become a significant factor?*

ANNA: Oh, intention and theme and scoring all go together. What are you developing the movement *for*? What are you doing all this *for*? And so you had to have an intention, there had to be a theme, and I didn't know what to *do* with this intention and theme until the scoring.

NANCY: *So how did you answer that question—What are you doing it for?*

ANNA: It depended on what the intention was. Okay, the intention of the "Chief Seattle Run" [in *Circle the Earth*][1] is that enough people have to be unified, and they have to be committed to say, "We want to heal this earth and it's gonna take a hundred of us to do this. It's gonna take 50 of us to do this. It's going to take the willing commitment of enough people to say we will heal this earth. Every step is a prayer, and we must all pray together for the healing of the earth." And the mandala that we do this in must be unity itself, which is a circle. The circle is an act of unity, and the four directions give it stability. It's the squared circle which is the archetypal mandala of harmony. And in order to achieve this unity, it has to be a very closed score.

NOTE

1. The "Chief Seattle Run" referred to here is later referred to as the "Earth Run."

And a score like the "Vortex" score, also from *Circle the Earth*, has to be an *open* score because the intention there is—How do we honor differences? How do we honor diversity, and still find our commonalities?

NANCY: *What is the score for the "Vortex Dance"?*

ANNA: The first part is very open. It begins with everyone walking through the space, looking at each other, looking to find a common beat. Once that beat is found, it begins to break up into each person evolving their own dance, breaking up more and more into individual dances and smaller groups until it's almost chaotic. This part honors diversity. Then at a certain point in this 20-minute score, we feel—Now is the time to do something *together*, in order to honor the commonality. And it will be through making something vertical in the center of the space. And that's the score. That's all a hundred people have to work with.

NANCY: *So you've been given an amount of time and an intention.*

ANNA: Yeah. Which is to honor diversity and then to find a way of working together where you can also honor a commonality. And every time it's done, whatever they build in the center is totally different. Here in Marin County we use the mountain image, but in other places they don't. In Australia, they had streams of trails and they had people *walking* up the trails, on each other's bodies, up to the top. They came down and just made a beautiful kind of flower pattern with petals opening up on the floor. It's always different. So that dance has to be a very open score. Do you see?

NANCY: *What do you mean exactly by "open" score?*

ANNA: In scoring, we have a scale. If you have from one to ten, and openness is 1, I'd say the "Vortex Dance" was about a 2. Because they're told how to begin and how to end.

NANCY: *Do you actually think of the scores in this way—numbering them?*

ANNA: Oh yes. I actually mark them in the *Circle the Earth Manual*. Because I tell people, "I want you to know beforehand this is going to be a real closed score," so they don't say, "Oh, you turned me on to exploring in this free way and now you're shutting me down." I know by now not to do that. And in a more open score I say, "Please don't expect to be told what to do."

NANCY: *What number would you give a ballet?*

ANNA: Well, ballet dancers do all closed scores.

NANCY: *But then you have to consider at what level it is closed or open. Can it be open* emotionally *but closed* physically? *"This is what you're going to do but you can feel it any way you like."*

ANNA: But you can't tell somebody how to feel.

NANCY: *No, but as you said, certain movements will evoke certain feelings. And some more than others.*

ANNA: Yeah, yeah, I hear what you're saying. It's true. The more the movement is closed, the more it closes the emotional responses. See, people doing the "Chief Seattle Run" are very unified emotionally, because the score is so closed.

NANCY: *So is scoring where you're feeling your growth now, your growing edge?*

ANNA: Yeah. More in relation to Myths and Rituals. But I couldn't do that until I developed the scoring system. And scoring offers an objective process for valuacting.

NANCY: *Evaluating?*

ANNA: Yes. You can go directly to scoring from the resources or I can "valuact" these resources first—What happened? What did you like, what didn't you like, what is it saying to you, where does it go from here? I could say, "In terms of my intention, these are the best resources to use. I'll use these, and *now* I'll score."

NANCY: *So the intention is already there before you begin?*

ANNA: Yeah. But sometimes you can do a score in which the intention of the score is to get clear about what the intention is.

NANCY: *That sounds like a familiar score for doing Contact Improvisation. How would you scale Contract Improvisation as a score?*

ANNA: It depends on what direction you give to the performers. Scoring defines activities. It tells people what activity to do, not how to do it. If you said, "I want the two of you to do Contact for five minutes and then stop wherever you are. Or you have five minutes to bring it to a closure." That's already closing it. Or you say, "I want you to do Contact Improvisation within this red space." You've closed it again.

NANCY: *It's interesting, because I think that often in Contact a lot of these things are assumed. I've often asked people in my Contact classes what their assumptions are about the form. Does it have to be only two people together, do you have to be in physical contact all the time, is it supposed to be smooth, do you have to be giving weight, or support if you're given* *weight, and the list goes on. And then you realize that in fact what once seemed very open had become quite a closed score. Or your attitude can switch and you can say, "Gee, all I'm saying is that dancing is 'based on the physical contact of moving bodies and their relationship to the physical forces that govern their movement,' that's a very open score."*

ANNA: Yes—that's an excellent model for an open score. What makes it an open or closed score is how *you* define the activity, in space, over time, with people. Doing Contact Improv *itself* isn't open or closed.

MYTHS AND RITUALS

NANCY: *So, let's get back to your beginning to work with Myths and Rituals.*

ANNA: Where I'm at *now* is that it's been helpful for me to define the myth and ritual as coming from a symbol. So I have to do *Circle the Earth* in a workshop form. I try to have people understand that the symbol of their myth, of peace, is their own body, on a personal level. And that what they experience in their body, *how* they experience their body, is going to be their story. And *that* story is their myth, and that everybody has a different story, a different myth. How they *perform* it is their ritual. And everybody has a personal ritual. *Circle the Earth* is the collective myth and ritual, and the earth is our collective symbol. And the score that has been evolved is the *story* of that earth. And the *collective score* that they do is the collective ritual. And it is possible, and this is what we work very hard on, to have the collective score going on at the same time that the individual myth is being acted out. Because of the scoring I was able finally to make it. Because you *can't* have a collective myth that is going to be meaningful to everybody in the same way without having something . . . very serious.

NANCY: *. . . fascism.*

ANNA: You got it. I was going to say that you have something very serious. You have either a guru, which can be a form of fascism, or you have a dictator—Here it is, feel it like this, do it like this. So you have to have this done as a workshop. I can't do the dance any other way, because I need people to find out—What does "circle the earth" mean to *you*? Personally. And that takes time to experience and discover.

NANCY: *You need a process.*

ANNA: I need a process to do that so that the two things go together: the personal and the collective. And that's why I think we can do it with non-dancers. I've never done it with just all dancers. I'd love to do it sometime. I think it could be *wonderful*. So far I've been very lucky that so many beautiful dancers are attracted to do it.

NANCY: *Do you have a sense of where you are in this scoring process—are you in the middle or towards the end of your exploration of it?*

ANNA: I don't know. The *Planetary Dance* [which happened on Easter Sunday] just blows my mind. I don't know where to go with that. There were *actually* people in 37 countries doing that dance, starting at sunset and going through dawn, so it was like rippling, a mantra. I know it means that people want to be connected. Very much. And they want dance to count in the world today.

NANCY: *They want to use movement as a vehicle for that connection.*

ANNA: That's right. See, they were all encouraged to do something of their own, but to do something alike. So we all either did the "Peace Dance Meditation," or we did the "Chief Seattle Run," but other things that they did would be more local.

NANCY: *Was the* Planetary Dance *just an event for that one day?*

ANNA: Yeah, that was just something I wanted to do on that day.

Why I want to keep doing *[Circle the Earth]* more is that I want to keep testing if it *is* a Peace Dance. The only way you can test it is by seeing if you experienced anything that you can describe as a peaceful state of mind or feeling in yourself. And also by doing it in different cultures, I want to find out more ways of doing it.

NANCY: *Changing your score?*

ANNA: Yes, I'm open to that. The scores do change a little bit but slowly. And every time I do them we all do a valuaction. I get all the participants' ideas of what worked and didn't work for them. I remember the last time I did it I felt that I needed to get more voice in it. So I tried to do it this time. I brought Susan Osborne in. And I have to think that through, how that worked. Yeah, the scores change each time we do it. I'm trying to get people to use the score with kids, or with teenagers. It's clear enough that it could be like a play. Different directors do it and get different things. Alice Rutkowski learned the scores and did it in Philadelphia last year. And Melinda Harrison has done parts of it in Colorado.

NANCY: *Yeah, it's like a movement play in a sense. But you see it as a ritual and call it that. What do you think the difference is between a ritual and a performance?*

ANNA: Your attitude when you're in it. These people, even afterwards when it was all finished, they really needed to consider what was not peaceful in their life, what were they going to do about it. They had to stand up and say—This is not peaceful in my life and this is what I commit myself to do. What are you going to commit yourself to do about peace in the world? So it's not enough to have done this dance.

This dance is meant to simply awaken your interest in peace—to take it as a metaphor and make it real in your life. If it were just a piece of choreography you wouldn't necessarily have that agreement with people. I have that agreement with people before we start—this is a ritual and a ritual means that you're going to change something and that you're doing something that's bigger than yourself and you're not doing it for yourself *only*. It only works *through* you. I wouldn't have the right to say that to anybody if I were doing a piece of choreography.

NANCY: *Although I often feel that performance attempts that depth of connection to its material.*

ANNA: Yeah, but these people really have to get up there and say, "I am going to do dah dah dah." I made a commitment, for example, after I heard all their commitments. I said, "One of the hardest things in the world for me to do is to ask people for money. And I'm going to start asking for money when I feel very strongly about people who have it and people who don't, who need it to be able to live a more creative and peaceful life." After the dance I announced, "I would like you all to make a real money contribution for the Pomo tribe so they can build a roof for their roundhouse and so they can feed some of the families there that really don't have enough food to eat. And I want you to give as much as you can." And that was the hardest thing in the world for me to do. And I got $375. I would *never* have done that before. So that dance, as a ritual, gave me permission to do that. Also, it gave me responsibility to look at my life and deal with a relationship which is not peaceful, and to do something about it. To find my strength and my power from the dance itself. What I have to do is go into my warrior stance [from the "Confrontation Dance" in *Circle the Earth*] and say I've got to be a powerful warrior and I've got to have the courage to do what's necessary in this relationship. And to get not only my inspiration but my *know-how* to do it from the dance. That's what makes it a ritual.

NANCY: *Do you mean from dance in general or from this particular dance?*

ANNA: From this dance. I've gotta find my stance in that. I've gotta find my inspiration and vision from "I Am the Earth," I've got to find my determination from the "Chief Seattle Run." I've gotta find my own restoration from the "Restoration Dance." I've gotta go to that dance and say, "I've gotta have this and this is what I've gotta do and these are the consequences and this is what I may have to sacrifice." So in that sense it's a ritual. Also it's a ritual in the sense that I am required to make a connection between who I am and what I'm doing. I'm *required* to do that.

I never used to do that. When I was called an avant-garde artist in the '60s and early '70s, I used to do dances because I wanted to . . . I wanted to take my clothes off, I wanted to see what it was like. Or—Forget about the proscenium arch, who cares about it, I want to get out there and do that and see what that is like. I mean, I just did things because I was an adventurer and I wanted to break down all these confining rules. "Why do I have to dance *there*? Why can't I dance outside? Who says I have to dance in the theater?" I was really being an adventurer and I didn't have to say—What am I doing, or *why*. And that was fine for me then. I don't regret it. But it was *different* than a ritual. So rituals are, to me, different. And I didn't really start making *that* commitment, as you know, until I had cancer and then I thought—What am I *doing* with my life?

NANCY: *A search for meaning, in a sense.*

ANNA: Yeah, yeah. And I think what's true for me is not necessarily true for anyone else. I think each person has to go through their own evolutionary process in their own way and in their own time. The important thing is that they're true to their nature and true to where they are in their own evolutionary process. And I just have to be true to mine. And one of the things that I wanted to be very careful of is not to become an aging dancer. I don't want to be 67 years old dancing like I'm 21 when I'm *not* 21. I can't move like I'm 21 and I don't think like I'm 21. But I don't want to see somebody who's 21 or 35 trying to be an elder, either, when they're not. When we're each true to where we are in our process, that is *so beautiful*. That's *life*, you know? And I have to step lively and challenge myself every minute so I stay true to where I am in my process and not just relax and do the same old thing because it's comfortable and because that's the way I made my reputation. I have to be real careful of that.

NANCY: *I appreciate that you're doing that.*

ANNA: You know, I'm getting an Honorary Ph.D. I'm just *thrilled* about. I mean, I can't use it, but what I'm thrilled about is that the academic label is being put onto movement. That's an acknowledgment to the field. Dance is being acknowledged as having wisdom and intelligence and is in itself education. That's so wonderful.

MOVING TOWARD LIFE:

A DANCE SERIES FOR PEOPLE CHALLENGING LIFE-
THREATENING ILLNESS

This manual is written for students of dance in the hopes that they will be encouraged to use their skills as dancers and teachers to assist people living with cancer.[1] It
is also for caregivers, health professionals, and people who have had cancer or are
living with it now. This work is an extended application of my explorations of the
Life/Art Process, the Five Stages of Healing, the PsychoKinetic Visualization
Process, and my personal studies of the integration of mind, emotions and
sensations.

I am very careful to make no claims that the work I am doing with people
with cancer and other life-threatening illnesses is a treatment or can extend life, but
I am certain that it does expand and transform the *quality* of life. There is intriguing
evidence that some people who undertake healing processes that *make sense to
them* can extend their lives as well as expand them.

I follow this particular path because it is through dance that I have learned my
most vital lessons, and have come to respect the inner and mysterious power of the
body to name its injury and to heal. Dance, by its very nature and intent, is a holistic form, and the approach to dance which I take links movement, feelings and
images in a holistic manner. The body has deep wisdom within it—memories,
ancient knowledge, and personal and collective experiences beyond anything we can
imagine with our conscious minds. I continuously refer to this wisdom, encouraging participants to learn to listen to the body and its deep wisdom. This aids in a
process of reclamation of the body and often releases fear. When the body is in

NOTE

1. This essay is a chapter from my manual entitled *Moving Toward Life* which documents an eight-week series of classes I teach to people with cancer, AIDS, and other life-threatening illnesses, and to their caregivers and friends. Other
chapters focus on prayer, play, dance in the environment, the immune system, our belief systems, and self-portrait
work. The manual is descriptive, detailing each lesson plan, and includes specific applications and possible adaptations
of the work.

crisis, it is right for us to return to it and do whatever we can to tap into its natural capacity to heal.

ANIMAL ALLIES

When man [sic] sought to know how he should live, he went into solitude and cried until an animal brought wisdom to him. Thus were the sacred songs and ceremonial dances given to my tribe through the animals.

Pawnee Chief

The connection between animals and people, found in myths and folk tales, stretches back to the beginnings of human existence. From prehistoric times, we have cave drawings depicting animals as humans, and humans as animals. This primal bond is so strong that animal dances persist into modern times. Perhaps this is evidence for the origins of dance, and part of dance's function in the lives of early peoples.

Something uncanny, and perhaps even instinctual, happens when we imagine the transformation of our human selves into an animal nature. This action captures the imagination, and inspires us to tap into deep unconscious feelings and psychic needs. As we embody an animal image through movement and dance, we can actually experience and express certain qualities we may not have access to in our ordinary lives. We can come to understand the fierceness of the lion, the strength of the boar, the aggression of the tiger, the playfulness of the monkey, the patience of the turtle. Embodying the movements of an animal can give us permission to call up censored emotions, or the hidden and blocked emotions that are precisely what we must integrate into our lives as a vital force in our healing.

Finding Your Animal Ally (or Bush Soul)

Theme of Session:	Animal allies
Intentions:	Allow participants to experience qualities and attitudes of animals which will support them in their day-to-day lives.
Check-in:	Each session of *Moving Toward Life* begins with a brief check-in.
Preparation:	A set of physical exercises will acquaint us with a wide range of movements that correlate with animal-like movements.
Evolutionary Movements:	From ground to air

Suggestion for presentation: Evolutionary movements are generally unfamiliar to the average person and may be tiring. For that reason, it is a good idea to divide the group in half and let one group witness as the other group performs the movement. Alternate back and forth. This gives time for people to rest as well as observe different movement ideas.

. Moving on the ground without the use of arms or legs.
  At first participants may be stumped by this notion but eventually find fascinating ways to ripple their spines, or coil and recoil like snakes or caterpillars.

. Move through space remaining on the ground, using elbows and knees.
  This will promote the full action of the spine as it twists, rotates and extends.

. Crawl on hand and knees.
  This will require coordination of arms and legs.

. Move through space on hands and feet.
  Free movement of the pelvis and lower back should be encouraged.

. Continue and move on feet with hands low, barely brushing the floor like an ape.
  The legs need to have a wider stance for balance.

. Continue lifting the body a bit higher, yet still bent forward.

. Walk upright and notice the tremendous change in one's feelings.

. Extend the spine and elevate the body towards the sky.

. Lift the body high off the ground into the air, like a bird.

The last movement in the evolutionary cycle tends to be vigorous, as people attempt to fly and leap and jump. It will feel like a relief to lie down afterwards and rest, and this will take us into our guided breath meditation.

Guided Breath Meditation

The participants are lying down for this exercise.

Allow your mind to become a witness to your breath, rather than a director. There are four intervals of rhythms in the breath:

. Breathe in.

. Pause.

. Breathe out.

. Linger in the space of stillness. Wait, and your breath will enter your body again on its own.

Imagine the breath as an ocean wave. The rising of the wave is the inhalation, followed by a peak and a pause before the wave falls and flows back into the smooth ocean water. The ocean is moved by the tides; the breath is also moved by something other than the will. It is being activated by the life force.

Guided Visualization and Drawing: Finding Your Ally

. Use your breath to enter your body.

. Visualize a blue dot in your mind's eye. On each inhalation of your breath, the dot expands. It expands until your entire vision is a clear blue sky.

. Begin to fill in this sky with a landscape. Imagine a lush rain forest, a jungle, an expansive plain, a water hole, a desert, a mountain.

. Imagine you are in one of these places in the natural environment.

. What sounds do you imagine you can hear? What smells? What colors do you see? What textures do you feel? What time of day or night is it?

. An animal enters into your landscape. How does the animal move? What does it look like from all angles? What kind of sounds does it make? What does the animal feel like?

. Gradually transform yourself into your animal—your face, your hands, your feet, your whole body. You are your animal.

. Explore your animal movements and sounds.

. Interact with others.

. Draw a picture of how you imagine your animal looks.

. On another piece of paper, write down words you associate with your animal: how it moves, what it does, how it feels.

. Circle four words you have written that you are drawn to.

. Use these four words to make a chant or a poem or a story. You can add prepositions. See what your animal has to say to you.

. Dance your animal ally in groups of three: A, B and C:

> A: dances her animal
> B: is her partner in the dance, echoing and supporting
> C: chants A's words, repeats, adds something, improvises

. Switch roles.

. In all three roles, there is room for improvisation. This dance is done so participants can gather more information about their animal allies.

. Ask your ally a question: How will you be able to help me in dealing with my illness/issue in my life? What quality in my life do you represent? How can you support me? Give the animal a name.

. Check out by sharing your experience with the animal ally.

Conclusion

These experiences have greater meaning when the participants are encouraged and given some clues about how to use this material in their daily lives. For example, one woman who had drawn a turtle came back to class the next week and told us her doctor had given her devastating news. Essentially, he said her "time was up," and she immediately called upon her ally to support her in that moment. She said, "My turtle shell protected me from his harsh and brutal words and besides, my turtle is a lot older and wiser than he is. I'm not ready to die." It is important to emphasize different ways that the material of movement, writing and drawing can begin to become part of the participants' new lifestyle as they deal with their illness.

EARTH DANCES:

THE BODY RESPONDS TO NATURE'S RHYTHMS

When I was a little girl, I had a tree as a special friend. It was a big elm tree, which I could climb, and snuggle my body against its branches. I would go to my tree when I wanted to be alone, or hide, and there I felt unthreatened by problems I had at home or at school. Sometimes I would bring a friend, but mostly I would go alone, to dream and fantasize. In my tree, I felt completely at home and peaceful. Birds and squirrels and little insects were part of my tree world. There were delightful and unexpected sounds, wonderful smells, and a whole community of tree beings of which I was a member. The tree felt strong and enduring, a part of me and a powerful extension of my own being. I used to tell my tree my secrets and hurts, and I would ask the tree questions about life. The tree was so important to me that I gave it a name. In some childlike way, I knew the tree was my friend. It was a real living being and we had a true relationship.

When I grew up and had children of my own, we lived in a house surrounded by a redwood forest. When the girls were upset, they would run away into the forest. I knew they were safe in their special place among the trees and that there they found the same solace and comfort as I had when I was a child. And when their children would come and visit, I would take them on walks in the forest and delight when they played in the trees, fantasizing space ships, monsters, and fairies with lacy moss dresses.

I knew then that what had been true for me was also true for them and that there must be a commonality in the relationship between all humans and the natural world. Our kinship with the natural world, and the inspiration we derive from it, seems to be a central part of the human experience. I have come to see, as Rosebud YellowRobe said: "Nature, and all that is in it, is also in each of us."

In exploring these ideas, I have looked to native and indigenous peoples and seen that many other cultures maintain a close relationship to nature. Many

We dance in a circle,
like the orbit of the
earth.

Photo by
Coni Beeson.

indigenous people believe that every tree, every stone and every mountain has its own guardian spirit. In ancient times, if one cut a tree, or moved a rock, or dammed a river, it was important to ask permission or placate the spirit in charge of that particular element. Before the advent of science, many believed the earth was a living entity, personified as our Mother. There is a saying among the American Indians: "Walk lightly upon Mother Earth for you are walking on grandmother's back." This idea—that, the earth is a living entity, a goddess—is foreign to the white West, which has related to the natural world as an inanimate object to exploit and control.

On the Northern Californian coast where I have a home, my neighbors are the Pomo Indian Tribe. Over the last thirty years, I have befriended members of the tribe, learned their dances and their customs, and spent many hours listening to their stories. These dances are done in the round house, their sacred communal space. Here we dance on a dirt floor with our bare feet, praying directly to mother earth. A large fire always blazes, sending the message of our dance in a spiral of smoke through a large opening in the roof and up to the Great Spirit. This hole brings the sky and the moon and the stars into the round house with us. We dance in a circle, like the orbit of the earth, and we circle around a center pole, a tree which connects our bodies to the body of heaven and the body of earth.

The Pomos *live* their experience of nature, not just in thought, but in their daily interactions and in their worship. Their dance expresses their belief in the sanctity of nature, and their dance consecrates the world. I have been attracted to their ways not because I have wanted to imitate their life or their rituals, but rather to understand better something I believe is true for all of us, as human beings in relation to the earth.

As a dance artist, I am propelled towards the natural world by three beliefs. One is the notion that the human body is a microcosm of the earth; the second is that the processes of nature are, for me, guidelines to my aesthetics; and the third is that nature is a healer.

THE HUMAN BODY IS A MIRROR OF THE EARTH'S BODY

Our bodies are composed of the same elements as the earth. For example: we are 70% salt water; the earth is 70% salt water. (Our planet could be called "Water" instead of "Earth.") The elements that make up our bones also make up stones. Our heart works the way rivers, streams, brooks or tributaries return water to the ocean. The heart, the ocean of our body, is the place where all the fluids of the body arrive, and an aerial view of rivers and streams looks much like a picture of the veins and arteries inside us. There are other ways the human body reflects the body of nature. Our breathing mirrors the winds of the world; our metabolism is akin to fire. When

*We respond to nature as
being beautiful and right
because we ourselves are part
of its making and we
empathize with its order.
Anna Halprin at Sea Ranch,
1983.*

Photo by
Coni Beeson.

we take in nourishment, we build a little fire out of it to assimilate the food into our systems. Our skin continually renews or sheds, like leaves falling in the autumn. And our body moves and changes in a cyclic way, just as the earth does. We cycle between darkness and light, sleep and waking. We experience seasons, just as the earth does, and the seasons are comparable to the cycle of human life itself, with spring being the time of beginnings and children, and winter, the time of endings and death.

NATURE IS PURE PROCESS MADE VISIBLE

We respond to nature as being beautiful and right because we ourselves are part of its making and we empathize with its order. My own empathy is intense; I receive physical, emotional and spiritual nourishment from nature, as I imagine we all do. I also look to nature to discover what is both meaningful in form and content for dance as art. I often ask myself: What are the "right" patterns?

The interacting forces in nature generate artistic forms. Water moves and swirls, as waves crash and tumble down the banks of a river. Water heaves and undulates as the tides pull and release. The wind skips across the surface of the water, the sun flickers and sparkles, and the full moon traces a long pathway on the back of the sea. Rock forms carved by wave actions move me as great works of art do; the edges of waves leave linear markings by chance on the sand. They are wonderful models for dances. The windswept cypress trees along the coast line have unique and fanciful shapes. When I look at tide pools and observe the arrangement of the stones at the bottom, they seem to me like perfect compositions.

If the results of the natural process seem so inherently right, and if we find them dynamically exciting and beautiful, then, in my view, they form a basic source of our aesthetic sensibilities. The question seems to be: how can we utilize these resources— creatively, individually and collectively—to produce an art expressive of our lives and our sensibilities? How do we make dances reflecting the principles of nature?

Rather than imitate the outward forms of nature or use nature as a backdrop, I identify with its basic processes. My work in nature is not representational; I do not seek to represent nature inside myself. Rather, the work is reflective; I seek to understand the natural world as a reflection of my human experience. Although this work is generated primarily by a kinesthetic connection, it also includes the feelings, associations, personal and communal images, and life scripts that are part of our human nature. In that way, the interface between our human ways and the ways of nature are integrated. Just as the ancients danced to call upon the spirits in nature, we too can dance to find the spirits within ourselves that have been long buried and forgotten.

*There are many ways the human
body reflects the body of nature.*

Photo by
Paul Fusco.

*Rather than imitate the outward
forms of nature, I identify with
its basic processes.*

Photo by
Coni Beeson.

To share my interest and enthusiasm with this process, my husband and I began to give workshops over 25 years ago. These teachings have evolved into a yearly four-week retreat at Sea Ranch on the Northern Californian coast which I continue to teach. At Sea Ranch, we have ocean, sand, cliffs, rocks, meadows, trees, rivers, birds, deer, raccoons, skunks; we have the sun and moon and wind and fog and mist and rain to surround and support our dances. We work outside in the natural environment, and we search for the reflections of ourselves that can be found in trees, clouds, and water.

NATURE AS A HEALER

Nature as a healer works on many levels. The story used to illustrate the process is Rick Lepore's, who used his interactions with the natural environment to come to terms with the untimely death of his partner. Rick experienced this process as a healing; others may use it to discover their own personal mythology, or to gather information about their lives in other ways. The following description is of both the workshop process and Rick's story.

Week One: Sensory Awareness

We focus on sensory awareness. By isolating each of the senses—sight, touch, smell, taste, hearing—we sharpen our ability to use them fully in response to our environment. We do a series of blindfold walks to isolate and fine-tune our kinesthetic sense. Taking out the dominant sense of sight intensifies the kinesthetic sense. We use drawing as a way to concentrate on what it is we are seeing. All of this is done in silence in order for the stimuli, especially sound, in the environment to be the sole focus of our attention. Rick speaks of this experience:

When I explored in the natural environment through touch, sight, smell, taste, sound and movement, a connection occurred between me and the world. This was the beginning of realizing my grief and loss. I was opened up emotionally by the sheer beauty of nature. One moment of smelling the sea, or hearing the ocean waves roaring and crashing, or touching thin blades of meadow grass, so perfectly formed, made me joyful inside. From this place, I began to slowly grieve the loss of the beautiful love Brian and I had shared. Engaging in the natural environment through my body was the bridge back into my own feelings.

Week Two: Explore Elements in the Environment

We begin to explore the specific elements of nature and choose one upon which to focus. It may be rock, water, sand, air, or sun. We discover characteristics of this element that resonate with our own human experience. We make contact with the element, and from that contact, we explore movements that are an integral part of the element. From this connection, we begin to find feelings, associations and content, and from this, personal myths and rituals grow in an experiential cycle. In this way, myths and rituals are "recognized" rather than "made," "discovered" rather than "created." Rick writes of his experience in this way:

EARTH:

In my exploration of earth, I found a place to burrow, to dig into, as if the earth were some-one's torso. It yielded to my movements. The movements came from my pelvis, and engaged my sensuality. I became like a snake, curling and undulating into the musk-scented soil and I became intoxicated by this. I realized there would never be a replacement for Brian; what we shared was too special. Sensuality was an important part of our relationship, and so it was an integral part of my healing. Nature offered me a sensual experience of us together.

TREE:

I found support from a tree, and a place to rest. In my drawing, Nature is sharing itself with me, covering me, making me one of her own. I am cloaked in the bark of the tree. I felt as if the tree were absorbing my grief, sharing it with me. I felt the compassion and understanding I had been searching for. I imagined that the tree had its own grief and could be with me in mine. I did not fear my emotions were too much for it, as it stood tall and strong and quiet. I simply rested.

Week Three: Opposite Elements

We find the opposite polarity of the element we had explored the previous week. If you first selected rock, your next choice might be water. In a three-part process that includes contact, exploration and response, we make contact with our element through the whole body, and repeat the last week's process. We then explore this new element until our responses lead to further development. We begin to incorporate other people in our dances, both as witnesses and performers. This enlarges and extends the possibilities of the dance. We draw our elements to become conscious of what we have been doing and we try to understand what our seemingly random movements mean. The drawings we make begin to include not only the element itself, but our response to it. It is this connection that begins to reveal the content and message of the element, and make its mysteries more conscious. We create scores for other dancers and teach them to people so we can gain objectivity on what we have learned, and we do different scores simultaneously to discover new relationships and possibilities. This is how nature operates—a variety of elements exists in continuous and simultaneous relationship—and all of our scores are modeled on the processes of nature.

Rick's experience during Week Three was a transformative ritual and a cathartic release.

DRIFTWOOD:

My ritual was developed as I was given two words by chance: one was "driftwood" and the other was "dragging." I began by dragging a lifesized piece of driftwood. The physical location in which this took place was an extremely steep, thirty-foot rock cliff connecting the beach to the meadows above. On a spontaneous impulse, I began the difficult task of dragging the driftwood to the rock cliff, placing it in careful arrangements, and returning to the beach below to continue. This lasted for an hour, and I placed twenty pieces of driftwood on the cliff.

The ritual was repetitive and simple enough so that I could immerse myself in it. It became familiar to me, inseparable from my psyche and part of the natural world where I performed it. I did not know at the time but part of the familiarity of the ritual was in what it contained—an enactment of traveling to be with Brian during the last six months of his life: For six months, each weekend, I drove over a mountain range to visit Brian. The trip lasted for one hour. I made the trip approximately twenty times.

The ritual was a series of journeys marking each period of the end of Brian's life; each of the twenty pieces of driftwood contained particular memories of our time together. It was strenuous to perform. Often, I almost lost my footing and was terrified by the possibility of falling off the cliff, desperately clinging to the driftwood. The task was relentless and the way was so hard. How long would this go on? It was as if the ritual contained all the emotions involved in being Brian's support, partner, friend and lover as he was dying. I discovered these different connections and the meaning of my dance by making a drawing of my experience. The drawing brought the connections to consciousness.

The ritual contained its ending. I chose from the assortment of driftwood one piece, beautifully formed like Brian's body, and placed it on the sand. I put stones around it, to protect and honor him, and laid with it. In my drawing, the driftwood is surrounded by a skeleton and above it, an orange figure which looks like a spirit, watching from above.

The ritual, its enactment, and the final burial all released images and emotions about what it was like to lose Brian. The next day, I took my drawing of a cat and enacted it. I found myself pushed off the ground, my body flung into space. I would land on all fours, spine flexed, only to feel pushed off the ground with even more strength and effort. It was as if something were underneath me, pushing me up off the ground. In this dance, I finally vocalized my anger about my loss and heard myself scream, "You little shit, why did you have to go and die?" My grief included all the selfish demands of wanting him back, and of blame. From the quiet enactment of the burial came the release of anger and pain. The dance

"The moment I put the seaweed on my head, I believed it was a monster that had engulfed me." Sea Ranch, 1993.

Photo by
Coni Beeson.

ended with me, exhausted, whispering to him in the meadow, believing without a doubt that he could hear me, that he was just on the other side.

Week Four: From the Self to the Collective

We look for various ways to close. One is to find a blend of our opposite elements by choosing a third element. By now, we have many tools to guide us in our contact, exploration and response to the environment. We can draw about our element, write about what we see in the drawing, create a score from this and include others, perform it and then recycle the performance. Before he was able to find this blend, Rick needed to confront his grief and loss, and he used his experience of nature as a healer in this confrontation. Nature offered him the images he needed to synthesize all the learning he had been doing in the previous three weeks of the training.

I made a drawing of very dark images, and expressions of anger and fear emerged. Again, we worked on the beach and this time, I came across a huge mound of seaweed with which I covered my body. It became an embodied expression of my fear. I created a dance confronting this fear, and the moment I put the seaweed on my head, I believed it was a monster that had engulfed me. I screamed and ran in terror and confusion. I stumbled under the weight of the seaweed, fell to the ground, and then rose up under its weight. I was guided to destroy it and survive. I got hold of the monster, tearing and beating it, and finally threw it and myself into a crashing wave, where it was carried away from me. It was a dance which transformed my fear into a fight against the helplessness of watching death take Brian away. Through nature I was able to make this confrontation physical. Death became as real as the seaweed covering my body.

This confrontation with the dark side is an essential part of the healing process. Once he had taken this step, Rick could experience the harmony found in the blend of elements. Rick found his blend in the tree.

I began to seek ways of receiving comfort, finding quiet spaces in the natural environment which could soothe and restore my sense of balance. One day, late in the afternoon, I was watching some shadows on the tree trunks above. I suddenly felt the presence of something alive in that tree and when I looked more closely, I realized it was Brian's face smiling down on me peacefully and calmly. It was, for me, a moment of resolution about the integrity of his spirit. Brian had always been there, in the realm of nature, and only now, could I see him.

The last days of the workshop are a collective rather than a personal experience. Everyone creates a dance together. By now, the group has evolved a common creative language, a set of values, and with these new resources is empowered to create communal experiences fed and stimulated by the environment. This invariably results in spontaneous community rituals with both primitive and contemporary qualities. We become connected to nature in its most evocative forms, and these

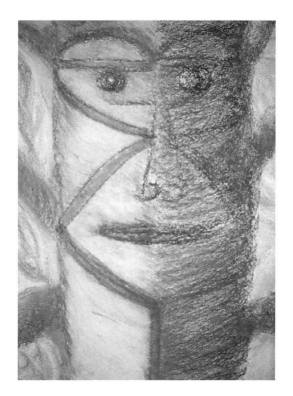

TREE: I suddenly felt the presence of something alive in the tree and when I looked more closely, I realized it was Brian's face smiling down on me.

Rick Lepore, 1993.

CAT: I heard myself scream, "You little shit, why did you have to go and die?"

Rick Lepore, 1993.

Lawrence Washington
enacts a personal ritual.

Photo by
Paul Fusco.

rituals emerge as creations of the earth itself. This connection between human nature and biological nature, when magnified by the collective, creates a community healing. Rick's closing ritual brings his personal experience of nature as a healer into a larger relationship to the group and the world. He uses the group as a touchstone, to help him synthesize his understanding of the entire process.

I returned to the end of the ritual of dragging driftwood, where I lay with Brian surrounded by stones. It was now time for me to leave the place of his burial. The others in my group sat around me for a while, and then began to open up the circle of stones to form a path. Slowly, I began moving towards the path and out into the beach. I was followed by my friends, each of us turning back toward the burial, and back again to the open beach. The sky was infinite, the ocean was calm; and because the tides had receded, a whole new beach of cliffs and rock formations I had never seen had been created. It was as if the four of us were entering a new world, moving forward in a way I could not have done alone. I was being shown exactly where to go from the place of his burial: out into the largeness of the world.

Clearly, there is a close and ancient rapport between humans and the natural environment. We have become too separate from this innate relationship, and we suffer a spiritual loss because of this. The human need to live within the context of nature remains in our physical bodies, encoded in our biology and our mythology. I believe that reconnecting to nature will lend us a vocabulary for our art and our lives, and a key to both our ancient and new mythologies. I think back on my childhood and my tree friend and I realize how rooted my experience was in these deeply human needs. It is my hope that this experiential contact with nature and its inner manner of operation will inspire in us enough love and move us, in our art and our lives, towards a deeper understanding of the sanctity of the earth and our place on it.

PLANETARY DANCE

Because the world is round, it is always sunrise somewhere and sunset somewhere else, always noon and also the middle of the night. When my phone rang on 17 April 1987 it was midday in California. I was about to leave for the final rehearsal of *Circle the Earth*, a two-day dance ritual which was to culminate at sunrise on the 19th with our participation in a planetary dance.

It was Amanda Levey calling from New Zealand and she sounded very excited. "We have just done it. We danced the *Earth Run* at sunset. I think we have started the worldwide dance!" On the other side of the planet it was April 18th and night. And while we were still rehearsing our turn of *Circle the Earth*, the dance had already begun.

When I arrived at rehearsal and told the performers of Levey's call there was stunned silence, some quiet tears, a sense of awe, and then a spontaneous celebration. The *Planetary Dance* was moving in a wave around the globe, going west with the sun while the news had reached us coming east by the telephone. In these split seconds of joy we understood that the world was indeed round and also connected, each part to the other. Inspired, we went on with the rehearsal, preparing for our part in the ritual.

I felt especially fired inside. I had been rehearsing and preparing for this kind of dance for over 60 years but only seemed to be realizing it now: a dance that mattered, a dance that could contribute to the quality of life, a dance of power.

I have always called myself a dancer and called my work dance because that was my own training and history and, if you really look into it, also the history of dance. Dance has a magical and transforming power. Some cultures understand this; so do some people in cultures that don't. I have found the dance world is often out of touch with this power. The Western notion of "progress," of "later is more developed than earlier," is barely tolerable in science, and completely out of place in art.

The all-too-common practice of identifying what you are doing by its place in some nonexistent, smooth time continuum creates false categories and false under-standings of interrelationships. I began as a "modern" dancer. But how long can anything keep calling itself modern, or postmodern?

Books on the "history of modern dance" sometimes lay out an elaborately con-structed family tree based on who came before and who came after and who studied what technique with whom. As firmly entrenched as I sometimes am in these modern dance histories, my fall off the family tree took no more than a small breeze. All I had to do was create a dance (*Apartment 6*, 1965) in which the performers wore shoes (horrors!) . . . and not even ballet slippers or jazz shoes, or bare feet, but high heels! I had not realized that being barefoot was already such a sacrosanct tradition. Suddenly I was no longer modern. And soon, not even to be considered a dancer.

When an artist begins to work outside the officially recognized context of her discipline, the established artistic community will often ignore her. If this doesn't work (because the artist is either persistent or good, or both) she may be called "avant-garde," meaning that she is ahead of the times or so far behind that she seems to be ahead (which is what happens when things move in circles).

The dance community in the '60s was too conservative to have an official avant-garde; the theatre world, however, was not. So my work began to be thought of as theatre and my strongest artistic rapport was with theatre people like Jerzy Grotowski, Lee Breuer and Ruth Maleczech, Julian Beck and Judith Malina, Richard Schechner, San Francisco's Actors' Workshop, and the San Francisco Playhouse on Hyde Street. In the '60s much of the work I did was innocently avant-garde, which is to say that it was controversial, but I was not always certain why. At times there was enormous hostility from audiences.

I was concerned that we had some kind of power that stirred people up. If we could generate this kind of magical power in dance, how should we use it? This power came from within the dance and also from that space between the spectators and the performers. The power was not contained and, in fact, could not be con-tained within the confines of a stage that was separated from the spectators. Not only could it arise from the whole of life and affect the whole of life, it was most powerful when it did so.

So we were tapping into some source, but did we really know what to do with the connection once we made it? I don't think so. The resulting hostility and con-frontation with audiences, although exciting, often fun, and sometimes dangerous, was not what I wanted.

I wanted to know what else we could channel the power toward and how to channel it. So when the riotous atmosphere of the '60s calmed down, we contin-ued a steady exploration based on those two questions. For several years I made no distinction between audience and performers. I preferred designing structures for all kinds of people who would become performers. These structures, or scores as we later called them, explored notions about a group mind, male and female separations and rejoinings, environmental influences, ritualistic initiations, interpersonal relations, and others. Some structures were improvisational while others were formal.

The chief intention of my works at this time was to understand how the process of creation and performance could be used to accomplish concrete results: social change, personal growth, physical alignment, and spiritual attunement. This necessarily involved studying the relationships between audience and performers, between a person's life issues and the performance content, between performance skills and life skills. In other words, developing an integrated life/art process.

While in the middle of this, in 1972, I got cancer. For ten years I withdrew from public performance. I didn't stop working but the work became internally oriented. This was only natural: I was working to regain my life and using the work process in my own healing.

During this time, whatever remained of my classical, external aesthetics were of little concern. How a dance looked or how it might be received by an audience was not on my mind. More important was how it felt to the performers and how they were able to use the experience of its creation and performance in furthering their own personal, artistic, and communal growth.

When I gradually began to return to public works I had different interests. First, I wanted to create dances that would influence change. I wanted to apply what I had learned about healing myself to other people and to whole communities. From 1972 to 1986, I explored this idea with an intimate group in a training program. Secondly, I had a strong interest in working with the general public, with large numbers of people who were untrained in dance or any type of performance. I had an opportunity to do just that in a series of community dance classes I led. Each session was attended by 60 to 100 people.

In these large group dances I noticed an exceptional phenomenon occurring time and time again. When enough people moved together in a common pulse with a common purpose, an amazing force, an ecstatic rhythm, took over. People began to move as if they were parts of a single body, not in uniform motion but in deeply interrelated ways. This recurrence of spatial and interrelated movement is no accident. It is an external version of the geometry and biology of our inner life—our bodies extended in space. In this sense, such movement is contained within us. People form circles. They make processions. Spirals. Entrances and exits. They orient themselves in space by using the four directions. They create a central axis. They move linearly in processions. In the same way we move from one to the many, from alone to couples, to family, to tribe—leading, following, blending.

In these archetypal movements people seemed to be tracing out the forms and patterns of a larger organism, communicating with and being moved by a group body-mind or spirit. This phenomenon of tapping into a deep collective force needs 50 to 100 people to break through individual limitations and even cultural preconditioning. The time it takes to generate such a dance depends on the diversity of the people, their purpose and the guidance they are given. It can take as little as 30 minutes to all day or night.

Had I discovered something new? Of course not! This large-scale group movement is an ancient phenomenon in dance. Cultures everywhere in the world have channeled the power of such a group spirit to help them bring rain, hunt, raise crops, and initiate the young. It is a power that can renew, inspire, teach, create and heal. What was exciting was that we were learning how to generate this same tribal spirit and energy, this same sense of group ritual with people whose culture contains little of such tradition in dance performances. We were learning how to return to performers and spectators power which in this culture had often been taken from them and placed in the hands of scientific experts and official artists.

The point has been raised that this collective power can be destructive, as it was for Hitler, Jim Jones, or any fanatical cult leader. I have gone to considerable lengths to develop a process that safeguards participants from this potential. By virtue of making a score (scenario) visible, learning and evaluating it, and then modifying it with their own images, the performers become empowered as cocreators of the dance. In other words, the leader does not require obedience but rather creative involvement. Furthermore, it's crucial that the purpose of the score is clearly stated so that each performer can agree to the purpose and can determine whether the score realizes that purpose. If it doesn't, there is a mutual responsibility to recycle the score until its purpose is fulfilled.

More and more, in both workshops and public rituals, I encouraged people to work with their own lives as material, to use real-life issues so that the transforming power of dance would have the opportunity to effect real-life changes for them. On a personal level my experience in ridding myself of cancer showed me that it was possible to use the power of dance for a higher purpose, that we could channel the power to experience interconnection with a life force, and that this experience was nourishing and necessary—the right of all living beings, not just artists. This power could be channeled for healing, of our bodies, our psyches, our communities, and for the healing of the planet . . . for peace.[1]

NOTE

1. See Lawrence Halprin, *The RSVP Cycles: Creative Process in the Human Environment.*

It was in this context in 1980 that my husband and I began a project called *Search of Living Myths and Rituals through Dance and the Environment.* I didn't know then that it was going to last five years. From this workshop, we made a performance called *In and On the Mountain* (1981). This was not the kind of dance I had done in the past. The idea for it had emerged from the six workshops Larry and I had led during the year. In these workshops hundreds of people from the community had taken part—exploring the environment, moving together, sharing reactions to their experiences. They had drawn pictures of images that came to them, and what was amazing was that Mount Tamalpais kept reappearing. When we noticed this recurring image we knew we had found the myth we were searching for. It wasn't only that the trailside killer had terrified the people in the community—he had defiled, denied, threatened the very heart of our community. For the community the mountain became a symbol of our spiritual identity—our responses to the mountain individually and collectively became our story or myth—and how we would enact our myth would become our dance, our ritual.

In and On the Mountain took place in the theatre at the College of Marin, overlooked by Mount Tamalpais. The theatre became the symbolic cave, like a native American kiva.[2] The dancers invoked the spirit of the mountain and enacted the killings. The urgency and the realness were intense. Friends and family of the women who had been murdered were in the audience. Someone called the police because they imagined the killer was present. During the night after the performance a series of ceremonies and events took place in preparation for the second part—*On the Mountain.* The next day witnesses and performers went to the mountain peak and walked down the trails where the killings had taken place. For the first time in two years a group of people returned to the mountain and reclaimed it.

A few days after the ritual, the police received an anonymous phone tip and the killer was captured.

Often people get upset when I tell this story because they get caught up in "cause and effect" or "who gets credit/blame for what." Am I really saying that the ritual caused the capture of the killer? If I say yes, then the discussion immediately moves to the question of how. But it is of no use to quarrel about how the two events are related; it is important to understand that they *are* related. In one sense we performed a prayer and our prayer was answered. Why argue about the power of prayer? Rejoice and try prayer again. Which is exactly what we did.

And in any event, it seems to me that the real miracle was not the capture of the killer but what happened with the people who performed the ritual, what

NOTE

2. A native American ceremonial structure that is usually round and partially underground.

*Witnesses and performers
went to the mountain
peak and walked down
the trails where the
killings had taken place.
For the first time in two
years a group of people
returned to the moun-
tain and reclaimed it.*

Photo by
Jay Graham.

happened in the community. They found a meaningful myth, and reclaimed the mountain. That was their purpose. Catching the killer was an added bonus. The performers felt that they had taken an active part in bringing the terror to an end. They had transformed themselves from victims of violence to creators of peace. It was no less and no more than an act of magic.

Inspired by this, we continued to dance on the mountain each spring for five years, not just for peace on the mountain but in the world: *In and On the Mountain* (1981), *Return to the Mountain* (1982), *Run to the Mountain* (1984), *Circle the Mountain* (1985), and then *Circle the Earth* (1986, '87, '88). During those years many people came from other parts of the country and the world to participate. They returned home eager to share the experience with their own communities.

So the rituals began to "go on tour." Of course this was not a tour in the ordinary sense because there was no permanent company. What traveled from place to place was not the performers or even a particular performance, but the scores, the recipes for creating the rituals. In the beginning, I was always present as a facilitator and I brought along some of the ceremonial objects which had been used in San Francisco as a kind of material continuity. After a while the rituals began to take on lives of their own. People wanted to take them back to their own communities. I began to receive letters and calls asking permission to do all or parts of *Circle the Earth.*

Out of this response grew the idea of the *Planetary Dance,* of uniting, on 19 April 1987, all the groups touched by *Circle the Earth.* This letter went out in 1987:

Dear Friend of Circle the Earth,

You are invited to help create a very special event this Spring: our first Planetary Dance of peace. On April 19, 1987 all the people and places that have touched Circle the Earth are invited to join in the world-wide performance of this special score. Hopefully, over 2,000 people in 25 countries around the world will participate in this event, gathering the family of Circle the Earth in the spirit of peace, unifying us in dance, prayer, and meditation.

THE SCORE:

We will be performing the Earth Run portion from Circle the Earth. In Marin, we will begin at sunrise at the foot of Mt. Tamalpais. You can join us by performing the Earth Run in your own community at any time between sunrise and sunset on April 19th—the time of Easter, Passover, and especially Spring, the time of renewal and hope. The Earth Run has been called a moving mandala of peace. Since the time of performance will vary from place to place, our Planetary Dance will "ripple" or "run" around the world with the passage of the sun.

A DANCE WITH VARIATIONS:

   Although the performance will focus on the Earth Run, there is also ample room for you to create a unique event—one that will express the character and imagination of your culture. You can do this in two ways:

1. Frame the score (preparation and closure) in different ways—a ceremony, ritual, blessing, or dance pertaining to something special in your community or culture; a group of spiritual leaders of different backgrounds offering inspiration; processions; spontaneous group dances and singing; meditations; etc. Many groups are planning to do a preliminary workshop.

2. Change some of the resources used in the Earth Run score—within the score, we encourage you to explore narrations appropriate to your group or culture.

SHARING THE EVENT:

   We would like as many groups as possible to photograph their performances. Document your community's participation in the Planetary Dance—slides, photographs, writings, graphic scores, valuactions, visualizations . . . any way you can think of. Send a copy of this documentation to us at Tamalpa and we will combine and edit them. This rich set of resources can also serve to stimulate growth for a world-wide awareness of dance as a powerful expression for people's visions for peace.

   We know that for many people it may be difficult to organize a Peace Run. For this reason, we invite you to do the Peace Dance Meditation, either alone or with family and friends. In this way your participation will add to the power and magic of linking together with the Planet for Peace.

   That's the basic idea. Your questions and ideas are important in shaping this event, so I eagerly await your response. I am very excited about our first Planetary Dance, excited about what we will create together and what we will learn about creating peace from each other. Please let me know how you and your friends or community can take part.

Yours,
Anna

   We had very little sense of how many people and places would do it. So when Amanda Levey called from New Zealand, that was the first hint that it was happening on a global scale. Slowly, over the next few days, we began to receive phone calls, letters, and other materials from these "peacemakers around the world." Sometimes from people we had never heard of who had learned of the Planetary Dance from intermediaries. My letter became a kind of chain letter finding its way to unexpected places. After six months, we still received documents of these events. Some of the events were large, with hundreds of people; some were small and private, like a father and son in Japan who sent us a stunning graphic design of their dance.

I am still amazed at how easily it all happened, so easily that it is obvious that *Circle the Earth* and the *Planetary Dance* must in some way embody something already at work. We did not create the wave that moved around the globe on 19 April, we simply rode on it.

Is there not a growing vision in the world today? More than ever before, people all around are uniting to express their highest aspirations for life, and in the process learning that they have both the power and the responsibility to create a world without war, free of hunger, respectful of each other, of all life and of the environment. We have Live Aid, Hands Across America, a marathon run around the world, Instant Cooperation, and Harmonic Convergence.[3] This spontaneous and popular movement has its parallel in theatre and dance. Call it Global or Planetary Art.

What I find new and particularly challenging in this global art is its scale. That scale is largely unexplored. For now the biggest artistic problems seem to be the logistics of working over great distances. So we continue to work by the principles developed on a smaller scale, though we know that they will be transformed, even abandoned, once we come to understand the potentialities of the global scale. The scale is new, but newness of form does not mean that it is unconnected to the past. It is the latest—and not the last—stop for us on a continuous trail. The *Planetary Dance* was a natural outgrowth of *Circle the Earth.* There was nothing new about *Circle the Earth;* it was a natural outgrowth of *Search for Living Myths.* And *Search for Living Myths* was not new either, that was an outgrowth of societal art developed with our multiracial dances in the '70s. And that wasn't new either, that was an outgrowth of the '60s when we were busy breaking every boundary we could find to redefine our values and rediscover authenticity. And did we find new values or just rediscover old ones?

Of course art on a global scale is developing in many different directions and embodying many different values. The arts merchants of the world, who deliver symbols and images in much the same way and for the same kinds of profits that they manufacture and deliver other commodities, recognize that there is a global market. They visualize global art as a one-to-many configuration. The central source is also characterized by assumptions about superior creative abilities, technologically and culturally. This is just a large-scale version of "artist-as-elitist."

The global art I am interested in developing does not take a one-to-many configuration. It has many sources or centers and no audience. It is completely interac-

NOTE

3. These were all large-scale popular events initiated by a variety of people with the purpose of mobilizing people around the world to speak out about peace in a nonpolitical manner.

tive and difficult to characterize because there is no separate stage from which to view it and no neutral, cultural stance from which to criticize it. It may appear at times to be shaped as many-to-many; it may at moments take the form of many-as-one. It is a highly flexible form because it is not sharply defined by cultural bias. In many respects it has the same shape as the nuclear nightmare: all will be involved and it will not be confined to a single moment in time or a single place. All our seeming differences will seem inconsequential in the face of our overwhelming commonalities.

So what's the next step in developing *Circle the Earth* as a global or planetary dance? Letting go of it. Re-creating it. Realizing that as exciting, inspiring, exhilarating as its many performances have been, it is still full of racial and cultural bias and necessarily so. It was created from a very specific, local concern and gradually enlarged in scope and intention. And there is certainly no single artist nor any one community or culture that can alone redefine the score to make it fully work on a global scale. There is no one among us with that much vision. The vision must arise from the interaction of many different sources. A new score for *Circle the Earth* must be collectively evaluated and re-created by diverse participation. And it probably won't and shouldn't even be called *Circle the Earth* anymore. Even the title implies traveling, going from one location to another, a separation of the planet and her many people. *Circle the Earth* was where the dance was going, the direction it took. Now is the time for a new direction.

There is a discernible trend for people to by-pass governments, cross over boundaries, and unify for the common good—for survival. *Circle the Earth* is my contribution to that process. Art and dance can take a lead. It is necessary for art to express visions that political systems resist. In a world where war has become a national science, peacemaking must become a community art, and even more importantly, a planetary art in the deepest sense of the word: An exemplification of our ability to cooperate in creation, an expression of our best collective aspirations, and a powerful act of magic.

EPILOGUE

In 1994, I made little effort to repeat the Planetary Dance, *and at times I was even unsure if the dance would happen at all. In the end, however, I was amazed at how the event generated itself and how so many people contributed to its creation, either because they had been doing it for years or because they wanted to join in an event that had, over the years, become a customary spring celebration.*

What had begun as an experiment in 1984 started feeling like a tradition by 1994. And with this shift from experiment to tradition, the stage upon which the dance was performed expanded from the stage of the mountain to the stage of time. This enactment of the ritual was connected to the first enactment and to every successive enactment of the dance.

Suddenly, the canvas upon which we were painting was enormous, encompassing the past and the present and the future, expanding the potential and possibility of the Planetary Dance *itself.*

This year's Planetary Dance *made me think a good deal about the relationship between tradition and experimentation, and how contemporary rituals need to maintain an experimental attitude if they are to be authentic. The* Planetary Dance *is a synthesis of contemporary forms of dance, the creative process, and dances of traditional cultures, and it stands at a balancing point between tradition and experimentation. In order to make rituals that create change, we need to remain in an experimental mode, while holding fast to the elements of our rituals that are weighted in time. There are many ways to maintain an experimental mode, including recycling aspects of the rituals that work and reframing elements that don't; initiating new members into the circle of the community; telling the myth over and over again so the community knows its story; and creating opportunities within the context of the ritual that allow everyone to participate and contribute.*

The Planetary Dance *is a global dance form: a dance that transcends cultural and temporal barriers, a dance that speaks to the needs of the community that makes it, and a dance that addresses contemporary issues, such as peace, illness, and the needs of children, as they are experienced by all people on this planet. The* Planetary Dance *is dance for the benefit of others; the* Planetary Dance *is a prayer in which we ask a higher power to bring about a particular result. The* Planetary Dance *is a means through which we can bring our everyday life—relationships, concerns, and work—into the context of a spiritual life.*

THE "EARTH RUN" FROM *CIRCLE THE EARTH*

TO BE PERFORMED AS THE PLANETARY DANCE BY PEACEMAKERS AROUND THE WORLD

DESCRIPTIONS OF SCORES FOR THE "EARTH RUN"
FROM *CIRCLE THE EARTH*

In the beginning formation, the performers kneel along the sides of a square aligned with the four directions. The square should be big enough to enclose a running track. (The square may be elongated into a rectangle if necessary to provide adequate running space.)

The kneeling performers focus on the center of the space, concentrating on the earth and its inhabitants. Each performer will then choose a life form to whom they wish to dedicate their run. It can be a person they know, a human grouping, an animal, a plant, etc. When they begin their runs, they will call it out. For example, "I

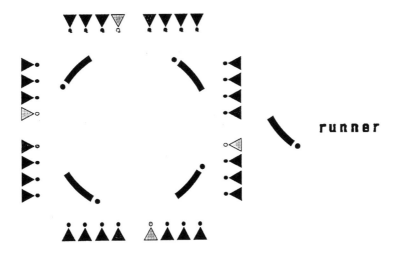

runner

run for the people of South Africa," "I run for the whales," "I run for the rain forests," "I run for my mother," etc. Drummer starts a pulse beat.

One by one, each person dedicates their run by speaking their intention, and then starts running counterclockwise to the pulse of the drum. Allow time intervals between the starting of each person's run.

As the circle of runners becomes established, a runner may turn to the inside of the circle and reverse direction, forming a smaller clockwise circle of runners within the larger counterclockwise circle. The inside runs will maintain the pulse of the run, but will be traveling at a slower velocity by taking shorter strides.

As the circles fill up, two other options become available: a fast outer lane circle and four resting stations within the running circles. The fast lane is entered when runners choose to lengthen their stride and peel off toward the outside from their original circle, and reverse direction so they are now running clockwise. Runners in all three circles maintain their relation to the pulse, making an effort to keep the circles evenly spaced.

Anyone wishing to stop running can turn toward the center of the circle and come to rest at any of the four direction points within the innermost running circle. Both exiting and re-entering the run must be done through the innermost circle. In this resting place, runners can stand still, keep the rhythm, run in place, but stay concentrated on the intention of the run.

Once many have entered the run, the narrator begins to read a speech or poem which meaningfully makes a plea for humankind's care of the Earth. Chief Seattle's address is the poem which has been used in many performances.[1] This speech can

NOTE

1. In 1853, Chief Seattle of the Puget Sound tribe wrote his reply to the "Great White Chief in Washington" who had sought to acquire two million acres of land for $150,000. This reply is a profound statement about the environment and love for Mother Earth.

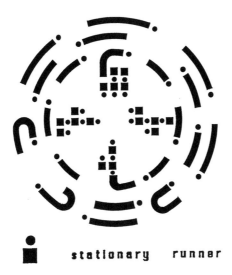

stationary   runner

be read anywhere, but a regional favorite can be substituted. The reading may be repeated again and again until the end of the run.

The length of the run will vary, depending on the number and endurance of the group running. The run needs to last long enough to develop a sense of effort and determination for the participants and a sense of the timelessness of the process.

The end of the run is signaled by a sudden stopping of the drum beat. Those still running stop and listen to the narration, then join the groups standing at the four directions. With everyone in place, all make a symbolic gesture of touching the Earth with any part of the body, i.e., hands, forehead, belly, chest, feet, etc. Then there is a three minute period of silence, or humming, or personal prayer.

CIRCLE THE EARTH: A PHILOSOPHY

There is quite a long tradition of using ritual dance for the purpose of affecting the world. In fact, Western civilization is one of the few cultures that doesn't. In ancient times and in traditional cultures, dance functioned as the means by which people gathered and unified themselves in order to confront the challenges of their existence.

When the members of some hunting cultures needed food, they danced a hunting dance, preparing themselves for the rigors of the hunt and supplicating the divinities and animal spirits to bless their undertaking. Often the dancers enacted the whole ritual of the hunt, bringing it to a successful conclusion. It was believed that when the dancers entered the dance, they actually became the hunters and the prey. By enacting the hunt, they believed they invoked a sympathetic magic and that the correct completion of the ritual ensured the successful completion of the hunt. They believed there was no difference—the hunting dance and the hunt itself were the same spiritual event, seen from two different temporal angles.

Among many of the planting societies, dance rituals are also said to dissolve space and time. They allow the dancers to re-enter the sacred reality that existed before the beginning. In that reality, the dancers re-enact the magical events by which their divine ancestors created their people and their way of life. The dancers do not portray their divinities; rather, they *become* the divinities and participate directly in the birth of their society. The dances usually tell the story of how food came to the people. It was often held that the growth of the crops for that year, and thereby the survival of the people, depended on the exact performance of the correct ritual. Through these performances, the people were renewed and the cycle of life began again.

To celebrate birth and marriage, to initiate the young into adulthood, to initiate adults into the scared mysteries, to prepare for war, to celebrate victory or lament defeat, to heal the sick, to help the dying on their journey into the land of the dead, to maintain the life of the community on its proper path, the people sang their songs and danced their dances. Dance was the most important language people knew. It was a magical language of power. It was the language of the spirits. It was the language in which were told the myths and stories that provided the people with the correct way to make sense out of their experience.

In the evolution of Western industrialized urban culture, people gradually lost the language of dance even as they lost the consciousness of spiritual and natural participation. By now, we have heard about the various problems and crises birthed by the alienated consciousness of this millennium. Insulated from nature by a special world of mechanical, technological construction, Western culture has deeply disrupted the delicate fabric of life to the extent that we now face a serious threat to our continued existence. Within the culture, we also confront a thorough dislocation stemming from the same roots and manifesting in crime, disease, confusion and the constant threat of war.

The re-discovery of the lost language of dance now offers us the very vehicle which people traditionally used to form their cultures and face their crises. And, strange to say, the dance we will recover has been purified and renewed by its long burial in the West. In a sense, ancient dances held their people captive, and tradition had to be preserved for a society to survive. It is probably almost as true to say that the dances created their people as it is to say that the people created their dances. Now, we can use dance to re-create our culture.

During more recent times, the great artists of Western culture, freed from the compulsion to repeat the past, have discovered and taught much about the process of creation. However, the medium they used for their exploration was the medium of an art increasingly separate from the economic, political and social realities of most people. We have gained many tools from the exploration of these artists and now we must learn to use dance in a more integrated way.

You may believe that the power of the ancient dances came from the coordinated imagination of a unified people, or you may join with those early dancers in the belief that the dances actually channel a subtle, all pervasive spiritual energy controlling physical manifestation. In either case, there is no denying that the dances had the power to cohere and maintain societies for hundreds and, in some cases, thousands of years. Now, in our time of need, we have the opportunity to bring that power to bear on our task of transforming, reuniting and renewing our society so that we may find harmony among and between the people of the earth. It is in this context that we at Tamalpa Institute have chosen to focus dance upon the central issue of our time: how to bring peace to ourselves, to our local communities, to different regions, and to the whole world.

We believe peace is more than the absence of war between nations. Peace is a powerful, creative way of life through which people cooperate to solve their problems and realize their potential. The threat of nuclear devastation emerges out of a war- and conflict-oriented culture. It is clearly very important to work on ending the arms race and assisting oppressed people to attain liberation and social justice. However, it is equally important to build a strong, peaceful reality. We want to help create a strong culture of peace.

People need to be at peace within themselves, in their families, in their schools, and throughout their communities. People should be able to work in an economy that encourages the development of peace-releated products and services. Likewise, people ought to be creating and witnessing music, art and drama portraying the challenges and opportunities of attaining peace. Can we really say that we live in a state of fully flowering peace, with the crime and unemployment and poverty and disease that exist here, even though we live in a region spared from the devastation now visited upon so many regions of the world? If we could bring about a significant development in the peace that exists here, imagine what we would learn about encouraging peace in other places around the world.

To make our contribution to this vision, we hope to develop a new kind of dance. Based on our understanding of the traditions of dance, and on our own experiments, we are exploring a simple form which we call Peace Dance. A Peace Dance begins with the invocation of the appropriate spiritual powers, and a request for their blessings. Then the dancers enact some important conflict and its resolution, leading to a strong, creative peace. Finally, the participants take some actions in their everyday lives which will contribute to the actual realization of the peace they desire.

CIRCLE THE EARTH

Circle the Earth evolves from an intensive experience of creativity between myself and a group of 100 workshop participants in the seven days and nights before the performance takes place. Their creativity is based on an open-ended score that guides the group in an experience of gradually intensifying creativity, and culminating in the actual performance.

The enactment of a collective "myth" is a central part of *Circle the Earth*. "Myth-making" is not a task we generally recognize as being part of our contemporary culture. One tends to associate "myth" with ancient people, or with a fable, an untruth, or "make-believe." However, considered in its original meaning, a "myth" embodies a personal and collective vision of how we experience ourselves and the world.

The *Circle the Earth* workshop consists of movement and sound exercises and imagery processes designed to generate the performer's creative imagination.

We join as a whole in the center of the space, to build a symbol of our collective strength. The "Vortex Dance" from Cirle the Earth, *1985.*

Photo by
Paul Fusco.

Although the collective myth has been already named and scored, the workshop enables the performers to re-create the score in a way that embodies their personal responses and leads to the unfolding of their own mythology. In this way, it is hoped that the workshop experiences will infuse the performance with shared visions, intentions, ideas, and images that reflect a passionate commitment arising from mutual involvement. People of different ages and diverse backgrounds are encouraged to participate in the workshop. No formal training is required.

Circle the Earth premiered as *Circle the Mountain* on April 13, 1985, in Marin County, California, and the theme of the dance over the last five years has expanded from peace on Mount Tamalpais to peace throughout the world. The underlying objective is to make a vivid statement for mutual understanding and peace, one that can be taken from the performance in Marin and shared with many people in many places. Since April 1985, *Circle the Earth* has been taken to the United Nations Plaza and Central Park in New York City, Boston, the Southwest, Los Angeles, and San Diego. It will go to Switzerland, Germany, Australia, and Russia in 1986. By involving people in this performance, it is hoped that another spark for peace and global community can be nurtured.

ANNA HALPRIN: A LIFE IN RITUAL

INTERVIEW BY RICHARD SCHECHNER

SCHECHNER: *Why do you feel more comfortable in the theater world than the dance world?*

HALPRIN: The theater world is more inclusive than dance in Western culture. Particularly when it comes to using movement connected to feelings. In the dance world the reaction I often get is that "this is therapy, not dance." I've never found this prejudice in the theater world. I search for real-life-as-art. I want the personalized self-body to become the metaphor for the big collective body. I don't like the way ballet, modern, or even postmodern dance armors the body personality by abstracting feelings, content, and physical movement. It becomes formalized art, feels distant from life, and doesn't involve me. I can be momentarily entertained, excited, even elevated like anyone else that goes to dance performances, but it doesn't last.

I often visit the Native American Pomo Roundhouse. The Roundhouse is partially underground—the entrance is a narrow passage that opens up into a round space with a dirt floor, an open fire, an opening in the roof for the sky to enter and the smoke to leave, a center pole, and a rhythmically pounded drum made from a log over a resonating hole in the ground. It's a mystical theatre. The people dance their prayers, their stories, their healings, and their dreams. They joke and feast, the young and old. Some dances outsiders can join; other dances are only for the initiated. When Loren Smith, a Pomo Healer, comes to *Circle the Earth* he understands what is happening, even though it's nothing like his dances, and he is a great critic. He knows when the power is present, when it isn't, and why. I'm comfortable, at home so to speak, with this kind of "theatre" as well. What interests me is how

NOTE

Richard Schechner is a teacher, theater maker, and chief editor of The Drama Review.

completely interwoven the many threads of cultural life are—social, political, spiritual, and aesthetic. It's more than just dance.

SCHECHNER: *What is it that puts you where you are?*

HALPRIN: Everything that has happened to me in my life puts me where I am. My interest in social issues may very well come from my background as a Jew. Particularly since my impressionable years of growing up were during the time the Nazis ruled most of Europe. Or my enchantment with my grandfather—my first dance experience was seeing him pray when I was four years old. He was a Hassidic Jew who would pray by singing, jumping up and down, and flinging his arms in the air. He had a long white beard and I thought he was GOD, and that GOD was a dancer. To this day, I still have vivid memories of his religious ecstatic dancing.

Fritz Perls, pioneer Gestalt therapist, was interested in theatre and would often conduct sessions around the pieces we were doing. He made a tremendous impact on me and broke the barriers between the "artist" and the "person." He showed me ways to humanize, if you will, the artist and art. My dance professor at the University of Wisconsin was Margaret H'Doubler. She was originally a biologist and taught dance objectively from a scientific perspective. That was a wonderful eye opener. I could learn an approach to movement based on the nature of movement and its inner operation. This released me from learning a set vocabulary of movements based on imitation or copying my teacher. Instead, to the degree movement was objectified, I could subjectify, creating my own movement experience according to my own expressive mind. From her teachings I think I got a real strong foundation on how to generate creativity. She instilled in me a passion for true movement, and a fierce dedication to dance that people can do in their own way.

My husband, Lawrence Halprin, has impacted on me in so many ways I have lost track of our mutual boundaries. But certainly one area is an appreciation of the environment. Raising a family in the country kept me well-grounded, and led me to teaching children for years, and eventually brought me into community interaction. My battle with cancer has been an ever present lesson in my life. And this has been reinforced by the work I'm currently engaged in with people challenging AIDS. Someone summed it up with the expression: "Enlightenment—at gunpoint."

SCHECHNER: *What makes you angry when people freeze you in a historical box? How do you feel?*

HALPRIN: It has taken me a long time to find my place, my location in the arts, in dance, in theater. It has been a long journey. I get angry when people take one or another episode in my journey and use that episode to locate me. I want them to understand where I am now and to engage me in a healthy challenging dialog.

SCHECHNER: *I want to know who in the performance world and outside the performance world you feel close to. I don't want to embarrass you and have you tell me who your enemies are but who your friends are. Not your personal friends so much as the people whose work you admire.*

HALPRIN: When I was in New York City in June 1988, the International Arts Festival was going on. I saw several pieces that intrigued me. Among them were two that I'll mention: Martha Clarke's *Miracolo d'Amore* and the Gardzienice Theatre Association's *Avvakum and Gathering.* In Clarke's dance I liked the exquisite, lyrical, sensuous beauty of the images contrasted by the horror of the content; the skills of the performers in integrating movement, voice, imagery, in highly creative ways. I tolerated the proscenium arch but would have preferred the performance to take place in the plaza in Venice. Uptown at St. John the Divine, in one of the small chapels, the Polish group Gardzienice was performing. I felt the rage and intensity of Poland in political crisis in their bold, violent, gross, crude, and raw power. The women took the same physical risks as the men. Certainly the opposite of a ballerina who depends on men to support her. The women not only supported themselves but asserted themselves as they took giant attacking steps, like warriors, across the floor.

As I felt a strong female quality in Clarke's piece, I admired the powerful masculine thrust of the Polish piece. The men in Clarke's work were able to express femaleness just as the Polish women expressed maleness. This yin and yang is important to me. I want to see that balance and the ability to embody both male and female.

Just this past July at Redwood High in Marin County, California, Joseph Chaikin did a 30-minute monolog called *The War in Heaven* that he and Sam Shepard wrote. He performed this piece after his crippling stroke which affected his vocal chords so that his speech must be formed very consciously. The piece was profound in itself, but the eloquence, courage, and nobility of Chaikin's performance was inspiring—to see him use his illness as a teacher was a truly spiritual experience.

I read about Robert Wilson featuring a deaf and dumb boy in one of his pieces and I recall attending a rehearsal of his and being so pleased that he was incorporating a very large heavy-set woman in his dance. I was impressed that he showed an open mind about what a dancer's body should look like.

I missed Peter Brook's *Mahabharata* but I like the idea that he has a company of performers from many different cultures because I think this is a challenging concept, attempting to maintain cultural identity while moving toward some kind of universality. I identify with Jerzy Grotowski and Eugenio Barba because I believe they too are continuing to explore new ways to create a living theater—one connected to real life in a cultural context.

I like the idea that Liz Lerman has a dance company of elders and that they go to schools performing for children. That kind of diversity is a wonderful social statement of respect. Suzanne Lacy's work sounds great—I like her social, visual, and environmental connections. I feel deeply connected and have a sense of reverence for nature when I view the dances of Eiko and Koma. I admire their adherence to what is true for them in their Japanese culture. It's important to me that dancers be true to their culture, whatever that may be. When I had our multiracial company with Asian, Chicano, Latino, black, white and native Americans creating and performing together, the conflicts and creative resolutions we encountered came from a place of cultural diversity. It was incredibly exciting. The excitement led to unexpected new forms.

SCHECHNER: *Say a young person of 18 comes to you and says, "What should I do with my life?" and they won't take "I don't know" as a response. What response would you give them?*

HALPRIN: What a huge question! My response would be: Go on a vision quest in the wilderness. Stay there alone until an answer comes. If the answer is to dance, then find a way to dance that is purposeful. If you choose dance in your life, then make sure your life is integrated into your dance. Go other places and witness the great ceremonial dances of India, Bali, Africa, or, closer to home, American Indians, and get a broad perspective. Then find a teacher or teachers who inspire you. Don't forget that you are being nurtured from life itself and, if that is cut off, ultimately what's left is just a flashy technique, usually imitative of someone else's idiosyncratic style.

SCHECHNER: *Which dancers are you talking about?*

HALPRIN: I really don't like any way of training the body that is based on some preconceived stylization.

SCHECHNER: *But where do you see that? Do you see that, for example, in Martha Graham's technique?*

HALPRIN: Yes. The movement was real when Martha Graham, Doris Humphrey, Charles Weidman, and Hanya Holm revolted against ballet and the Denishawn, and developed another style. It was a major breakthrough. But because it was based on their personalities, it was subjective and idiosyncratic. Their followers imitated them and soon we had companies of look-alikes. When the next generation of modern dancers began to imitate them and blend ballet into their technique it became slick and glitzy, losing all the original intention. Now we have postmodern, the newest fashion. Dance styles are like skirts that go up and down.

Imitating someone else's personal style produces an army of clones. This offends me—it offends my fierce loyalty to the uniqueness of the individual. Even those I consider the very best of our dance artists today—some who have made a major contribution and who, by the way, happen to be good personal friends, are examples. They have evolved a beautiful personal style—like Merce Cunningham, etc.—but their companies are full of look-alikes.

I prefer to have people told *what* to do but not *how* to do it. Certainly there are many ways to find our commonalities and to explore the basic principles of movement. I feel very encouraged that so many dancers are now turning to the work of Bonnie Bainbridge Cohen, Moshe Feldenkrais, Mable Todd, and others who approach movement from the point of view of origin, evolution, and structural integration.

SCHECHNER: *I'd like you to deal with what I think are some difficulties with your work. One difficulty is the gap between the actual experience of doing your work and how that feels for the performer in contrast to how viewing your work feels for the spectator.*

HALPRIN: I don't want spectators. Spectators imply a spectacle that takes place to entertain and amuse and perhaps stimulate them. I want witnesses who realize that we are dancing for a purpose—to accomplish something in ourselves and in the world. We are performing our best attempts to create authentic contemporary theatre rituals.

The role of the witness is to understand the dance and support the dancers who have undertaken the challenge of performing. Spectators often come with their own personal aesthetics. They sit back and watch and judge to see if what is done lives up to their preconceived notion of a particular, very culture-bound idea of a certain kind of "art."

If they have a hard time with my work it is because they don't belong. They don't know what they are supposed to do. They tend to get confused and embarrassed. I deal with this by doing my best to tell people what we are trying to accomplish and how they can help—what role we want them to perform. We have clear standards, clear values, but they are the values of a community engaging with an idea, seeking to accomplish something. Playing the role of witness in this kind of ritual is deeply engaging but very different from being a spectator.

In the end I just have to tell people what I'm up to and what I want, and hope for the best.

Stomping rhythmically on the ground, lines of Warriors urge the Monsters to emerge from the group. Circle the Earth, *1985.*

Photo by
Paul Fusco.

During a workshop rehearsal, participants confront their monsters. Taira Rester, Circle the Earth, *1986.*

Photo by
Paul Fusco.

SCHECHNER: *Another difficulty is trying to create an efficacious act, a dance that really makes rain, saves the world, or catches a murderer.*

HALPRIN: I don't really know whether dancing produces results per se, but I'm willing to find out. It brings out awareness and focuses us on issues of human need and concern, that much I do know.

SCHECHNER: *Well, that's not the way it sounds. You talk about the capture of the Tamalpais killer. You say, in effect, "Look, it worked for my cancer, it worked for Tamalpais, and it will work for the world." I have no problem with you believing that—but do you? You seem to waffle on this question of efficacy.*

HALPRIN: What I care about is that a group of people focus on something of mutual concern—on the effort.

SCHECHNER: *Is that "mutual concern" a shared belief that dancing is a ritual act that can do something? When a group of business people get together it's not just a "mutual concern" that they can make money but they believe certain actions will make money. If they make money they're happy—if they don't, they're fired. I really want you to face this head on.*

HALPRIN: I don't know whether dancing will work or won't. Maybe it will—and in this threatening world it's worth a try!

SCHECHNER: *But I want to know when you ask people to come together, is it in order to enjoy dancing, making dances, or is it to "change the world"?*

HALPRIN: I don't know the answer to this question yet. We are engaged in an experiment and we are by no means finished with it.

There is a very basic principle that underlies traditional rituals. The people enact in the ritual what they want to have happen in their lives. This principle has been around for a lot longer than our more recent notions of how to make things happen.

I'm just going back to this hypothesis and testing it out again, only with contemporary rituals. This is almost a scientific perspective and so I feel very reinforced by what has happened.

If a collection of communities dance together in a planetary dance all around the world—releasing their fear of war and enacting their desire for peace—and then if all these people agree to take specific actions for peace in their own lives and in the life of their community, this is pretty likely to help and not likely to be harmful.

And who knows, it may even turn out that there is some truth to the belief of traditional cultures that an unseen—energy—dimension does play a role in

*Witnesses participate by
donning masks to protect
themselves from the
Monsters during* Circle
the Earth, *1986.*

Photo by
Paul Fusco.

causing—or at least clearing the way for—manifestation in the physical dimension, and that ritual dance is a way to make an energy pathway to guide physical reality. That certainly would offer an explanation for how dance could help capture "the killer on the mountain" and heal cancer.

If this were even partially true, it would become even more significant and important for us to keep up this ritual of dancing for peace and for healing.

SCHECHNER: *I'm asking you to go one step beyond that. Look into your heart, and answer: If you found out it wouldn't change things, would you stop dancing?*

HALPRIN: No, because whether it rains or not isn't the purpose.

SCHECHNER: *What is the purpose?*

HALPRIN: For me, dancing can be a prayer. Would the Hopis stop doing the Snake Dance every August if it didn't rain? They would do it again next year. Do we stop praying if our prayers aren't answered, or do we pray again?

Efficacy in this sense is not cause and effect. The purpose is to awaken people to peace and move them to concrete peaceful action in their lives. For *Circle the Earth* there is a score designed for performers and witnesses alike to do the next day as a closure—*Peace Bird.* They mold a huge bird image in the sand by the seashore and then, one by one, place a rock in the circle as, aloud, they make a commitment to do a specific act for peace during the year. Like-minded people come together to do this dance because they care about peace and they have chosen dance as a way to give voice to their feelings; to take an active stance, to be counted as it were. Some people do civil disobedience, protest marches, whatever—we dance!

FOUNDING AND DEVELOPMENT:

DANCERS' WORKSHOP/TAMALPA INSTITUTE

The San Francisco Dancers' Workshop was founded by Anna Halprin in 1959 as a nonprofit organization created to promote innovative, contemporary art. The workshop began modestly as an experimental laboratory with a mix of dancers, musicians, architects, poets, and psychologists. Within a few years, the impact of its collaborative experiments attracted the attention of the avant-garde art world. The company was invited to perform at major international art festivals in Canada, Sweden, Poland, Italy, and Yugoslavia as well as at colleges, theaters, and universities throughout the country.

Dancers' Workshop was concerned with the training and development of a multiethnic, cross-cultural community of performing artists and community leaders. It developed forms of collective creativity, exploring and establishing creative technologies that work with the whole individual, the group, and community. It was theater in its broadest sense. Dancers' Workshop created new ways in which community life can come together through dance, deriving an approach to movement based on the natural and organic structures of the body rather than on artificially imposed stylistic forms.

Tamalpa Institute, founded in 1978 by Anna Halprin and Daria Halprin-Khalighi, is a center for the study of movement, dance, the healing arts, the creative process, myths, rituals, and community art. Designed as the nonprofit research and educational arm of the San Francisco Dancers' Workshop, Tamalpa was established to research the implications of the work of Dancers' Workshop, including the workshops' explorations in broadening the scope of dance/theater to address real-life issues and to deal with more of what is genuinely meaningful in people's lives. At Tamalpa, people are trained in a creative process which integrates psychology, body therapies and education with dance, art and drama.

Anna Halprin created an approach to dance that synthesizes personal and artistic growth through a unique process which can develop and heighten our natural sense of creativity. This approach is called the Life/Art Process because it functions on the premise that as life experience deepens, our art expression expands. This generates an art based on personal and collective content. The Life/Art Process emphasizes and revitalizes the whole person through the integration of physical, emotional, mental, and spiritual dimensions.

The mission of the Tamalpa Institute is to use dance and the expressive arts to teach people to release the creative spirit as a vehicle for healing and transformation. This is accomplished by using dance, healing, and the expressive arts to explore human needs, resolve personal and social conflicts, and serve ecological concerns.

CHRONOLOGY:

ANNA HALPRIN, SAN FRANCISCO DANCERS' WORKSHOP, AND TAMALPA INSTITUTE

The development and direction of San Francisco Dancers' Workshop (SFDW) and Tamalpa Institute can best be seen as having four phases, highlighted by specific works:

PHASE I: **Breaking the Barriers, 1955–1965**

· Founding of SFDW in San Francisco in 1955 by Anna Halprin with a small group of multidisciplinary artists. Making free use of elements in visual art, poetry, architecture, music, theater, and dance, Halprin formed a workshop to explore new perspectives in art and created a form called "total theater."

· A piece from this period, *Five-Legged Stool*, broke the tradition of the proscenium arch and used all spaces in the theater, and sometimes moved outside the theater as well.

· *Exposizione* was produced as an opera and introduced the use of the voice, both for singing and speaking. This work was a collaboration with the Italian composer Luciano Berio.

· SFDW, in the forefront of the American avant-garde, was invited to participate in international art festivals in Rome, Venice, Zagreb, Helsinki, Warsaw, and Stockholm, as well as cities in Canada and the United States. Its highly publicized and well-documented works had a major influence on the direction of the performing arts in America.

· Major works from this period:

THE FLOWERBURGER, 1959
Choreographer: Anna Halprin
Performers: Anna Halprin, A. A. Leath, John Graham

Artistic Director: Jo Landor

Collaborator: Richard Brautigan

Lighting: Patric Hickey, Jo Landor

Locations: Jay Marks Contemporary Dance Theater, San Francisco, Calif.; International
Avant Garde Arts Festival, Vancouver, British Columbia

RITES OF WOMEN, 1959

Choreographer: Anna Halprin

Performers: Anna Halprin, A. A. Leath, John Graham, Simone Forti

Artistic Director: Jo Landor

Poetry: James Broughton

Lighting: Patric Hickey

Location: San Francisco Playhouse, San Francisco, Calif.

BIRDS OF AMERICA OR GARDENS WITHOUT WALLS, 1960

Choreographer: Anna Halprin

Performers: Anna Halprin, A. A. Leath, John Graham, Daria Halprin,
Rana Halprin

Artistic Director: Jo Landor

Composer: LaMonte Young

Lighting: Patric Hickey

Locations: International Avant Garde Arts Festival, Vancouver, British Columbia; Opera
House, Venice, Italy; San Francisco Contemporary Dance Theatre, San Francisco, Calif.

FOUR-LEGGED STOOL, 1962

Choreographer: Anna Halprin

Performers: Anna Halprin, A. A. Leath, John Graham, Lynne Palmer

Artistic Director: Jo Landor

Composer: Terry Riley

Designer: Patric Hickey

Location: San Francisco Playhouse, San Francisco, Calif.

FIVE-LEGGED STOOL, 1962

Choreographer: Anna Halprin

Performers: Anna Halprin, A. A. Leath, John Graham, Lynne Palmer

Artistic Director: Jo Landor

Composers: Morton Subotnick and David Tudor

Lighting: Patric Hickey

Locations: San Francisco Playhouse, San Francisco, Calif.; Rome, Italy; Zagreb, Czechoslovakia; Helsinki, Finland

EXPOSIZIONE, 1963
Choreographer: Anna Halprin
Performers: Anna Halprin, A. A. Leath, John Graham, Daria Halprin, Rana Halprin, Lynne Palmer
Artistic Director: Jo Landor
Composer: Luciano Berio
Lighting: Patric Hickey
Sculptor: Jerry Walters
Stage Manager: Ken Dewey
Assistants: Members of the Marin Dance Coop
Location: XXVI Festival Internazionale di Musica Contemporanea, Opera House, Venice, Italy

PHASE II: **Audience Participation, 1963–1978**

· The reaction of audiences to this new and iconoclastic art form led to the second period which began with *Parades and Changes.*

· Audiences were invited to participate. Scores were written to be performed by the audience together with the company.

· Workshops were held to research processes whereby a large group could collectively produce a work of art.

· Public events were staged with hundreds of participants.

· *Citydance* was an annual dance event which involved countless numbers of people from sunup to sundown all over San Francisco.

· Major works from this period:

APRIL 1962 EVENT, 1962
Choreographer: Anna Halprin
Performers: Anna Halprin, SFDW, A. A. Leath, John Graham, Simone Forti
Composers: Terry Riley, LaMonte Young
Designer: Patric Hickey
Location: University of California, Los Angeles

VISAGE, 1963
Choreographer and Performer: Anna Halprin
Composer: Luciano Berio
Designer: Jo Landor
Lighting: Patric Hickey
Locations: Muzicki Biennale, Zagreb, Yugoslavia; Rome, Italy

PROCESSION, 1964
Choreographer: Anna Halprin
Performers: Anna Halprin, A. A. Leath, John Graham, Daria Halprin, Rana Halprin, Lucy
Lewis
Artistic Director: Jo Landor
Composer: Morton Subotnik
Lighting: Patric Hickey
Sculptor: Charles Ross
Location: University of California, Los Angeles, Calif.

PARADES AND CHANGES (12 versions), 1965–67
Choreographer: Anna Halprin
Performers: Anna Halprin, A. A. Leath, John Graham, Daria Halprin, Rana Halprin, Lari
Goldsmith, Paul Goldsmith
Composers: Morton Subotnik, Folke Rabe
Lighting: Patric Hickey
Sculptor: Charles Ross
Locations: Stockholm, Sweden; Poland; University of California, Berkeley and Los Angeles,
Calif.; San Francisco State, San Francisco, Calif.; "On the Mall," Fresno, Calif.; Hunter
College, New York, N.Y.

APARTMENT 6, 1965
Choreographer: Anna Halprin
Performers: Anna Halprin, A. A. Leath, John Graham
Artistic Director: Jo Landor
Designer: Patric Hickey
Sculptor: Charles Ross
Locations: Helsinki, Finland; San Francisco Playhouse, San Francisco, Calif.

THE BATH, 1967
Choreographer: Anna Halprin
Performers: Nancy Peterson, Kathy Peterson, Karen Ahlberg, Daria Halprin, Peter Weise, Morris Kelly, Michael Samuels, Joseph Lange
Composer: Pauline Oliveros
Locations: Atheneum Museum, Hartford, Conn.; Dancers' Workshop Studio, San Francisco, Calif.

MYTHS (Series of 10 Performances), 1967–68
Choreographer: Anna Halprin
Performers: Anna Halprin, SFDW, audience
Composer: Casey Sonabend
Lighting and Collaborator: Patric Hickey
Location: Dancers' Workshop Studio, San Francisco, Calif.

OME, 1968
Choreographer: Anna Halprin
Performers: Anna Halprin and SFDW
Composer: Casey Sonabend
Lighting: Patric Hickey
Location: University of Oregon, Portland, Ore.

LUNCH, 1968
Choreographer: Anna Halprin
Performers: Anna Halprin, Norma Leistiko, Larry Reed, Annie Hallet, Kim Hahn, Daria Halprin, Rana Halprin, Gary Hartford
Composer: Charles Amirkhanian
Lighting: Patric Hickey
Location: Hilton Hotel, San Francisco, Calif.

SAN FRANCISCO STATE UNIVERSITY C10, 1968
Choreographer: Anna Halprin
Performers: Anna Halprin, SFDW, and audience
Composer: Casey Sonabend
Location: San Francisco State University, San Francisco, Calif.

LOOK, 1968
Choreographer: Anna Halprin
Performers: Anna Halprin, SFDW, and audience
Composers: Performers
Designer: Patric Hickey
Location: Museum of Art, San Francisco, Calif.

CITYDANCE, 1976–77
Choreographer: Anna Halprin
Performers: Anna Halprin, SFDW, Allan Stinson, Jim Cave, Soto Hoffman, people of the
Bay Area
Locations: City streets of San Francisco

PHASE III: **Third World Involvement, 1969–1982**

· James Woods invited Anna Halprin to hold a workshop for a group of all-black artists at
Studio Watts in Los Angeles shortly after race riots in Detroit and Watts in Los Angeles.

· *Ceremony of Us* showed the confrontation process between the black and white groups. It
premiered at the Mark Taper Forum in Los Angeles and later toured northern California.

· SFDW was reborn as a multiracial performing company.

· The Reach Out Program was initiated at this time to provide leadership training in the arts
to minority and indigenous peoples. Students in the training became members of the performing company, the teaching staff, and went on to professional careers in the arts.

· Documentation of this program became a credible standard for minority training in the
arts.

· Major works of this period:

CEREMONY OF US, 1969
Choreographer: Anna Halprin
Performers: Anna Halprin, SFDW, Studio Watts
Designers: Patric Hickey, Jo Landor
Locations: Mark Taper Forum, Los Angeles, Calif.; Pacific College, Fresno, Calif.; Merritt
College, Oakland, Calif.

EVENT IN A CHAPEL, 1969
Choreographer: Anna Halprin
Performers: Anna Halprin, SFDW
Composer: Casey Sonabend
Designer: Patric Hickey
Location: Pacific University, Stockton, Calif.

NEW TIME SHUFFLE, 1970
Choreographer: Anna Halprin
Performers: Anna Halprin, SFDW Reach Out performers
Composers: Richard Friedman, Bo Conley
Designer: Patric Hickey
Locations: Soledad Prison, Calif.; Harding Theater, San Francisco, Calif.; Civic Auditorium, Oakland, Calif.; Civic Auditorium, Richmond, Calif.; Arts Center, Sausalito, Calif.

KADOSH, 1970
Choreographer: Anna Halprin
Performers: Anna Halprin, SFDW Reach Out performers
Collaborator: Rabbi Samuel Brodie
Designer: Patric Hickey
Locations: Beth Sinai Temple, Oakland, Calif.

INITIATIONS AND TRANSFORMATIONS AND *ANIMAL RITUAL,* 1971
Choreographer: Anna Halprin
Performers: Anna Halprin, SFDW Reach Out performers, students at the American Dance Festival
Composer: James Fletcher Hall
Lighting: Patric Hickey
Stage Management: John Muto
Locations: University Art Museum, Berkeley, Calif.; Williams College, Williamstown, Mass.; Museum of Art, Richmond, Va.; George Washington University, Washington, D.C.; New York City Center, New York, N.Y.; Connecticut American College Dance Festival, New London, Conn.

RITUAL AND CELEBRATION, 1977
Choreographer: Anna Halprin
Performers: Anna Halprin, Reach Out performers, and audience
Assistant: James Nixon
Location: Berkeley, Calif.

MALE AND FEMALE RITUALS, 1978

Choreographer: Anna Halprin

Performers: Anna Halprin, SFDW, audience

Composer: Kirk Nurock and Natural Sound

Locations: City Center Theater, New York, N.Y.; Museum of Modern Art, San Francisco, Calif.

ARCOSANTI ALIVE, 1978

Choreographer: Anna Halprin

Performers: Anna Halprin, with architects and Arcosanti residents

Collaborator: Paolo Soleri

Location: Arcosanti, Ariz.

CELEBRATION OF LIFE—CYCLE OF AGES, 1979

Choreographer: Anna Halprin

Performers: Anna Halprin, SFDW, Norma Leistiko, Daria Halprin, Rana Halprin, Mr. and Mrs. I. Schuman, Benito Santiago, and a company of 50 people

Composers: Rod Marymor, Sandy Hershman

Designer: Patric Hickey

Location: Hilton Hotel, San Francisco, Calif.

PHASE IV: **Formation of Tamalpa Institute, 1978–Present**

· Tamalpa Institute was born when a formal training program replaced the workshop format. The methodology through which individual life issues could be transformed into professional quality original dance art had been tested and refined through the Reach Out workshop trainings.

· Students of the trainings had received university credit for their work and now could receive B.A., M.A., and Ph.D. degrees through Tamalpa Institute's association with International College and Sonoma State University.

· In 1980, the methodology for creating original art from real-life issues was tested. A six-month series of workshops culminated in the performances *In and On the Mountain,* done with a large community group.

· "A Search for Living Myths through Dance and the Environment" in 1980 was the first in a series of workshops which involved public dance events and performance. The performances of *Circle the Earth,* 1986–89, were the culmination of this phase.

· The creation of workshop formats for people living with cancer, AIDS and other life-threatening illnesses, including Positive Motion, Women with Wings, and Moving Toward Life.

· Major works of this period:

SEARCH FOR LIVING MYTHS AND RITUALS THROUGH DANCE AND THE ENVIRONMENT, 1980
Choreographer: Anna Halprin
Collaborator: Lawrence Halprin
Participants: People of the Bay Area
Designer: Patric Hickey
Locations: College of Marin Fine Arts Theatre and sites in Marin County, Calif.

IN AND ON THE MOUNTAIN, 1981
Choreographer: Anna Halprin
Performers: Tamalpa Dancers and workshop participants
Artistic Director: Jo Landor
Lighting: Patric Hickey
Set Design: Joseph Stubblefield
Music: Kirk Norwick
Poet and Narrator: Kush
Location: Mt. Tamalpais and College of Marin Theatre, Kentfield, Calif.

THANKSGIVING, 1982
A spontaneous gathering of people on the mountain to celebrate the freedom of the mountain from the grips of the killer.
Poet and Narrator: Kush

RETURN TO THE MOUNTAIN, 1983
Choreographer: Anna Halprin
Performers: Tamalpa Institute dancers
Set Design: Joseph Stubblefield
Guest: Don Jose Mitsuwa
Musicians: Weldon McCarty, Shakti, Bo Connley
Masks: Annie Hallet
Narration: James Nixon and James Cave
Location: Mt. Tamalpais and Redwood High School Gym, Larkspur, Calif.

RUN TO THE MOUNTAIN, 1984
Choreographer: Anna Halprin
Performers: Tamalpa Dancers and Norma Leistiko
Set Design: Joseph Stubblefield

Poet and Narrator: Kush
Location: Mt. Tamalpais and Redwood High School Gym, Larkspur, Calif.

CIRCLE THE MOUNTAIN, A Dance in the Spirit of Peace, 1985
Choreographer: Anna Halprin
Performers: 100 participants
Musicians: Brian Hand, Suru
Set Design: Joseph Stubblefield
Co–Workshop Leader: Jamie McHugh
Poet and Narrator: Kush
Location: Mt. Tamalpais and Redwood High School Gym, Larkspur, Calif.

EARTH RUN, 1985
Choreographer: Anna Halprin
Performers: People from around the world
Locations: United Nations Plaza, New York, N.Y.; Big Sur, Calif.

CIRCLE THE EARTH, A Dance in the Spirit of Peace, 1986
Choreographer: Anna Halprin
Performers: 100 people from the Bay Area and around the world
Musicians: John Gruntfest, Grand Rudolph, Weldon McCarty
Guest Composer: Terry Riley
Poet and Narrator: Kush
Set Design: Joseph Stubblefield
Altars: Eeo Stubblefield
Location: Redwood High School Gym, Larkspur, Calif.

CIRCLE THE EARTH, A Peace Dance with the Planet, 1987
Choreographer: Anna Halprin
Performers: 100 performers from the Bay Area and around the world
Guest Singer: Susan Osborn
Musician: Brian Hand
Set Design: Joseph Stubblefield
Altars: Eeo Stubblefield
Location: Redwood High School Gym, Larkspur, Calif.

THE PLANETARY DANCE, 1987
Choreographer: Anna Halprin
Performers: People of the Bay Area, and people in communities all over the world
Location: 63 cities around the world

CIRCLE THE EARTH, Dancing Our Peaceful Nature, 1988
Presenters: Anna Halprin and Guest Artists
Participants: People of the Bay Area
Location: Marin Headlands, Calif.

CIRCLE THE EARTH, Dancing with Life on the Line, 1989, 1991
Leaders: Anna Halprin, Jamie McHugh and Tamalpa facilitators
Collaborators: Brian Hand, Mark Katz, Jason Serinus, STEPS Theater Company, Allan Stinson, Joseph Stubblefield, Carol Swann, Women with Wings
Location: Mt. Tamalpais and Redwood High School Gym, Larkspur, Calif.

CARRY ME HOME, 1990
Choreographer: Anna Halprin, with Allan Stinson
Dancers: Positive Motion participants
Musicians: Jules Beckman and Norman Rutherford
Location: Theatre Artaud, San Francisco, Calif.

BIBLIOGRAPHY OF BOOKS, FILMS,

VIDEOS, AND RECORDS

ARTICLES AND BOOKS

Baigell, Matthew. "Close-Up of Modern Dance Today: The Private Teacher." *Dance Magazine,* December 1957.

Broughton, James. *She Is a Moving One.* San Francisco: Pennywhistle Press, 1988.

Cahill, Sedonia, and Joshua Halpern. *The Ceremonial Circle.* San Francisco: Harper, 1964.

Danon, Marcella. *New Age and New Sounds: Il Directtore d'Orchestra.* Venice: Edizioni Multimedia, 1994.

Feuerstein, Georg, and Trisha Lamb, eds. *Voices on the Threshold of Tomorrow.* Wheaton, Ill.: Quest Books, 1993.

Halprin, Anna. *Collected Writings I.* San Francisco: Dancers' Workshop, 1973.

———. *Collected Writings II.* San Francisco: Dancers' Workshop, 1974.

———. *Collected Writings III.* Kentfield, Calif.: Tamalpa Institute, 1986.

Halprin, Anna, with illustrations by Charlene Koonce. *Movement Ritual I.* Kentfield, Calif.: Tamalpa Institute, 1979.

Halprin, Anna, with Allan Stinson. *Circle the Earth Manual: A Guide for Dancing Peace with the Planet.* Kentfield, Calif.: Tamalpa Institute, 1984.

Halprin, Anna, and Jim Burns. *A School Comes Home.* San Francisco: Dancers' Workshop, 1973.

Halprin, Anna, James Nixon, and James T. Burns. *Citydance 77.* San Francisco: Dancers' Workshop, 1978.

Halprin, Lawrence. *The RSVP Cycles: Creative Processes in the Human Environment.* New York: Braziller Press, 1969.

Halprin, Lawrence and James T. Burns. *Taking Part.* Cambridge: MIT Press, 1974.

Halprin-Khalighi, Daria. *Coming Alive! The Creative Expression Method.* Kentfield, Calif.: Tamalpa Institute, 1987.

Highwater, Jamake. *Dance Rituals of Experience.* New York: A. W. Publishers, 1978.

NOTE

The Anna Halprin Archives will be housed in the San Francisco Performing Arts Library and Museum, and the New York Performing Arts Library Dance Collection. Both archival libraries will house portions of the archives pertaining to Halprin's work done in those cities. The San Francisco archives will house the majority of archival materials, including films, video tapes, press materials, documentation of classes, workshops and special events, photographs, and Halprin's extensive notes, journals, and written explorations.

Jean, Norma, and Deak Frantisek. "Anna Halprin's Theatre and Therapy Workshop." *Tulane Drama Review* 20 (March 1976).

Kostelanetz, Richard. *Dictionary of the Avant Garde.* New York: a capella books, 1993.

———. "Metamorphosis in Modern Dance." *Dance Scope* 5 (Fall 1970).

Luger, R., and Barry Lane. "When Choreography Becomes Female, Part 2: A Talk with Anna Halprin." *Christopher Street,* December 1978.

McDonagh, Don. *The Rise and Fall and Rise of Modern Dance.* New York: Outerbridge and Dienstfrey, 1970.

Renouf, Renée. "It Could Be This or It Could Be That: An Interview with Ann Halprin." *Genesis West* 1 (4) (1963).

Roose-Evans, James. *Experimental Theatre from Stanislavsky to Peter Brook.* London: Routledge and Kegan Paul, 1984.

———. "James Roose-Evans Meets Ann Halprin in San Francisco." *Dance and Dancers* 21 (March 1970).

———. *Passages of the Soul, Ritual Today.* Dorset, England: Elemental Books Ltd., 1994.

Rutkowski, Alice. "Development, Definition and Demonstration of the Halprin Life/Art Process." Ph.D. diss., 1986.

Steinberg, Janice. "Anna Halprin: Ritual Keeper." *High Performance Magazine* 9 (1) (1986).

Van Tuyl, Marian, ed. *Anthology of Impulse.* Brooklyn, N.Y.: Dance Horizons, 1969.

Woolger, Roger J. *Other Lives, Other Selves.* New York: Dolphin Doubleday, 1987.

Young, Alan. *The Cancer Puzzle.* Portland, Ore.: Frank Amata Publications, 1993.

VIDEO TAPES

Circle the Earth: Dancing with Life on the Line. Documentary. Produced by Media Arts West, 1989. 40 minutes, color.

Embracing Earth. Directed by Anna Halprin, filmed by Ellison Horne and Abrahams-Wilson Productions. Four sections, with Simone Forti, Sam Yip, and other dancers. One hour, color.

Inner Landscapes. Directed by Joan Safer, filmed by KQED-TV, 1992. One hour, color.

Positive Motion. Documentary. Abrahams-Wilson Production, 1991. 30 minutes, color.

The Power of Ritual. An interview with Anna Halprin by Dr. Jeffrey Mishloff, 1988. One hour, color.

Ritual of Life and Death and *Dance for Your Life.* Two documentaries on one tape. Filmed by Ellison Horne, 1989. 40 minutes, color.

FILMS OF ANNA HALPRIN AND DANCERS' WORKSHOP

Ann: A Portrait. Filmed and directed by Coni Beeson, produced by American Film Institute, sound by Richard Friedman, 1971. 21 minutes, black and white film.

NOTE

*Impulse Magazine, founded by Anna Halprin in 1948 and published by her for three years, was the first dance journal to be published on the West Coast. Murray Louis, a student of Halprin's at the time, served as editor of the magazine. In 1952, Marian Van Tuyl became the acting editor. This anthology is a compilation of that work.

The Bed. Directed by James Broughton, 1963. 20 minutes, black and white film.

The Bust. Produced by KQED-TV, 1971. 10 minutes, black and white film.

Children's Film. Produced by KQED-TV, 1954. 20 minutes, black and white film.

Four in the Afternoon. Directed by James Broughton, 1963. 30 minutes, black and white film.

How Sweet It Is. Directed by Lawrence Halprin with Paul Ryan, 1975. 12 minutes, black and white film.

Parades and Changes. Directed by Arne Arneborn, produced by National Swedish Television, 1966. 40 minutes, black and white film.

POW. Produced by KPIX-TV, 1968. Black and white film.

Procession. Produced by University of California at Los Angeles, 1964. 30 minutes, black and white film.

Right On (Ceremony of Us). Produced by KQED-TV, 1969. 30 minutes, black and white film.

RECORDS

Ceremony of Us. Produced by the Delexi Foundation, Dancers' Workshop Company, and Studio Watts, February 1969.

References to illustrations appear in bold type.

UNIVERSITY PRESS OF NEW ENGLAND publishes books under its own imprint and is the publisher for Brandeis University Press, Dartmouth College, Middlebury College Press, University of New Hampshire, University of Rhode Island, Tufts University, University of Vermont, Wesleyan University Press, and Salzburg Seminar.

Anna Halprin, author, is a long-time pioneer and innovator in the universal language of dance, chipping away steadily at preconceived ideas of what dance and art can be. Her career developed in northern California and has been influenced by that natural environment. She is the founder of the San Francisco Dancers' Workshop and Tamalpa Institute and the creator of Movement Ritual, the Psycho-Kinetic Visualization Process, and the *Planetary Dance*, the first global peace dance. She works with large groups around the world and creates community-specific rituals. She teaches internationally and is the recipient of numerous NEA grants, a Guggenheim Fellowship, and many awards and honors for her work. In 1995, Anna Halprin will be seventy-five years old.

Rachel Kaplan, editor, works as Anna Halprin's personal assistant. Alternately, she is a performance artist, an art critic, a teacher, and a community organizer. She lives and works in the San Francisco Bay Area.

Find a way to dance that is purposeful. If you choose dance in your life, make sure your life is integrated into your dance. Don't forget that you are being nurtured by life itself. Ceremony of Us, 1969.

Photo by
Tylon Barea.

Library of Congress Cataloging-in-Publication Data

Halprin, Anna.

    Moving toward life: five decades of transformational dance / by
Anna Halprin; edited by Rachel Kaplan.

       p. cm.

    Includes bibliographical references and index.

    ISBN 0–8195–5284–4 (cloth : alk. paper). — ISBN 0–8195–6286–6
(pbk. : alk. paper)

   1. Halprin, Anna. 2. Dancers—United States—Biography.
3. Modern dance. 4. Dance therapy. I. Kaplan, Rachel, 1963– .
II. Title.

GV1785.H267A3 1995

792.8'028—dc20   95–1696

  [B]